I'll Always Carry You:

A Mother's Story of Adoption Loss, Grief, and Healing

Linda L Franklin

Copyright © 2019 by Linda L Franklin. All rights reserved.

No part of this publication may be reproduced, stored in a retrieval system, or transmitted in any form or by any means, electronic, mechanical, photocopying, recording, scanning, or otherwise, without the prior written permission of the author.

Limit of Liability/Disclaimer of Warranty: While the publisher and author have used their best efforts in preparing this book, they make no representations or warranties with respect to the accuracy or completeness of the contents of this book and specifically disclaim any implied warranties of merchantability or fitness for a particular purpose. No warranty may be created or extended by sales representatives or written sales materials. The advice and strategies contained herein may not be suitable for your situation. You should consult with a professional when appropriate. Neither the publisher nor the author shall be liable for any loss of profit or any other commercial damages, including but not limited to special, incidental, consequential, personal, or other damages.

I'll Always Carry You
A Mother's Story of Adoption Loss, Grief, and Healing
By Linda L Franklin
1. Family and Relationships / Adoption and Fostering 2. Family and Relationships / Death, Grief, Bereavement 3. Social Science / Marriage and Family
Paperback ISBN: 978-1-949642-15-5
eBook ISBN: 978-1-949642-16-2

Cover design by Lewis Argell

Printed in the United States of America

Authority Publishing
11230 Gold Express Dr. #310-413
Gold River, CA 95670
800-877-1097
www.AuthorityPublishing.com

I loved this book! Not only does it honestly depict so many aspects of the experience of being a birth/first mother, but it makes that experience available to all members of the adoption community in a manner than can be heard and understood. Linda Franklin is courageously truthful in the telling of her experience as a young woman who became pregnant, who was coerced by society into giving up her baby, and who then set out to find him again. There are many obstacles to adoptees and their first/birth mothers finding one another that are so arbitrary and unnecessary, but which instill fear and paralysis in many of those wishing to do so. I hope that Linda's example of courage and tenacity will instill hope in all those who have been separated and wish to be reunited. This book is full of courage, dedication, love, and inspiration. READ IT!

—Nancy Verrier, LMFT, mother, lecturer, and author of *The Primal Wound* and *Coming Home to Self*

As a mother and a therapist, Linda Franklin writes with passion and authority about the loss of her first child to adoption, the long-term impact of that tragic separation and her resultant grief. It takes courage and insight to share this life-defining experience with others in a style which is both personal and educational. Her book poignantly illustrates the psychological and emotional significance of appropriate grieving.

—Evelyn Burns Robinson, author of *Adoption and Recovery: Solving the Mystery of Reunion* (2006) and *Adoption and Loss: The Hidden Grief* (2003, 2018)

Linda Franklin has added her voice to a surging chorus: women speaking out against the social brutalities designed to facilitate the loss of their children to adoption. Franklin traces her own 20th century experience and the decades of suffering and recovery that followed. Franklin offers her story as a cautionary tale, clarifying the limits and damages that continue to characterize adoption today.

—Rickie Solinger, author of *Wake Up Little Susie: Single Pregnancy and Race before Roe v. Wade* (1992, 2000) and *Reproductive Justice: An Introduction* (2017), among other books about reproductive politics.

A river of grief runs through Linda Franklin's writing as she deftly chronicles the era in which we both lost children to adoption. Yet her story is also one of hope and healing as she navigates through reunion and the difficulties that ensue. A story that first mothers will recognize and adoptees appreciate.

—Lorraine Dusky, author of *hole in my heart, a memoir and report from the fault lines of adoption.*

Franklin gives a painstaking account of how she comes to be one of the millions of unapprised and ultimately exploited girls of this infamous era. She captures with vivid, excruciating detail the day she signs the adoption papers, under the guidance of a creepy attending psychologist, Dr. Malone, who weeks later tries to seduce her. Franklin tells this part of her story with such honesty that we cannot doubt her adolescent innocence and vulnerability.

Even more importantly, Franklin helps us understand adoption's aftermath: the undercurrent of regret, sorrow and guilt that birthmothers carry for submitting to closed records and permanent separation.

Franklin exposes the emotional toll of a particular American Era as well as its ongoing legacy. Rather than simplistically representing adoption as a social and moral good, she demonstrates the ongoing error of a heartless policy and its detrimental effects not just on birthmothers but on families: children, siblings, parents, and spouses.

—Janet Mason Ellerby, Author of *Following the Tambourine Man: A Birthmother's Memoir* (2007) and *Intimate Reading: The Contemporary Women's Memoir* (2001)

To my three sons — Chad, Jared, and Lee

TABLE OF CONTENTS

PART 2

PART 3

Part 4

Part 5

Part 6

ACKNOWLEDGEMENTS

Among those who have contributed to this book, I count friends and members of valuable organizations, including Concerned United Birthparents, Post-Adoption Center for Education and Research (PACER), and American Adoption Congress, whose voices have informed, educated, and given me courage and motivation to share my own story. In addition, I have "met" dozens of first mothers and adoptees on Facebook and Twitter and learned from each of you.

I have benefitted from friendships and participation in my local Gold Country Writers' Group. Shelley Buck, Paul Comiskey, and Marianne Barisonek generously read and offered criticism on manuscript excerpts, as did numerous members of Gold Country Writers' weekly critique groups. Margie Yee Webb offered support in technology, helping me reach a wider audience. Friends, including Linda Ankeney, Janie Evans, Rose Kraft-Bo, Julia Mullen, Barbara Tellman, Marcia Martin, and JoAnne Jones donated their hours reading and giving feedback on my story, as did other first mother authors, Carol Schaefer and Janet Mason Ellerby.

My book could not have begun without the searcher, Marilyn, who reached out to me. It may never have progressed without the support of the caring post-adoption social worker, Cathy. They have generously allowed me to share portions of their emails, as have my sons. Letters and email messages have been lightly edited for punctuation, clarity, and brevity.

I cannot overlook the value of my two editors, Rachel Howard and Margaret C. Murray. In Rachel's capable hands, my story became the right one to tell. My work with Margaret has been more in the nature of a needed knife to carve excess from my creative endeavor and reveal the essential story. While at times I've wished her knife to be less sharp, I believe she has made my story pop.

Most especially, I must thank my discovered son, Lee Yates, who both read and commented on my progress and who has allowed me to reveal some of his story in telling my own. My husband, Dave Judd, read and gave more positive feedback, on multiple manuscript versions, than I could possibly deserve. I am indebted to all of my family members whose stories are featured in this book – Chad, Jared, Lee, Terra, Maddie, Gwen, Marcia, Ellen Kaye, Judy Ellen, Stephen, and Dave.

Other than the use of names with permission, all other names have been changed or restricted to non-identifying first names. Any similarity to other persons is coincidental and unintentional.

PREFACE

Almost two decades ago, I began writing to help me release the overwhelming feelings I experienced upon discovering that my son I'd given up for adoption thirty-five years before was alive. That discovery opened a deep well of feelings I had buried in order to survive his loss. The journal I began then transformed into this story.

I became driven to reconnect with him. I opened to the world of what is known as the adoption triad – the birth family, adoptee, and adoptive family. I became aware that the voices of original mothers such as myself are rarely heard. Our pain is easy to ignore and discount. I hope my readers, within and out of the adoption triad, will gain appreciation for the perspectives of mothers like myself, many of whom still do not know if their children are dead or alive.

Many women of my era faced pregnancy crises, though not all lost their children to adoption. Many hurriedly married and raised their children. Some pursued then illegal abortions. Yet they also faced painful choices within the then unbending expectations of family, culture, and society.

Younger women today may know little about the limits of that earlier time. Yet they too are caught in a maelstrom of differing views and opportunities for women. I hope my story may inform them to protect their rights, hard-fought and gained.

My title, *I'll Always Carry You,* contains multiple levels of meaning. We mothers are said to carry our babies during pregnancy. We parents carry our children in our hearts forever. A client once shared a beautiful proverb with me: "When our children are little, they sit on our laps. When they're grown, they sit on our hearts." How much more this is true for first/birth mothers whose adoption loss is wrapped in grief and often carried in secret.

But connections between mother and child are even deeper than we know. Scientists now know that mother and child are linked at the cellular level[1].[2] Fetal cells cross the placenta, allowing our babies' DNA to become part of our bodies. These fetal cells are not only circulating in our blood; they are embedded in our brains, often for a lifetime. They can migrate to various areas in our bodies needing help to repair tissues, heal heart damage, stem cancer tumor growth, and even reduce the likelihood of Alzheimer's disease. In other circumstances, these cells may set off undesired autoimmune reactions as well.

Now we know that even when our babies leave our bodies, we mothers carry their traces. Is it any wonder we never forget them or completely recover from their loss?

What should we call a mother like myself? Since I first discovered support through Concerned United Birthparents, I applied their label of "birthmother" to myself. I have since learned that many others prefer to call themselves "first mothers," "natural mothers," "real mothers," "mothers of loss," or simply "mothers." It appears to me that there are no labels that will not be felt as an affront to someone in the adoption triad. The public recognizes the term "birthmother" to describe a woman who gave birth to and did not raise her child. The fact that I did not raise the child I gave birth to is the source of deep sorrow for me, but the use of the term "birthmother" neither causes nor worsens that pain. It is also true that I am my son's first mother, so I have decided as much as possible to refer to myself and others in this story as first/birth mother or simply birthmother when needed.

---

1 Laura Grace Weldon, "Mother & Child are Linked at the Cellular Level", June 12, 2012, *lauragraceweldon.com*, https://lauragraceweldon.com/2012/06/12/mother-child-are-linked-at-the-cellular-level/.

2 Robert Martone, "Scientists Discover Children's Cells Living in Mothers' Brains," *Scientific American*, December 4, 2012, https://www.scientificamerican.com/article/scientists-discover-childrens-cells-living-in-mothers-brain/.

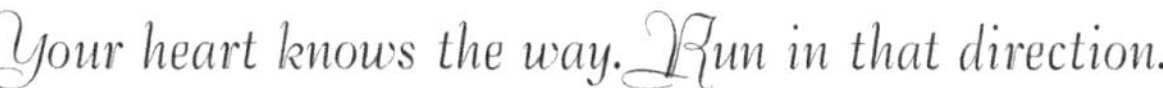

Your heart knows the way. Run in that direction.

—Rumi

PART 1

1

JARED STARTED IT

These pains you feel are messengers. Listen to them.

—Rumi

APRIL 7TH, 2000

My son, Jared, and I cram into our American Airline seats. The stewardesses scurry up the aisles, adjusting luggage in the overhead compartments and snapping them closed. Jared buckles his 300 pound, 5' 9" heft into the window seat while I squeeze into the middle seat. I'll have to struggle over the woman on the aisle to make my way to the bathroom.

Jared will probably doze and not want to chat a lot; so, I've decided to write the letter I'll bring to the post-adoption social worker during our five-hour flight to Texas. Under my eyelids, I sneak a peek at my aisle mate. She is at least twenty-five years younger than my five-and-a-half decades, with a face that appears untroubled. I make a quick decision not to strike up a conversation. My abdomen tightens at the thought of her peeking over my shoulder while I write. This young woman can't imagine the world I felt trapped in before she was born or the shame that still keeps me locked in its grip.

I turn and look past Jared out the tiny window. There's the Northern Sierra Nevada mountain range rising 7,000 feet to rim the Central

California Valley. I've loved trekking up and down many of the challenging trails, often washing away dust and sweat at the trail's end in a frigid lake. But today the craggy peaks show rough and sharp-edged.

What am I getting myself into?

A memory, the loneliness of lying flat on the hard labor table staring up at the dark ceiling, trembles through me.

I glance toward Jared and notice him smiling. His characteristic sweet smile curves like a crescent moon. He's happy I invited him to accompany me on this rare trip to Texas. The sun coming in behind him on the plane makes his curly brown hair gleam. He was always sensitive, but now there's an innocence engendered by his disease that slowed his thoughts and words yet made his heart more visible. Despite or maybe because of his chronic disability, Jared has the facility seen in children that points to the essence of truth. Only Jared would have encouraged me to come back home to Texas to begin this search.

It was January 2000, only a few months ago, and Jared and I were at home in Davis, California when he asked me, his olive-skinned face immobile, "Why don't you look for my brother?"

With his flat expression, he might almost have been inquiring about the weather. I'd stood frozen, staring at his penetrating green eyes. There was only one time I'd told him and his older brother Chad about my firstborn, and that was twenty years ago.

Jared, always slow to speak, just waited and watched me. My special, most vulnerable son had just dropped a bombshell. A faint image of the baby I'd seen only once, decades before, burst into memory, while my mouth clamped tight like a rusted hinge on a tiny coffin.

Adrenaline rushed through my body. Had I failed Jared by not searching for his brother? Had I let myself down as well? Maybe I'd done more than conceal my lost son. Maybe I'd buried a vital part of myself along with him.

I looked at the clock. Four-thirty, it said. I decided it wasn't too early to pour myself a screwdriver cocktail. When I returned from the kitchen, Jared hadn't moved.

"Why should I look for him?" I asked at last, holding my drink and my breath.

Jared's voice came back clear and definite. "Because you'd be a good mother for him to know."

Tears sprang to my eyes. Tears of gratitude at his praise choked me. The loss of his brother must have been on Jared's mind all these years. All of the dedication and support Dave and I gave Jared had paid off. Serious, intense, his expression pinned me on a knife's edge.

"Maybe he wouldn't want to know me," I finally replied. "Maybe he wouldn't like me. I don't know. Maybe I'd just upset his life." I didn't relay my other, worse fear. Maybe he inherited schizophrenia like you. What if I found another disabled son? Could Dave and I handle that?

Yet Jared's question pushed open the door to my past, just enough for me to squeeze through. I can't let it slam shut again. I have to dare. I have to find out if my son still lives. What is his name? Where is he? How can I reach him? Maybe I could meet him. Maybe I could get to know him.

I can't stop until I find what I lost.

The plane lurches into turbulence and the 'Fasten Seat Belt' light blinks on. I grip the armrests and reach beneath my feet to pull out the packet of paper I've brought with me. The seatbelt digs into my stomach. I had better write the best letter of my lifetime.

But how to write this "message in a bottle" and how long will it float after I leave it in the murky ocean of the Gladney Center for Adoption, which I knew back then as an unwed mothers' home? It will probably be yellow with age if my firstborn son ever sees it. Still, my shaky hand poised over the paper, I begin.

"Dear Biological Son,

It is very hard to know how to begin this letter or even how to address you. After all, I saw you only one time and that was thirty-five years ago."

I look down at the nearly blank paper on my tray. My throat aches and a tense emptiness fills me. Still, I continue.

"I held you in my arms for only fifteen minutes."

I turn to stare out the tiny airplane window. Beside me, Jared's eyes are closed. He'd been a cuddly baby, quick to nestle his warm body into the curve of my arm. Would his brother have been the same? The nurse had brought him to me wrapped in blue flannel. His eyes were closed that morning, too.

I lean back in my plane seat and close my own eyes, remembering how the nurse had leaned over and gently rubbed his cheek. My baby opened his eyes. "He's just been fed," she told me. Wisps of dark hair stole from beneath his blanket.

I stare down at my empty hands, then pick up my pen with heavy fingers and write two more lines.

> "You were sleepy, and I remember you finally opened your eyes briefly. I looked down into the deepest blue eyes imaginable and you seemed to peer up into my hazel eyes."

Did that instant of eye contact create some unconscious connection for my baby as well as me? I doubt it. I am flying to leave a letter for a grown man who, as far as I know, may not even still exist. How strange that he may be carrying on a fully formed life somewhere while I, his mother, don't even know if he's alive.

Out the plane window, dark clouds scud across a gray sky, mirroring my recollection of the nurse reaching down to remove him from my arms.

"It's time to take him back to the nursery," she'd said. It was the only time I held my baby.

I watched as she carried him through the heavy wooden doors. They swung shut and he vanished, lost to me.

My throat squeezes the sob that threatens to escape. I cast a glimpse towards my seatmate, engrossed in reading a tattered copy of *Redbook*. With my sleeve, I rub away a tear and return to writing.

> "That is all the time we had together and perhaps it's all we ever will have. I am writing this letter not knowing if you will ever read it. I don't know if you will ever want to…or even if you are still out there somewhere. By the time you read it, if you do, perhaps I'll be gone."

Outside the airplane window, leaden clouds threaten an early-spring rain. We'll probably have a bumpy landing. Thinking of these memories I've closed off till now, I bite my knuckle. My stomach reels. What do I know of this lost son? Only those days inside me when he performed acrobatic feats beneath the coffee cup I held on my swollen belly, never knocking the hot liquid onto the carpet. We played Bridge together with the other girls in the Gladney apartment while their unborn babies tumbled too in their huge stomachs and Diana Ross crooned "Where Did Our Love Go?" from the little brown Philco radio. The Supremes harmonized behind her, singing our song as I hummed along.

Don't leave me, I begged my baby. Could he hear? Did he already know what I wouldn't admit, that I was going to let him go? Could some remnant of that 60's music reside in his subconscious? Did the accumulated, unspoken sorrow we four abandoned girls brought to the game permeate his cellular memory?

Perhaps he likes to play Bridge, I wonder?

I twist my legs in the cramped airplane seat, unable to get comfortable, as I imagine how my son, now grown, may feel. Maybe he thinks I abandoned him. What if he blames me?

Maybe if he hears how things were back then, he won't be angry at me.

I write more about myself, how I was only nineteen, a sophomore in college, grieving my mother's tragic death only a few months before, my grandmother's death shortly after. I was unable to turn to my father, always mentally unstable, and diagnosed after my mother's death with paranoid schizophrenia. I tell him of my lack of confidence in myself and in marriage. My parents had been so miserable together.

I don't mention that my baby's biological father abandoned me and encouraged me to give him up for adoption. I remember how impossible it seemed to consider bringing home my baby, how the shame of my unmarried pregnancy would have branded me, almost like the letter "A" the adulterer, Hester Prynne, was forced to wear for the rest of her life after having a baby out of wedlock in Nathaniel Hawthorne's *The Scarlet Letter*.

"It seemed unimaginable to present my father with a baby born 'out of wedlock,' as we said in those days."

I lean back in the airplane seat. My shoulders and chest feel weighed down like the lead-lined apron used when I have mouth X-rays at the dentist. I hear the Fasten Seat Belt sign coming on with a ping.

"Mom!"

Jared is pointing toward the aisle where the flight stewardess approaches. A red scarf tied around her neck, she leans over me to ask, "What would you like to drink?"

Did I not hear her the first time? "Oh, coffee," I say.

"Cream and sugar?" she asks.

"Yes, please. Sweetener if you have it."

"The yellow packet or the pink one?"

"Yellow."

Jared orders his favorite, Diet Coke.

I try not to spill the coffee when it arrives in its little white Styrofoam cup with the yellow Splenda packet. How complicated just to order a cup of coffee! How many ways can there be to imbibe carcinogenic chemicals while attempting to control my middle-aged waistline? If all of these diet drinks cause cancer, then I'll be gone if, or when, this letter I'm agonizing over ever reaches its intended recipient. I chuckle to myself in dark humor. Then, sighing, I return to my letter.

"Both my parents had very conservative ideas about premarital sex."

In case my son receives this, I need to write a compelling reason for him to return to my life. Our evangelical ministers told us Jesus had raised Lazarus from the dead after four days. Can I unearth him like Lazarus? Should I? If my child grew up in a strict religious environment as I had, maybe he'll judge me. Maybe his parents told him bad things about me.

Before stopping at Gladney, Jared and I are visiting my father again. No doubt he will welcome his favorite grandson. Instead of his usual endless criticisms and judgments, he shows a rare sweetness and even occasional light-hearted teasing with Jared. It's an affection he doesn't display with me, my sister, or brother.

A stewardess passes by, holding out the plastic bag for trash. I toss in my empty paper cup. These secrets I've been keeping for thirty-five years and the shame I've hidden behind are my trash. Aren't they the detritus of my painful past? I pick up my pen to tell my son how I released him for adoption as an "act of love," because I felt he needed something better than I could offer him then.

Maybe if the Supremes had warbled "Mommy, mommy, mommy; mommy, don't leave me," I could have found the strength to question if I must give up my baby. All those months in the unwed mothers' home, I'd ignored my inner voice trying to tell me this path was a mistake. Instead, I hoped somehow the moment of separation would never come. Plaintive feelings like an Irish blessing pour out in my next paragraph.

> "I hope you have had a good and happy life. I hope the parents who raised you were good to you and that you felt at home with them. I wish I knew more about you and that we could discover what we have in common. Perhaps someday we will."

I hope, I hope, I hope, I wish, I wish, I wish. I hope and wish so much for this stranger son. Will I ever find out the truth? My seatmate gets up to go to the restroom and I decide to do the same. Walking up the aisle, I glance at the other passengers dozing, reading, or watching a movie. No one else seems to be struggling.

How to describe the person I've become, how to convince my son I'd be someone worth knowing. Back in my seat, buckled up again, I take up my paper and pen. I tell him I now am married to a wonderful man who is an attorney and plays classical guitar and the violin. How I now have a happy life. How I became a Licensed Clinical Social Worker, have a job I enjoy at Kaiser in outpatient psychiatry, and always think of him when a client tells me they're adopted.

> "After a lot of struggles and mistakes, I have recovered from my own anxiety and depression."

Do I sound like someone he'd like? Could he understand those struggles and mistakes? I describe his two half-brothers, both of whom would like to meet him. Chad, thirty-one, who didn't go to college after high school, but has been one of his company's leading salesmen for several years and is the father of our darling five-year-old granddaughter, Terra Linda. Jared, twenty-nine, single, who works in construction labor and is a talented acrylics painter.

I pull out the pictures I've brought on the airplane to enclose in my letter. Jared's shows his full face like mine, green eyes close to my hazel ones. The curly ringlets that circle his face came from his father, as does his artistic temperament. His serious eyes fixed on the camera, he gazes out with his mysterious jumbled thoughts. It's Jared who seeks out family, calls every day, reports his latest activities, therapy groups, doctor appointments, medications, and painting projects.

Resting next to me, Jared opens his eyes, turns to look at his photo. "Are you giving my picture to my brother?" he asks.

"Yes, assuming he gets the letter. Is that okay?"

"Sure."

I pull out the photo of Chad, tall and slim, whose logical mind I can always count on to make sense of my emotional tangles. Chad stares directly at the camera with gray eyes, his blond hair falling all the way down to his shoulders. With his narrow face and strong triangular jaw line, he resembles his father, though he has my thick wavy hair and, when we're both in good moods, a wide smile. Chad wraps his arm around Terra with her blue eyes, red hair, and bright smile. Though Chad loves his partner, Marcia, it's his daughter who has captured his heart.

Then there's a picture of me and Dave with his short-trimmed beard and mustache, our arms around each other. Dave's ruffle of wavy hair curls on his neck and around his ears, circling his bald head. My dark wavy hair, maintained through Clairol, is not much longer than his. If these pictures reach my first son, will he recognize himself in my round face and the high cheekbones bequeathed by our Choctaw Indian great-grandfather?

I release a silent prayer and let my son know if he ever wants to meet us, we would all welcome him and his family members.

"If that never happens, please believe that I have always loved you and treasured your memory in my heart.

Love, Linda."

2

I BEGIN

Courage is resistance to fear, mastery of fear, not absence of fear.

—Mark Twain

JANUARY 2000

The mail arrives. In the clutch of bills, a corner of a glossy newsletter pokes out. I pull the Spring 2000 Gladney Newsletter edition out cautiously. I feel my heart race as usual and a vague pain through my chest, even though I've been receiving Gladney's newsletter ever since our visit in 1980.

I poke my hand into the glossy tri-fold paper and a loose staple embeds itself in my index finger. "Ouch!" A drop of blood collects from the prick. A memory flashes, the heavy pads I wore between my legs after giving birth.

The Edna Gladney Home for Unwed Mothers was what it was called when I went into hiding there in June,1964. I knew nothing of the history then, but later I learned that the Center in Fort Worth, Texas began in the 1880s to find homes for children sent across the country on what became known as "orphan trains." Edna Gladney's name became enshrined after she expanded to include services for unwed mothers and adoption for their babies. She was credited with the permanent placement of ten thousand babies. In 1941, MGM released a movie about her life, "Blossoms in the Dust," which received an Academy Award nomination for Best Picture of the Year. Many years later, I watched the touching story of Edna Gladney helping illegitimate children, presumably orphaned or abandoned by their mothers, receive happy adoptive homes.

By 1964, Edna Gladney was no longer there and Executive Directorship had passed to Ruby Lee Piester, who in 1980 would help to form the National Council for Adoption, with founding goals included to prevent opening of sealed adoption records retroactively and resisting allowing birth mothers at least two weeks before signing adoption relinquishment papers, even though these had been recommended as state models for adoption by an Advisory Panel of the US Department of Health, Education, and Welfare.[3] During Ruby Lee Piester's period at Gladney, she supervised the placement of seventy-six hundred babies. One of them must have been mine. Had she admired his little rosebud mouth? Probably not.

One of Ruby's social workers would have brought my tiny boy in to the prospective parents. I imagine him wrapped in the same blue flannel blanket as the one time I held him, his new parents sitting in the social worker's office dressed in their Sunday go-to-church clothes, nervous, palms a little sweaty, older than me. The worker hands him to the mother first. "Oh, he's so precious," she coos. She gawks at his round face, his dark hair, his eyes so blue. "He's beautiful." She turns to her husband to show him his new son. That father is tall, clean shaven, his hair brushed back, a whiff of Brillantine drifting from his scalp. He smiles at his wife, pleased she'll be a mother now. His hands shake just a tad as he reaches to trace a finger across my baby's forehead.

My baby.

Drops of blood continue to well from my finger as I examine "The Gladney Center for Adoption," newsletter. A new name with

---

3 "Mission, History," *National Council for Adoption*, Accessed Feb. 18, 2019, ttps://www.adoptioncouncil.org/who-we-are/mission

an admirable ring for a couple hungry for a baby and eager to trust the adoption services.

To me, even the word 'adoption' seems dangerous, as if saying it sends tiny slivers of glass into the sensitive tissues in my mouth. Ever since I'd given up my baby, that's how I'd treated adoption, wanting to eliminate the word from my vocabulary. Some of my professional colleagues specialized in adoption, but I never did. I passed by a lawyer's sign advertising "Adoption Services" once and wanted to kick it down.

One time at Kaiser Permanente Hospital, where I treated outpatients as a therapist in the psychiatry department, a social worker from California Child Protective Services gave us a training presentation. After telling us how stressful it was to work with cases of child abuse, she declared: "Most of my employees don't stay long. They go to work for something happy, like adoptions."

Happy! My colleagues chuckled in agreement, while my jaw tensed. I wanted to blurt out that their picture of adoption, the one with the happy couple receiving the fortunate baby, left out the mothers like me who'd given birth, given them up for adoption, and never seen them again. My picture had a dark empty cutout space where my baby would have been.

I made a fast retreat to my office and hid from my co-workers that day. To me, adoption was like a ferocious dog let off its leash. It might appear friendly, but if you got too close, it could lunge at you, dig sharp teeth in, and rip out a piece of your tender flesh. One of my colleagues, an Asian woman, had adopted a baby girl from China. Someone asked her what happened to the "real mother." "I'm the real mother," she pronounced, her voice sharp. I kept silent.

On the front page of the Newsletter is a picture of a girl about nineteen, the age I was when I entered Gladney. She is smiling broadly. Her face, framed by black hair falling down her shoulders, is unlined. In her hands, she clutches a pink plush pillow.

Beneath the picture is her testimonial. "I'm happy I made the right decision for everyone and didn't think only of myself."

Yes, that's "the loving thing" we were supposed to do. I did what the social workers told me. I bought the party line that my baby needed a mother *and* a father, and it would be wrong of me to keep it.

But did the neatly-dressed, young women social workers at Gladney think of what I would suffer? Their ring fingers sparkled with gold bands and diamonds and framed pictures of their children decorated their desks. How could they have imagined I'd ever forget?

I'd never been given a pink plush pillow to hold. They gave our babies to someone else to hold and praised us for not thinking only of ourselves when we let them do it.

Well, they didn't exactly *give* them to the new parents. Those adoptive parents paid a small fortune. They didn't call that selling babies, though.

How much did my baby cost? I hope it was a lot.

On the back page of the Gladney Newsletter, I am surprised to find an article about a Post-Adoption Department that now helps women who gave up their babies in the past. I never dreamed they might offer ongoing help to birth mothers.

I only have a vague memory of one phone call from some social worker at Gladney a month or two after I left.

"How are you doing?" I recall her asking.

Feeling numb and disconnected, I croaked out a lifeless sounding "Okay." When the phone call ended, I wandered listlessly over to the refrigerator and stared at the contents. The thought of food repulsed me.

I might have told the caller from Gladney that anxiety held me in its tight grip, as if a thick rubber band clenched my stomach tight. I might have said I looked good without that pooched out fat tummy that most women have after giving birth. I might have asked about my baby, but I didn't. I had sunk into a hole too deep to plumb, even if I'd been able to fathom what words I might have said.

In the newsletter today, a photo of a genial looking woman with curly dark hair and plastic framed eyeglasses looks at me. Cathy Bowman is her name, a Post-Adoption Social Worker. The thought of contacting Gladney again sends ripples of anxiety down my body and makes my limbs twitch, as if I've had too much caffeine. But maybe things have changed.

During my 1980 visit, the social worker informed me Gladney had developed an internal registration process where I could register. My son could also register when he turned eighteen. If both of us registered with contact information, Gladney might put us in touch with each other. I sent away for the paperwork then and I learned that a notary public had to verify my identity. Shock and shame stopped me in my tracks. Who would falsely claim an identity as a birth mother anyway? For two years, I imagined the notary's disapproving expression before I finally screwed up my courage, got the paperwork notarized, and mailed it off.

Once my son and I registered, Gladney required that we each have a counseling appointment before they'd give us identifying information. What if the counselors decided we weren't ready to meet? Would Gladney refuse to give me my son's name then? Where did their control end?

After these brief attempts to reconnect with my past in 1980, I'd done what most of my therapy clients did with traumatic memories—compartmentalized, poked, pushed, and shoved them into the deepest part of my psyche where I barely noticed them. Even though I'd spent six months in my own therapist's office sobbing through the clinical hours, grieving my childhood pain, I'd managed never to mention my lost son.

I look at Cathy Bowman's picture again. She has a nice smile. The article says she welcomes calls from birth mothers. I see her phone number. Taking the newsletter into my cluttered office, I lay it on top of the paper pile. It's too late to call Texas today. Tomorrow morning, I'll call Cathy to see what she's like. I can always change my mind.

Tonight, I'll watch an old movie with Dave and cuddle Girlie, my gray cat, while we hold hands.

3

TAKE A CHANCE

Perhaps it is better to wake up after all, even to suffer, rather than to remain a dupe to illusions all one's life.

—Kate Chopin

JANUARY 2000

I hear, "Hello, this is Cathy Bowman."

I take a deep breath and draw myself up. "Hi, Cathy. My name is Linda Franklin. I saw in the Gladney newsletter that you're the Post-Adoption Social Worker."

"Yes; how can I help you?" Cathy's voice sounds congenial, warm, and concerned. I also hear a hint of firmness.

I push the words out and then hold my breath. "I had a baby at Gladney in October 1964. I'm wondering if I might be able to find him. Or at least maybe find out more about him."

"Well, I can try to help you," Cathy answers. "I work with lots of women who are still having a hard-time decades after relinquishing their babies."

Other mothers have a hard time with this, too? Cathy, a social worker like me, sees this. My twenty years of professional education and experience make me want to challenge her. We're supposed to help people. If Cathy sees how damaging adoptions are to first/birth mothers, how can she keep working in the place that does them?

But Cathy sounds caring. I need her help. I mustn't challenge her. I know the rules. In 1964, we girls did what we were told. We didn't ask questions.

I remember my first interview at Gladney.

"You won't use your real name here," Mrs. Lewis explained. "All our girls have aliases they don't reveal to each other. What would you like to be called?"

I was stumped. Words that began with F ran through my mind. Findley, Fawcett, Fussbudget. She looked at me expectantly. "How about Farris?" she suggested.

"OK, sure," I agreed. Back then, I was innocent and compliant.

I went along with a system that thrived on secrecy, even outright lies. My baby received the name of the people who adopted him. A false name; not his original name. Even the laws on adoption created a lie and called it legal. The birth certificate would have been amended to show his adoptive parents had given birth to him.

"I'd like to find out anything you can tell me about my son," I tell Cathy.

"I can't really tell you anything," she replies. I expected this, though I don't believe her. I listen for sounds of her fingers tapping the keyboard or rifling through cabinets for facts about my son. Hmmm, records from 1964. Where would they be?

Cathy continues, "However, a law has been passed in Texas requiring adoption agencies to pass on medical information provided by birth parents."

I press my palm against my cheek and lean into Cathy's voice on the receiver in my other hand. "Do you mean I can write a letter to my son with medical information and you'll have to get it to him?" I can feel blood rushing through me.

Cathy hesitates, "Yes, I'll try to pass along any medical information you give me, but you need to understand I know nothing about your son's or his adoptive parents' whereabouts. I may not be able to find them."

Can I write an entire letter? How long? How much can I tell him? I draw a deep breath and rise taller in my swivel chair. "Well, can I include personal information? Maybe even pictures?"

"Yes," she replies. "Of course, we don't know if he'll want to receive a letter, but if we can locate him, I can offer it to him."

I feel as if I could almost jump up and whoop, but I swallow my shout. "Okay," I tell Cathy. "I'll be visiting my father in North Texas in four months. Can I bring you my letter?"

"Yes; I'll be happy to meet with you."

I could tell Cathy cared. She was a professional who used the laws and policies to do whatever she could to help struggling first/birth mothers. I could also tell that if my first son turned the letter down, she wouldn't encourage him to change his mind. She wouldn't try to persuade him. She'd respect his wishes above everything. As a social worker and now a psychotherapist myself, I know this is her proper role.

But back in 1964, the social workers told *us* what to do. They didn't offer *us* choices. They never suggested we could change our minds. We'd be selfish to keep our babies.

That was different. That was then. My heart speeds up, resentment and longing in tandem. I ask more questions. I'm not ready to hang up. Even though Cathy said she knew nothing of my son, I feel as if she has some magical connection to him. She is the umbilical cord. She holds the key to his identity. My son, if he lives, would now be a full-grown man of thirty-five. Yet the laws allow Cathy to know his name and deny it to me. Bitterness gnaws at me.

Being honest with Cathy, even over fifteen hundred miles of phone line, though painful, feels healing. The secrecy I've lived in for so long hides my long-ago loss. My husband Dave, sensitive and supportive, never brings up my lost son. It seems only Jared thinks about him and cares the most.

"Feel free to call me anytime," she offers.

Her parting words reverberate. My scabbed-over wound scratches open and I feel Cathy wanting to pour soothing balm on it. A part of me longs to let her; but a bigger part does what I usually do, retreats into distrust and vague anger.

Can I really accept help from what feels like the enemy camp? I doubt it.

4

TIME FOR CHANGE

Only I can change my life. No one can do it for me.

—Carol Burnett

1979

Training as a master's level social worker requires a lot of self-assessment. My three years in grad school felt like three centuries of personal development. After learning about assertiveness, setting limits, boundaries, communication skills, self-esteem development, conflict resolution skills, parenting skills, and recovery from codependency, I realized it was time for major changes at home. I hoped Don would want to work with me to create a faithful, sober, stable, and healthy home life for us and our children.

Choosing Don was the first indication of how my own adoption loss would influence later family choices; what I began to see as having caught and spread the "adoption virus."

Don, the kinky-haired, fun-loving man I married, not comprehending that his playfulness disappeared into gloom when not fueled by alcohol or marijuana. The husband I spent eleven tumultuous years with, swinging from intense love, joy, and passion to equally intense rage and conflict, exhausting us both.

In kindergarten, Don taught Jared to draw cartoons featuring rabbits and monkeys. Later, painting vivid flowers and jungle scenes caught Jared's imagination. In a street mural done through Turning Point Foundation for mentally ill clients, a local newspaper article featured Jared's charming green frog, his painting so much more expressive than any words.

The fact that we had both lost sons to adoption was part of the glue that attracted and bound Don and me. Don's first son had disappeared into adoption when Don was only fifteen. He got his girlfriend pregnant again, and though she kept that son, their parents refused to allow them to marry. The unspoken commonality Don and I shared was grief. Our lost-to-adoption sons became the ghosts in our family life, dragging unrecognized depression in their wake.

It turned out that Don wasn't interested in making changes - at least not with me. Right after I received my master's degree in 1979, we split up. I thought it was the worst thing that had ever happened, but after six months of heavy depression and therapy, my darkness began to clear. I realized it might be the *best* thing that had happened to me.

If I'd had family support, I'm sure we'd have separated sooner, but with my mother deceased and my father abusive, I felt I had nowhere to go. Now I realize I did have options, but then all I saw was subjecting myself and Jared and Chad to our chaotic, conflict-laden marriage. That had done us no good at all.

I bought a low-maintenance home with an indoor atrium and a Japanese garden, obtained a professional position with a living wage, and set out to make a better life for myself and our children who visited Don regularly, moving between two homes. I struggled with loneliness when they were with him and the new family he soon started. When they were with me, though, I started a ritual after work. It began at the kitchen counter. Before chopping and sautéing, I turned to my clamoring boys. "You first, Jared; how did your day go?" After discussing Jared's day, I turned to Chad. The next night, Chad came first.

Still, too many evenings I arrived home to find peanut butter smeared on the counter and ice cream melting down the cabinets. A friend suggested I draw up a list of chores with promised payment schedules for each.

"From now on, when you want money for a movie, you can earn it," I told Chad and Jared, showing them how much they could earn for daily, weekly, or monthly chores. Next time Chad asked for cash, I pointed to the chart. Soon after, I came home and found Chad wearing my paisley apron, the counters spotless, and a broom in his hand.

Jared got into the act. "What a good job you did cleaning the bathroom!" I encouraged him. "The toilet and sink look great! Maybe just wipe that corner a little more and it will be perfect!" What a change from my usual complaints! Now we could all feel good about positive things! I loved the looks of satisfaction on the boys' faces and sometimes even threw in an extra dollar for a Coke for a job especially well-done.

I learned to lower my voice to a whisper instead of raising it to a yell whenever our feelings grew heated. Both kids approached closer. It was far more satisfying than their former high-speed escapes from my attempts to impart parental wisdom.

The condition of our house and our relationships improved. I was making progress at raising future housekeepers, but Chad decided attending school was not in his plans. He had scored at a twelfth-grade level on the SAT given to all 7th graders. Chad, who had loved pre-school and found all the next grades boring, concluded he knew enough. High school became irrelevant to him.

In the mornings, I hurried off to my crisis caseload at Alta California Regional Center while the crisis at home built. "Get up!" I exhorted him. Chad lay prone on the mattress he'd put on the floor. I vacillated between being the extra-nice parent and punishing him, locking his stereo in the trunk of my car to deprive him of his heavy metal music while truant.

Nothing worked. Every day, my sense of helplessness grew.

One morning, Chad emerged from his bedroom in white Boxer briefs carrying a load of Legos. Evidently, he had plans for his day. He and I bumped into each other in the hall. His Legos scattered into a shamble of sharp-edged red, yellow, blue, and green squares and rectangles on the floor.

"Pick these up!" I demanded. He crouched down to gather the Legos. Gazing at his vulnerable back, his beautiful torso, his blond hair falling onto his straight spine and angular face, my heart softened. I bent down to help. I wanted to be gentle with my beloved fifteen-year- old son. But gentleness only supported the poor decisions he was making.

My voice tightened into the tone of tough love I'd learned. "All right, Chad. You get over to school today -- not tomorrow; today! Find out how you get back into classes. Either that or pack up and get out! If you don't need to go to school, you can get a job and take care of yourself somewhere else."

When I got home that night, Chad had registered for continuation high school, where it turned out he thrived, earning credits independently.

Then thirteen-year-old Jared, my talented cartoonist, began falling behind in academics. Jared had always been closer to his father, Don, while Chad got the lion's share of my attention. Jared had so many years of being the quiet younger brother, so affected by the verbal battles between Don and me. As a baby, Jared had been an early talker, speaking in whole paragraphs by a year and a half. Then, something changed. By three years, his language became halting. Yet it was Jared in second grade who stared at the stuck curtain rod in his classroom and then showed his teacher how to fix it.

Now every night Jared's middle-school teacher called to report a new problem and exhort me to be a better parent. Her tone of voice suggested Jared's problems must stem from presumed parental indifference.

"Ask him how his day went!" she advised. "Show him you're interested."

"I do!" I assured her. "He won't tell me. He walks away and hides out in his room. If I follow him, he refuses to answer." I pictured my curly-haired son with the hooded eyes, closing out my attentions. I felt my own deep sorrow.

The truth is that my attempts to listen to Jared's troubles usually failed. The same critical, judgmental words I'd heard from my own father came out in my voice all too often.

One day as Jared passed by, I was struck by his expression and stopped him. "Jared?" He raised his eyes to look at me from under his hoodie. I spoke slowly, softly, but deliberately. "Jared, you're just as important to me as Chad is."

Jared's face transformed somehow -- his cheeks, the lift of his forehead, the tightness of his jaw all softened. Dawning relief readjusted his features. "You matter to me just as much as he does," I assured him. His shoulders dropped. The set of his head on his neck straightened.

No miracles occurred after that. He continued to be withdrawn, seeming easily confused and overwhelmed. When he was younger, even an unexpected phone call would send him running to his room until one day I pointed out whoever was calling couldn't hurt him through the phone and he could even hang up if he wanted. He'd been tested as superior in intelligence, but now his teacher complained he couldn't concentrate, couldn't keep up.

At the school district's White House Counseling Center, his therapist said he was depressed, which I didn't have any trouble believing. Her words repeated in my head as I lay awake at night reviewing my failures. How I wished I could go back and change the way things were with Don and me.

5

DAVE

Love cures people - both the ones who give it and the ones who receive it.

—Anonymous

1986

Dave and I became friends while working together for five years for the State of California before I resigned to attend graduate school. Then we re-discovered each other when I was divorcing in 1980 after graduate school and dated for a year and a half before breaking up under the pressures of my single parenting and Dave's entrance into night law school. During our year and a half of dating, I made sure not to count on him or let him have much say in my struggling little family. We spent four years apart, both of us trying out other relationships, until I read Jared's scrawled message on a piece of torn newspaper, "Dave called."

It was 1986. I'd never expected to see Dave again, though Jared and Chad hadn't forgotten the camping trips, the movies, and the dinners we'd shared before. Every time I drove over I-5 and passed his Northgate freeway exit, I wondered where and how he was, but I kept in mind his "rolling stone" reputation. Dave had never married or had children, and none of his friends expected he ever would. The chances that he'd stick with me and my kids reeling from one challenge to the next looked little to none.

Still, I was excited to return Dave's call. My stomach sank when he told me, "I'm relocating to Southern California to be closer to my aging parents and to start an international law practice. I wanted to tell you good-by."

We met for lunch at our favorite Whole Earth Restaurant. I made sure to look my best in my brown fuzzy dress with the blue silk sash. Dave showed up in his usual crisp dress shirt, slacks and polished loafers. I'd always liked that he'd been a good dresser.

While I barely nibbled on my vegetarian lunch, Dave and I reviewed all we'd gone through since our break-up. I felt we'd both grown. Perhaps we might be ready for a healthy relationship based on mutual maturity and trust. Certainly, the attraction, the chemistry we'd always had still sizzled between us.

The next few months, while we renewed our dating relationship, Dave continued to make plans to move. Well, if this is all I get, I told myself, I'm just going to enjoy it. Chad and Jared were happy to see Dave again. My family problems continued though. Jared wasn't doing better in the private school I'd enrolled him in. Neither Jared nor I understood the Scientology terminology they used. Chad continued to earn independent high school credits, but most of the day he was free to follow whatever undesirable opportunities presented themselves.

With my burn-out from a crisis caseload at work, continuing ex-husband conflict, and lack of extended family support, my challenges seemed never-ending -- poor grades, discouraging teachers, principals who predicted the worst, indications of drug use, bad examples from my kids' friends with even worse problems. I dropped a hint to Dave. "Maybe it would be better to get them out of Sacramento."

Not long after, Dave took my hands in his. "I think we should all move down to Southern California, if you want to go."

"Yes, we'll come. Yes." I folded into his arms, ruffling his soft hair.

Dave's decision to take on my complicated family baggage was honed on the gritty stone of his disengaged family of origin that inspired his massive caretaking efforts. My great good fortune is that he turned those efforts on me, his pixie, as he fondly described me.

I learned Dave had grown up in a family of six, none of whom got the attention, support, and nurturing they needed. He wanted more connections with his nieces and nephew and siblings, but his now deceased parents set a family pattern of detachment that continued through the generations. He was cheated out of so many family connections.

His childhood, like mine, led him to adopt caregiving as a survival mode. Dave became an expert at supporting people in pain and I gave him plenty of opportunities to practice his craft.

He told me he saw no reason to bring more children into the world; certainly not his own. He inherited mine; a complicated brood indeed. Chad, the incipient outlaw who pulled Metallica and Iron Maiden muscle shirts over his slim, tall frame, wrapped leather, silver-studded bracelets around his wrist, and dyed his thick long hair a brassy, gorgeous gold. Chad's high school principal predicted a future for him of life in prison.

Jared's withdrawn, uncommunicative behavior made him hard to reach. No one yet understood that he had a serious brain disorder.

I packed up my brood and joined Dave in our little Los Angeles apartment. He'd stocked the fridge with a quart of milk, a small jar of peanut butter, a loaf of bread, one package of frozen vegetables, and a box of fish sticks. Gazing at my ravenous teenagers, I returned his warm hug and wondered if he had any idea what he'd gotten himself into.

The palm trees swayed in the ocean breeze in West LA, providing a soothing atmosphere, but Jared soon bombed out of his new school, resulting in calls from truancy officers, police, reports from Jared himself saying, "I wanted to buy marijuana from him, but he held a gun to my head." Finally, Jared's therapist recommended we send him to a residential treatment facility in Utah run by Mormons.

"He can't run away from there," the therapist assured us. "Not like residential in LA. He'd just hop on a bus here."

Jared, looking eager for a change, got on the plane and spent a year in rural Utah, where his excitement soon changed to disappointment. Still, he seemed to be improving, or at least safe. Meantime, Dave and I made a Thanksgiving trip in 1987 to Las Vegas, where we got married in the coral-colored room in The Chapel of Love.

After a visit home for Christmas, Jared went back to his previous high school. The school psychologist called me at work.

"Your son has schizophrenia. He's been hearing voices for years."

Schizophrenia – a neurobiological/psychological disorder usually characterized by auditory hallucinations, inability to separate reality from delusions, confusion, lack of motivation, inability to follow goal-oriented action or to experience pleasure, social withdrawal, inattention, apathy, and more.[4] These symptoms fit Jared. No wonder he hadn't done well for years and what were his voices telling him?

I closed my office door, roiled with shock. At least we had a diagnosis. I remembered how five-year-old Jared had shown me a little book he'd drawn one day, and I recalled puzzling at his words that seemed so profound. "Mom, sometimes I think life is a book and God is reading it to me." I also recalled how young Jared would suddenly burst out with piercing screams. What inner noises had he been trying to drown out?

Jared and I began weekly visits to Neuropsychiatric Institute of LA and anti-psychotic drugs he hated. There were psychiatric hospitalizations, six months at Camarillo State Hospital, board and care, home management, and enormous bills. Everything had to be prioritized around Jared's needs. Jared's seventh- grade teacher had described him as "an advanced self-taught artist," but three years later, he required heavy duty medications to quiet the voices in his head. His illness took all our energy and most of our money.

Dave, my endlessly supportive husband, and I have endured fourteen years of chronic crisis since Jared's diagnosis. Only recently has Jared become cooperative and medically compliant, allowing us to begin to focus on our other goals.

Dave, the "rolling stone," the one who never wanted kids, stuck with me and his two stepsons. He put aside his dreams of international law practice, shared his earnings and inheritance for Jared's care, joined in special education and private school meetings, and participated in multitudes of problems that arose with lack of services, unavailable

---

4 Dina Cagliostro, Ph.D., "Schizophrenia Symptoms and Diagnosis," *Psycom*, Accessed 2/19/19, https://www.psycom.net/schizophrenia

hospital beds, out-of-home placements, and drastically inadequate insurance coverage. He didn't turn away from Jared's pain or mine.

We'd had a plan for months to visit Kauai, but Jared seemed too sick to go. On the phone, I made desperate calls to the LA County Mental Health Crisis Team, begging for help to get Jared into the hospital. Dave was soothing Jared by helping him bake brownies. The chocolate aroma filled our apartment in the middle of our night's crisis, but the Crisis Team feared Jared was dangerous and wouldn't come. The Police Department said he *wasn't* dangerous, so they wouldn't come either. In the morning, Dave and I concluded it couldn't be any worse in Hawaii, so we dragged ourselves and Jared to the airport and boarded the Delta Flight. Dave and I had Scotch for breakfast and Jared stretched out across three seats and slept the whole way. When we returned, Jared's teacher said he wanted to send all his students to Hawaii. Jared was so much better.

Dave, the heart and spiritual seeker, the one who read Buddhist sutras on love and compassion and had received so little love himself growing up, stayed with me. We recognized our mutual childhood hungers for love and nurturing. We saw each other's maturity and wisdom struggling to emerge. We struggled to offer it to each other. Somehow, we held onto each other and held together onto something bigger than ourselves, believing love could hold it all together if we didn't give up.

Dave proved himself to be the "world's best stepfather" With his assistance, Chad, my rebellious teenager, turned from larceny to a legal, hard-working lifestyle. Chad referred to Dave as "a great stepfather." Jared, whose brain disease drained us emotionally and financially, became compliant and largely stable. When people asked if Dave had any children of his own, I only-half joked that "a Higher Power, probably a female one, cursed Dave and gave him mine." As the years have gone by, my sons *have* become Dave's family, too. They love and respect Dave.

There were times we barely made it. Dave tried the soft approach with both boys, and when that didn't work, he tried the strong "male" one. He and Jared got into a shoving match in our narrow apartment hall. Dave threatened Chad, saying nobody would care about him if Chad didn't show he cared about us. When Jared stole Dave's silver dollar coin collection to fund marijuana, he apologized. Dave forgave him. Chad started to help more, and Jared became more respectful.

In 1995, we relocated to Northern California, badly in need of financial security. Dave returned to his state job as a governmental program analyst and ultimately, an attorney. I closed my Southern California private psychotherapy practice and got employed at Kaiser Permanente Out-Patient Psychiatry Department as a psychiatric therapist. We bought a modest home in Davis and turned it into a cozy nest.

Chad married his girlfriend, Tonya, and they had our beloved granddaughter, Terra Linda. After they divorced, Chad and his new lady partner, Marcia, became the primary parents for Terra. I learned that Marcia was a first/birth mother who'd lost her daughter to adoption, too. "Marcia grew up in Texas. Her father was crazy, too," Chad told me.

"I was only fifteen, when I gave up my baby," Marcia told me. "Back then, I just thought it was a problem I had to get rid of, but now I wish I could find her."

One more connection to adoption. I felt my long-ago experience was sticking to me and my family.

6

BAD GIRLS

And the trouble is, if you don't risk anything, you risk even more.

—Erica Jong

APRIL 2000

For four months since talking to Cathy, I've felt lashed to a powder keg of dynamite that may injure me if it blows up and may hurt even more if it doesn't. Heavy ropes of hope, fear, and longing chafe and tie me in knots. I try to keep up with my demanding job, family, and friends, while thoughts of my upcoming planned visit to Gladney grip me. I obsess walking up the Kaiser Psychiatry Department halls to collect my psychotherapy patients. At home, I fight to stay focused on Dave while he talks about work and we prepare dinner. In phone calls with Chad or Jared, I try to concentrate on their news. Questions race through my mind like monkeys leaping from one branch to the next in a dark forest.

Will Cathy find my son?

Will he want my letter?

Will he like it?

Will he answer?

Is he even still alive!?

Back then, the sign read: The Edna Gladney Home for Unwed Mothers. That June 1964, I'd trudged up the hot concrete steps and tugged open the heavy door. Like the name, the building looked old-fashioned. Ornate trim dressed the upper story and the broad front girth and wide windows leant an imposing quality. The massive feeling that the building exuded seemed appropriate for the weighty secret I carried into it.

Back then, Gladney hid us mothers, really girls. "Bad girls;" that's what we were. "She's gone and gotten herself pregnant." That's how people talked about us then, as if it didn't take a boy at all. The father of my baby didn't have to sign any papers, didn't have to consent. Gladney didn't even ask his name. He was irrelevant. I gave away our son without a word from him, except to encourage me toward adoption. Adoption was Gladney's solution, too; the only one for the shame our whole culture tarred us with then.

Now I'll be meeting Cathy after visiting with my father and my brother, Steve. Even phoning Cathy felt like time travel back to a place it would be safer to avoid. What if my search proves as harrowing as my experience thirty-six years ago?

7

FRESHMAN YEAR

The only source of knowledge is experience.

—Albert Einstein

FALL 1962

When I began at East Texas State College as a freshman, I suddenly felt released from the unrelenting farm duties during my high school years, like a prisoner who's paroled, not fully free of the justice system but not behind bars either. Like a prisoner who has been over-controlled by harsh guards, I was ready to rebel from my mother's over-protectiveness and especially from the grim atmosphere created by my father.

Dating boys my mother would have called "wild," drinking beer they hid under blankets at loud football games and letting them touch me under those blankets seemed so exciting. I loved going out with a tall, dark-haired Phi Delta Theta fraternity boy and getting drunk on Everclear punch at his fraternity parties. I became the favored girlfriend of a sandy-haired, popular tennis player on campus. I relished the camaraderie with the other cloistered girls in our dorm when the housemothers ordered us to stay in our rooms and bolted the dormitory door, warning us against the hormone-crazed college boys outside intent on a panty raid. We peeked out our upper-story window at the clusters of laughing, bellowing boys and wished we could throw our pink, lace-trimmed panties out to them.

If my school friends from elementary and high school had seen me as the insecure goody-goody misfit I felt myself to be, my new college friends offered me a fresh start. That was the year I started to have fun for the first time. I loved being roommates with Ellen.

Ellen, slim with pale freckled skin and short red hair, was fun, friendly, and unabashedly sexual with her broad-chested West Texas boyfriend. I visited her home and practiced the 'barnyard dance' she taught me.

"You scrape first your left and then your right foot across the floor while you imagine sweeping cow patties out of the way," she explained, while her boyfriend, Dan, offered us swigs from the pint of Johnny Walker he kept tucked into his right back pocket.

I envied Ellen's good fortune in coming from the "wet" part of Texas where we could sneak a beer during the rodeo events that preceded the dance. The ice-cold beer seemed to cut through the congestion of white dust thrown up by the horses' heels as their slim riders chased after steers in the ring. The cattle tossed their heads, eyes bulging, trying to escape the riders' coiled, spinning ropes thrown over their heads.

"Billy Bob Murphy riding Apollo," blared the voice of the loud-speaker. "Three seconds and that steer is down!"

I was repressed, naïve, chronically anxious, quiet, studious, and gullible. Ellen was uninhibited and loved country music. Ellen told me about her sexual encounters with Dan and how to prevent pregnancy by douching with a Coke bottle filled with water. I wanted to be more like her. She seemed more interested in getting her M.R.S. degree than in worrying about the grades my mother wrote were important.

It was Ellen I wanted to be close to. In truth, I had a crush on her. She and I visited nearby small lakes, laying out our bright-colored towels on dry, gravel beaches. We had marathon study sessions, made possible by the "diet pills" the doctors gave out freely then. We compared notes on how little we'd eaten during these all-night stints and how flat our stomachs were as a result, then dashed to classes and filled in test answers with jumpy fingers and dry eyes.

On Sundays, we slept in and awoke ravenous at 4 p.m. Bed hair plastered to our heads, we'd take off to the Plantation Restaurant and gorge ourselves on platters of hot fried chicken, small ceramic bowls of canned green beans, corn niblets, and piles of mashed potatoes. We buttered the white rolls till they dripped yellow down our light, open-necked blouses.

Afterwards, we'd succumb again to our teenage bodies' cravings for sleep. Lying in our bunk beds, me on the lower and Ellen on the higher, night fell listening to the wails of George Jones' plaintive voice singing "She Thinks I Still Care."

My senior year of high school, our Howe Methodist Youth Fellowship group had made an epic trip to New York and Washington, D.C.

"Can I go?" I asked my mother, imagining my father's angry refusal to spend money. A few days later, my mother returned with good news. I could join my church group for the trip.

I flew in a jumbo jet for the first time, gazing down from the plane window awestruck at the lights of New York City stretching endlessly under the plane's wing. We visited Chinatown, the United Nations, and then the Russian Embassy in New York. We took the train to Washington, DC and visited the Washington Monument, the Lincoln Memorial, and the White House.

That year, Lyndon Johnson from our great state of Texas was Vice-President under President John Kennedy. Vice-President Johnson invited our church group to his impressive office. I stared at his craggy face, his bushy eyebrows over intense eyes. I had heard rumors about this powerful older man. "Let's line up for a picture before we leave," one of our leaders instructed. Johnson looked over to where I stood at the end of the front row.

"I want to stand next to that pretty one," he said, placing himself at my side as the camera clicked.

I discovered next fall it wasn't only Lyndon Johnson who thought I was pretty. Popular college boys who wanted to do more than stand by me asked me out. I finally grasped the latent power I had in my prettiness and burgeoning sexuality. Maybe I felt worthless inside, but they didn't know it. I needed to be wanted. My mother's letters exhorted me to preserve my virtue. "No good man will marry you if you're not a virgin," she warned me.

In the dorm, girls debated when to "go all the way." Many already had. We heard boys would make vulgar jokes about popping their girlfriends' "cherries." That freshman year, I let an insistent cowboy convince me to go all the way. Intimations of the illicit activities my mother counselled me against were mounting. I was discovering that they felt good. Still, after that, my freshman year, I limited my boyfriends to deep tongue kisses and heavy petting.

8

BACK HOME

In the little world in which children have their existence, whosoever brings them up, there is nothing so finely perceived and so finely felt, as injustice.

—Charles Dickens

APRIL 2000

At the foot of the escalator in the baggage claim area at the Dallas/Fort Worth Airport stands Steve, my brother, as tanned, slim, and muscular as he'd been when he was twenty. He seems the happiest I've ever seen him. He looks good wearing the jeans and plaid shirt he must have thrown on before dashing to his pick-up to come get Jared and me. With his thatch of blond hair and eye-catching features, everyone says he looks like Robert Redford. As Jared and I begin descending the airport escalator, Steve lifts his hand in a casual wave. I take a deep breath and pray the week will go well, or, at least not end up a catastrophe.

I know Steve has weathered a lot of disappointments. He'd wanted for a long time to return to farming. He'd gotten a degree in Accounting at North Texas State, but office work never suited Steve. Selling real estate in Denver had left him frustrated and dissatisfied. Now estranged from his former girlfriend and cut out of her son's life, I'm happy Steve can be back on the farm. "I couldn't come back to Texas until Daddy was too weak to get out into the pastures with me," he'd told me.

Steve turns off the farm-to-market road toward the house my father built and we grew up in. I glance toward the tumbling down old building on the corner that used to be the Cassidy Store. Before we were the first family in the area to get our own Philco television, we went to Cassidy's and sat on sweet-smelling hay bales to watch their black and white TV. Gathering with local men in overalls and work boots, their wives in house dresses and their excited children running around barefoot, thrilled me. I was sorry when my father brought home the big box and set up our own solitary 20-inch television.

Looking back, perhaps my father splurged on that revolutionary new device intending to please us kids. It sure made us happy those Saturday mornings spent lying prone on the carpet with our faces cupped in our hands to watch *Lassie* and *Sky King*.

As Steve drives the last mile on White Mound Road, I remember how the school bus used to drop us off at the Cassidy corner, then continue on its route. As we walked home, I'd searched the ditches for crimson and orange Indian Paintbrush, Bluebonnets, and Goldenrod wildflowers to clutch in my fist and take home to my precious mother. She'd put them in a mason jar of water, then hand me an ice-cold bottle of my favorite Hire's Root Beer. I'd force my tense jaw to open and let the sweet liquid ripple relief down my throat. I liked school, but many of my classmates jeered at my good grades and resented my Teacher's Pet status. I wished the teacher wouldn't put me in charge whenever she left the classroom. Once, I joined the other kids jumping out of our seats and chattering in a wild group. Mrs. Morton opened the door and remonstrated me. "Linda, I'm surprised at you!" I slunk back to my seat, my brief foray into childish hijinks squelched.

Approaching our house, I glance towards Steve and see his jaw tighten. Even with the cheerful jazz playing on the Sirius channel, seeing my father's John Deere tractor in the field causes a familiar dread to overwhelm me. I wonder if Steve feels the same.

My father is in his eighties now. Daddy recently spent a couple of weeks in the hospital after trying to castrate a bull calf in the field and being thrown violently to the ground. He lay in the pasture till help arrived. The doctor must have gotten fed up enough with Daddy's constant orders to have put him on an anti-depressant. Now Daddy sounds a little more docile, at least on the phone.

We pull up the gravel driveway to a cacophony of barking from Steve's German Shepherd and large white Great Pyrenees. "Hello-o-o," Daddy's gruff voice greets us as we drag suitcases up the concrete steps.

The metal porch door bangs our arrival. My father's pink face is still smooth above the rosy triangle below his throat where the sun had outlined the V-neck of his shirts during those stifling days bouncing on the tractor seat.

My father leans over the washing machine that sits at the boundary of the kitchen and the living room. He points the TV remote toward the now 40-inch RCA television blaring a football game. Avoiding eye contact, he directs his eyes to the game, clicking the remote from one station to the next.

"What's Chad up to?" Daddy asks. "How's Terra?"

"Terra's doing well," I tell him, "growing up fast."

"That girl's smart," he pronounces.

He doesn't ask about me. I don't volunteer. Once, when I told him I'd been hired for my first master's level social work job, he'd blurted, "Why would they hire *you*?"

Daddy turns his attention to the football game. "Get Jared something to eat!" he orders. The subtle softening in his voice signals he is as close as he ever comes to joking. "That boy looks hungry!" He smiles a rare mischievous smile and points at Jared, who flashes a smile back.

It seems whenever I walk past Daddy sprawling in his electric recliner in the living room, he barks orders. "Linda, get me the newspaper." "Take this dish." "Ah, run the dishwasher." "Warm up this coffee." "Did you get me some bread?" He's never smiling. I hold back my irritation, not wanting to make any waves, trying to maintain the peace with him and my brother.

Growing up, Daddy was always impatient. "Hurry! Hurry! Hurry!" and "Let's go! Let's go! Let's go!" my father shouted. Like a garden hose stuck on "jet," his orders were a continual stream of pressure. Every night I dreaded his clomping onto the porch, throwing his raggedy straw hat and leather work gloves onto the clothes dryer, and tramping into the kitchen in his bib overalls. I watched my mother's face tighten and knew she felt the same, both of us searching for clues to forecast Daddy's mood by paying attention to his scowl, how tightly drawn were his eyebrows, how grim the line of his mouth.

One night, when I was four or five, I forgot to pay attention. My Crayolas and coloring book were spread out on the maple kitchen table where I perched on bare knees in the chair, coloring. My father's beefy hand swept across the table with no warning, scattering the wax crayons onto the linoleum floor. My mother, in front of the stove, stood frozen until Daddy stomped past. "Get down and pick them up," she spoke, her voice low and cautious.

Not long after, I found my mother standing at the yellow Formica counter dusting flour and patting out soft biscuit dough. "Mama, why is Daddy so mean?" I asked.

I still can see the concern etched in her face. She paused, wiping her hands across her apron. "Because he's sick," she replied, her eyes trained on mine.

Jared and I inch through the six-day visit. One night I walk barefoot into the kitchen and almost step on a scorpion whose waxy translucent body and curled tail are almost invisible on the beige linoleum. Another time my father surprises me as I bring him dinner, raising his hand and clasping mine, squeezing it in a wordless gesture of affection.

Steve hurries in and out to the fields to look after crops and cattle. One day he drives me to the pasture. His pick-up jounces and bounces over the uneven hillocks. Round green patches dot the grass where cattle urinated. Steve jumps out to open the barbed wire gate that confines his huge shaggy bull whose clipped horns stick straight out over big ears from which dangle yellow tags. The bull and I stare at each other until I feel my bladder about to give out.

"Sorry, Steve, but I really need to go pee!"

"Go ahead. He won't hurt you."

I'm not so sure. I climb down from the high seat and circle to the other side of the pick-up, while Steve keeps watch.

"How much do bulls cost, Steve?" I ask as we leave.

"Too much," he says, "Three to five thousand isn't uncommon." He lowers his head, twists it to the side, and raises it again. I remember I've watched him make this neck motion for thirty-seven years, ever since he smashed face-first into the steering wheel, driving Mama in the accident that killed her.

What does my brother think about out here all day alone?

9
HORROR

When death comes it is never our tenderness that we repent from, but our severity.

—George Eliot

MAY 1963

Two teenage boys my family knew, Jerald Smithson and Sam Williams, decided May 13th to amuse themselves by racing their cars up a country road near our family home.

My mother and Steve had gone to Aunt Martha's and Uncle John's house to get a puppy from their litter to bring home. Steve was driving. Sam's vehicle sped by my brother's blue Plymouth, throwing up a thick screen of dust and wiping out visibility. My brother, who had swerved toward a ditch's edge, pulled back onto the gravel road. The impact of the second car, Jerald's '57 Chevy, on Steve's caused the front seat to come loose and fly forward into the dashboard. Steve's jaw was broken and his neck torqued, but the steering wheel protected his upper body. My mother, in the passenger seat, pitched forward and was impaled on the twisted metal of the mangled dashboard.

I hope Mama was cuddling that furry puppy when she was thrown violently into the dashboard. I hope his warm body was her last conscious memory.

The day before, Sunday, May 12th, was Mother's Day. I'd visited Mama that day. The next afternoon, my father called me at my dorm, "There's been an accident. It's pretty bad."

My first sight of Wilson N. Jones Hospital was flower beds of star-petaled white vinca glowing under street lamps, which struck me even at that moment as beautiful. A perky young woman in a white cap directed me to my father waiting in surgery. Daddy, who would turn forty-nine in three days, looked ten years older than yesterday. When I offered to get him some coffee, he snapped, "You don't need coffee!" I stiffened before asking a few cautious questions. We waited until a doctor pushed open the panel door at the end of the room. I knew by the professional look of compassion on his face that the news was bad.

For a few minutes, Daddy and I stood next to Mama in her hospital bed as she tossed and twisted in a thin sheet, grunting "uh, uh, uh" over and over, her face bloodless gray and crisscrossed with the scars the surgeons had sewn, each individually knotted with stiff black thread, the ends poking up like whiskers.

A machine with shining red lights and jagged blue lines at the foot of the bed began a rapid beeping. The lines were leveling out. It was the hospital staff who had the last moments with my mother, in some strange attempt to spare my father and me, though I did not want to leave. When the doctor emerged into the hall, saying, "I'm sorry. We couldn't save her," I went numb, somehow remaining erect leaning against the wall. My father managed to drive the ten miles home.

Entering the house, I passed each object in the kitchen: the maple table waiting to be set by Mama, the Woman's Day article opened where she'd been reading it, her limp housedress laid across the washing machine. I looked for her to come from the living room.

"I was worried about you," she'd say, relieved we were home, "You're so late."

That night, my father's voice, weak, piteous, and pleading, came through the bathroom door. "Linda, will you sleep in my bed tonight?" I cringed. Though I'd been allowed as a small child to crawl into bed with my mother, I'd always lain on the side away from my father.

I buttoned my pink robe over my shorty pajamas, padded down the hall, and slipped into the opposite side of the double bed. I fell asleep lying back to back with Daddy, neither of us speaking or touching, our two bodies a bulwark against utter desolation. I had the odd sensation of being - for once - important to him.

The next morning, ladies from our church, relatives, and neighbors traipsed in and out of our house, each carrying something to eat, their voices discreetly subdued. Casseroles of macaroni and cheese, chicken tetrazzini, and beef stew sat on trivets on the kitchen table. They all wanted to help, but I only wanted the casserole my mother could make.

Daddy and I went to the hospital to see Steve. Afternoon light glinted on his blond waves, highlighting the remnants of the baby ringlets Mama treasured so much she saved the barber's first clippings. Steve's eyes clouded with fear, both of us on guard for my father's condemnation. I have always been grateful my father held back the accusing words that would have destroyed my brother that day.

I went with Daddy to take care of the funeral arrangements, to select a satin-lined, richly polished casket more dazzling than any furniture we'd ever had in our home.

I procured my mother's favorite lilac dress with the tiny covered buttons from throat to waist. Feeling too embarrassed to bring her old stretched-out brassiere, I went instead to Penney's lingerie department. I lacked the nerve to tell the clerk who asked why my mother couldn't come in to select the bra for herself. Then I worried I'd bought the wrong size and condemned Mama to endure a too-tight bra around her chest for eternity.

The undertaker told me Mama wouldn't need panties, stockings, a slip, or her patent-leather pumps.

Daddy sent me to collect items from the ruined car. The windshield was shattered. The thin plastic padding on the dashboard was ripped, leaving jagged metal corkscrewed daggers that could have contained bits of the little puppy or even my mother's face.

Daddy, Steve, newly discharged from the hospital, and I went to the viewing that night. About forty people mingled in the mortuary room smelling of carnations. Uncle John and Aunt Martha approached with my cousin, Naomi. "I'm so sorry, Paul," Uncle John said. He rubbed his forehead and looked at the floor. I wondered if he was thinking the same thing I was. If only Mama hadn't wanted to get their puppy that day.

While we approached Mama in her coffin, the community of mourners hung back in respect. The embalmer had encased Mama's head in a hard, white Styrofoam helmet which completely encircled her forehead and cheeks, covering her ears and hair. He had sprayed a glittery coating onto the foam, weirdly suggesting cheerfulness or maybe the sheen of angels' wings.

I focused on my mother's face, warmed with embalmer's rouge and rosy lipstick, the subtle brown shadow on her closed eyelids.

Behind us there was a commotion. My sister had finally arrived, accompanied by our two aunts and our grandmother. Seeing the eerie crown that shimmered around Mama's distended head, Judy erupted. Her screams cut through the hushed group like a saw through metal. "That's not my mother! That's not my mother!" Judy cried.

"Close the casket! Close the casket!" my father bellowed. A funeral assistant in a dark suit whipped forward and lowered the cover over my mother's face. Now there were only tall sprays of white lilies and roses banking the blank cover beneath which my mother was hidden for eternity.

I felt robbed. I wanted to immerse myself into a last view of my mother's beloved expression; calm, gentle, and mild. My beloved and essential Mama, who I would never see again.

The next day, the Howe First Methodist Church was packed with mourners. My father sat next to me, the space between us crackling with wrongness. Our minister eulogized about the good wife and mother concealed under pink and white carnations in the coffin in front of us and asked the congregation to be of comfort to us in our loss. He assured us God needed our mother in his heavenly kingdom more than we did—more than I, more than my sister, more than my father, or my brother, who would carry the guilt of her death all his life and who would still weep in anger at God fifty years later. I choked back rage. It seemed God had proved to be as harsh as I'd feared growing up with our minister's threats of eternal damnation.

Afterward, Steve, Judy, and I spent a few days together with my father. We ate the church ladies' fried chicken, cornbread, and green beans cooked soft with bacon while the TV blared in the living room. We seemed to be no more able to speak about our feelings of horror than the fence posts that corralled the cattle grazing in the fields outside.

None of us had experience sharing feelings, especially not around our father, whose facial expressions conveyed his almost unvarying opinion that life was a grim and harsh business. We never heard him or our mother talk about any of the hurt, sorrow, fear, or disappointment that must have underlaid his rage. We learned to suppress our own resulting anger. To have done anything other than keep our confused feelings of grief inside would have been embarrassing, strange, and abnormal. A few times, I, the oddball, attempted to violate this unspoken understanding, which earned me a rebuke, "Linda, you live in the past!" spoken in a sure tone that brooked no discussion and proved my guilt.

When I returned to college to finish the last three weeks of my freshman year, I went through the motions of showing up for classes, turning in term papers, and taking finals. Since I had always been an excellent student, it was no surprise when later that summer my grades came, and, as usual, I received straight-As.

I did not discuss my mother's death with Ellen or Karen, who I knew had no experience with devastating loss. I didn't expect more than a few moments of empathy from them.

I was shrouded in armor, a petrified shell concealing my numb heart.

10
LAST NIGHT AT HOME

Every atom of me missed him.

—Anonymous

APRIL 2000

The last evening before I'll meet Cathy at Gladney, Steve and I pull rusty metal chairs onto the concrete patio at the back of the house. In the heat, the Texas dog-day cicadas sing "Gar-Gar-Gar-Gar-Gar-Gar" in loud harmony. I'd bought wine before leaving the "wet" Dallas area, because our home area was still "dry," offering nothing more soothing than Orange Crush.

Steve and I relax, chat, and sip the cabernet I hid behind the dying lilac bush, since Daddy disapproves of women smoking or having alcohol. He wouldn't be up to coming out and finding it. Once he'd caught me drinking one glass of wine and whipped out accusation with the speed of a rattler's tongue, "Linda, you're an alcoholic!"

Even when my family's fear and tension threatened, nature surrounded and protected me. The redbirds gathered in the hackberry tree, the gray-green clouds releasing a summer afternoon downpour, the sweet smell of the earth comforting me after the rain. At night, while the rest of my family gathered in the darkened living room watching *Ed Sullivan* or *Liberace,* I escaped into the dark outside. I felt myself falling up into the stars and planets stretched across the boundless sky like cold white diamonds. Were there other beings who might provide what I felt starved for? Each night when I eventually came back into the house, I felt the mute loneliness that separated each of us.

Now I tune into the backdrop sounds of the heat-loving insects. Buzzing, rattling, chirping, cheeping, almost purring, their sounds start low and build crescendo-like, repeating endlessly. Growing up, I'd absorbed their music in my bones, stored it in my cells. I'd spent hours wandering barefoot and lonely in the pastures, keeping an eye out for rattlesnakes and copperheads in dry grass. The cicadas, grass-hoppers, Guernsey cows, mud-caked pigs, banty hens that clucked me awake in the morning, pecan trees that shaded us. These were my family, too.

Now I long to find my firstborn, to bandage the wound ripped in me when I allowed Gladney to take him from me.

11

MEET THE SOCIAL WORKER

Normality is a paved road. It's comfortable to walk, but no flowers grow on it.

—Vincent Van Gogh

APRIL 2000

The three of us crowd into the cab of Steve's white Chevrolet pick-up. We are running late. My brother's farm duties assured us a delayed start. I try to control my impatience as Steve grips the steering wheel to navigate rush hour traffic. Gladney may be closing at five and I'll have no other chance for years to meet Cathy Bowman and drop off my precious letter. Jared and I are catching our flight home from Dallas/Fort Worth Airport after this meeting tonight.

Steve is anxious, too. I can see it in his tight shoulders. He wants to get me there on time. He's the one who walked by me as I had lain weeping on the cold ground in the dark outside our farm house just weeks after leaving my baby at Gladney. Keeping up the pretense of a happy Thanksgiving with my father inside had been intolerable. Steve heard my sobs.

"Oh, you poor kid," he said then. I'd never forgotten his caring words.

I reach into my purse to check the bulky envelope I'd prepared for Cathy. Six and a half pages. Would my son ever read it? Thirty-five years he'd been missing. I thought of the families whose service members never came home from Vietnam, Korea, or the World Wars and yet were never declared dead. It must be agonizing to never know the fate of a loved one who'd disappeared in war. I feel as if my son, too, is "missing in action." I'd read of the torment military families suffered, always wondering if their loved one might still exist somewhere. No relatives attending their funeral, no gravesite to mourn by, no dusty obituary notice folded into a drawer.

> Missing in action: "The designation for a member of an organization (usually military) with whom contact is lost and whose whereabouts are not known, but whose death is not confirmed."[5]

Later, I would learn the Pentagon operates an arm called the Defense POW/MIA Accounting Agency, tasked with finding and returning military personnel.[6] I read about a woman who burst into joyful tears when her uncle's remains were located after seventy-four years missing in action. Tears came to my eyes, too, sharing her joy after so much loss.[7]

By then I was familiar with the unspoken question I saw in people's faces when I told them I needed to find my own missing son. "Don't you think you may upset his life?" their expressions conveyed. But then my Twitter feed was clogged with anguished voices of adoptees whose need to find their biological families was similarly misunderstood. "Didn't you have a good adoptive family?" people asked them.

Steve steers off Highway 35 West and onto Hemphill, pulling up in front of a sandstone building. Where are the steps I remember dragging myself up in 1964? Where are the ornate trim and eaves?

---

5 "Missing in Action," *Wikipedia, The Free Encyclopedia*, accessed 2/19/19, https://en.wikipedia.org/wiki/Missing_in_action

6 *Defense POW/MIA Accounting Agency, Fulfilling Our Nation's Promise, Accessed 2/12/19,* https://www.dpaa.mil/

7 "A World War 11 Mystery is Solved, and Emotions Flood In," *The New York Times*, 5/28/18

Have I misremembered? Still, my heart flip-flops and my legs go weak. Steve tugs open the door. Thank God; the agency is still open.

Cathy Bowman, my lifeline to my unknown son, greets us looking slim and professional in her black dress with white trim. Her short, dark hair, perhaps owing its color to Clairol like my own, waves over her forehead above her plastic eyeglasses. "You two can wait over there," she motions to Steve and Jared.

She takes me through another door. I draw in my breath, momentarily paralyzed by a wave of grief. We are in Gladney's chapel, where I'd signed the relinquishment papers. Why aren't we meeting in her office instead? I catch a glimpse of Steve and Jared staring through the white blinds at my weeping face. Cathy draws the blinds. Behind us, polished brown pews gleam and late afternoon light streams through stained glass. Cathy directs me to a chair at the front of the pews, like that morning in 1964. "It often brings up a lot of feelings to come back here," she says, sitting across from me.

I pull out the thick packet from my purse and pass it to her. Would she redact any of it before sending it? I'd been careful not to include any identifying details. But why did there need to be such a wall between him and me, when both of us were now adults?

"You understand I don't know if I'll be able to get this letter to your son," Cathy says. "I don't know if I'll be able to find him."

Cathy passes me a box of Kleenex. Her eyes seem kind, interested. "Tell me a little about yourself," she says.

I relax and sit a little taller. "Well, as you know, I'm a social worker myself. I work at Kaiser as a licensed psychotherapist. I'm married to a wonderful man, but it has taken a while."

I think back to the decades of struggle, not willing to share more. I'd dressed up for this meeting in my black pants, silky blouse, and flowered jacket, trying to project the image of the proficient expert I use with my therapy clients and colleagues, my skilled self, the one who always looks competent and empathetic. Wasn't that what I'd done my whole professional life? How I'd kept my shame and stigma at bay? I'd become a sincere, caring, and skilled therapist, but keeping my secret had allowed my unacknowledged pain to harden into a brittle shell that seeped out as anger. Maybe some of those other birth mothers had just wept and wailed.

"I have two other sons, the one you saw just now, and another, my oldest, Chad." I wonder if Cathy noticed Jared's unusual weight that his anti-psychotic medications promote and add, "Jared has schizophrenia."

"That has to be really hard," Cathy looks at me with compassion.

"Yeah; we've had years and years of crisis. It has made it very hard to even think about my first son. I haven't had the energy."

"Well, it still seems like you've done better than most birth mothers."

Have I? I'm surprised at Cathy's comment. Maybe I'd have been more open if I hadn't felt the need to maintain my professional image.

"I always thought I couldn't find my son," I venture.

"As I told you on the phone, there's a law in Texas now that we have to try to get medical information to adoptive parents, if we can find them. I'll see what information we have and let you know what I find out."

Why only the adoptive parents? My son would now be thirty-five years old. Shouldn't he be the one to hear his medical history?

Cathy leans toward me. "There's a support group here tonight for birth mothers who relinquished more than ten years ago. Can you stay for it?"

I feel my eyes widen. My forehead rises and mouth drops open until I manage to answer. "Yes! When does it start?"

"Six-thirty. They're gathering now. I can introduce you, if you'd like."

"Yes," I breathe. At least I can sit in the first hour before we hurry to the airport.

Cathy ushers me toward a large windowless room where three women with friendly smiles have gathered for their meeting, then disappears. Marilyn, a dark-haired woman about my age, introduces herself, then Janet, a lean woman whose face suggests she's done a lot of sunbathing and Joan, maybe fifteen years younger.

"Come on in," Marilyn says, leading me to a chair with a brocade fabric seat. The four of us sit in a small circle.

"Cathy doesn't lead the meeting?" I ask.

"No, it's just us," Marilyn says. "We usually just talk among ourselves and catch up on what's happening with our searches or reunions."

Reunions? These women were in reunion with their sons or daughters! Where had I been all these years? Still hiding out in the shame of the sixties, I think.

"Would you like to tell us a little about yourself?" Marilyn asks, leaning towards me, encouraging me with her interest.

I glance toward the others. "I'm hoping Cathy will get my letter with medical information to my son. I don't even know if he's still alive or where he is or anything," I say. My voice trails off.

"Gladney told me they'd chosen educated parents for my child," I continue. "But they wouldn't tell me anything about what kind of education, just something in the science field. I never thought of myself as the scientific sort, at least not in the hard sciences. So, I wonder..."

"I found my daughter a few years back," Marilyn says. After a little while I realized she had a lot of problems."

My right hand goes to my heart as it does when clients tell me their sad stories. All those months at Gladney, the social workers telling us we weren't ready to be mothers. The mother and father they'd choose for our babies would be able to do a much better job raising them than we could.

"I'm disappointed my daughter's adoptive parents didn't set limits with her," Marilyn continues. "I feel like the children I raised have done better than her."

Had Cathy heard Marilyn's discouraging story? Is this all I can hope for from the life Gladney helped set in motion for my baby? My stomach turns hard and I almost forget to breathe.

"Tell us a little more about your story," Janet prompts.

I draw a deep breath. "My mother was killed in a car accident a year before I came to Gladney. My father, a total emotional wreck, was diagnosed with paranoid schizophrenia soon after. I was nineteen. I lived in the apartments with the older girls. My son was born the day before Halloween."

There's just enough time to share a little more before Jared and I have to rush off for our flight.

Marilyn hands me her card. "Keep in touch," she tells me.

"I will," I promise.

12

GOOD NEWS/BAD NEWS

It's no wonder that truth is stranger than fiction. Fiction has to make sense.

—Mark Twain

APRIL 2000

I come home to California after meeting Cathy at Gladney. Two weeks go by. Every day seems like a month. Finally, I call Cathy. Her voice rises in surprise as she asks, "Didn't you get the email I sent you almost a week ago?"

"You sent me an email? What address did you send it to?" How could it not have arrived?

"I'll forward it to you again right now," Cathy reassures me.

A few minutes later, her lost April 13th email pops up on my screen.

"Dear Linda,

I wanted to let you know what I know so far. It is a case of good news/bad news. The bad news is I cannot get an address for either your birth son or his adoptive parents. The good news is we have had contact with his sister, and we have her address. Yesterday, I wrote to her and let her know we have medical information for him and asked her to ask him to call me. I will let you know when I hear something.

Cathy"

"Oh my God, Cathy, how long do you think your letter will take to get to his sister?" Maybe she'll let slip what city she'd mailed it to.

"If she's in contact with him, it could be soon. I'll let you know the minute I hear anything."

With my hand shaking, I set the phone back into its cradle. I could have more news any minute. But maybe the sister wouldn't call my son. Maybe Cathy's next email would nose-dive too. Dave won't be home for an hour. I don't want to call him on the road. I run the hottest bath I can stand and pour half a box of Epsom salts in, hoping the near scalding heat will drain the tension from my frenzied muscles.

13

CONTACT

That great Cathedral space which was childhood.

—Virginia Woolf

APRIL 20TH, 2000

I drag myself home from my seventeen-patient day and click into my email. My eyes fixate on the subject line *"Contact!"* My heart speeds up and kicks out a few extra beats. Cathy has emailed that she has talked to my son and has given him all of my medical information. She says he asked her to send my letter to him.

Oh, my God! He's alive. She talked to him! It seems unreal. My lost son, back from the dead! I race through the next lines. Cathy cautions me that the hardest part is about to start, as there is no way to know when or even if my son will respond.

Even while knowing she is right, I want to ignore Cathy's words. The thought that it may take years for my son to respond feels unbearable. Maybe he never will. How can I bear it if he decides not to answer? I refuse to contemplate that. Excitement propels me to re-read Cathy's email.

> "He is a college graduate – he got his MBA...He opened his own restaurant a year and a half ago and from what he said,

it seems to be doing well. He has been married for five years and has two daughters – one two years old and the other six months old. He really is a very nice young man!"

My son's parents gave him the education Gladney promised. He owns businesses, restaurants no less, which I briefly dreamed of owning in my youth. All of this thrills me. But discovering his babies, his children, bursts into my consciousness like a pheasant that explodes out of hidden grass into the sky when discovered.

My grandchildren! I stare at the computer, longing for images of these two tiny girls to materialize on the screen. I love being a grandmother. When Chad's daughter, Terra, was only six weeks old, I took care of her. Carrying her in a pink cloth sling, Terra and I bonded chest-to-chest strolling in a neighborhood park that weekend while Chad and his wife, Tonya, searched for a new rental. Images of Terra float through my mind - her shiny wet body slippery with soap when Dave and I bathed her in the kitchen sink, her chocolate ice cream cone melting and dripping down her face and chin on her first visit to the Sacramento Zoo at William Land Park.

Maybe I can get to know these new granddaughters, enjoy their childish enthusiasms, play, giggle, read, sing, and skip with them. Not like their father – already grown, already gone.

I feel ready to leap up and set out to find my whole new family.

The front door bangs. "Dave! Dave! It's an email from Cathy. She's talked to my son! Come and read it!"

Dave looks over my head to read it, legal briefcase in hand. "Wow! That's fantastic!"

"And there are grandchildren! Oh, my God; he has babies!" I look up at Dave, wondering if he'll realize what this means to me.

My blood descendants. Two granddaughters I'd never dreamed existed! How ready can Dave be to take on more of my complicated family?

"Let's celebrate tonight!" he says, picking up his briefcase, trudging down the hall.

"Yes," I smile. I read Cathy's message twice more, savoring every word.

Where are my grandchildren tonight?

The coming Easter Sunday, a chance to bring the family together around our groaning dinner table, is also a perfect time to share my exciting news with Chad's family and Jared. Marcia, who lost her own daughter to adoption and has been Chad's lady partner for the last five years, is helping to raise Terra since Chad divorced.

Marcia and I both grew up in Texas with mentally ill fathers, strong religious backgrounds, and we both gave up our first babies to adoption. Chad must have recognized much of me in Marcia when they met working together at The Good Guys store; even her warm smile, full face, and dark, wavy hair.

As we pass around the potato gratin, pineapple salad, and ham, I wonder if Marcia will want to search for her child now that I've learned my son is out there somewhere. I can read the mixed feelings in her face. Is she about to cry?

Chad puts his arm around Terra. "You have cousins."

Terra's blue eyes shine. "I want to meet them."

"Yep, me too, but that may take a while. First, we have to find out their names and where they are."

Jared puts down his fork to join in. "Yeah, I want to meet my brother. I wonder where he is."

Dave, quietly observing his stepfamily, encourages. "Well, at least your mom knows he has contacted Gladney. Maybe he'll write back and tell us soon."

"Yeah. Maybe we can invite him to Easter dinner next year," I reply.

"Well, if he comes, I guess I won't be your oldest son anymore." Chad's expression reveals he's only half-joking. Losing his position as my indulged oldest son could be a shock. How would he feel at becoming the middle child, a position I was saddled with in my childhood?

"At least, I'll still be the youngest," Jared smiles and says.

"Well, now we know there's really young family," I say, looking at Terra.

"Yeah, Terra," Chad tells her. "You won't be the only granddaughter."

"That's okay. I want to meet my cousins."

Yes, I think. Everything could change; and not just for me.

14

MAMA

He who has gone, so we but cherish his memory, abides with us, more potent, nay, more present than the living man.

—Antoine de Saint-Exupery

1944 - 63

I recall my mother dressing up for church. "I need to lose weight," she'd say, sighing and patting her stomach. In fact, at the age of forty-three, she carried only one hundred and forty-two pounds on her five foot, five-inch frame.

She sewed most of her own clothes herself, but her favorite was a store-bought lilac dress, and that was the one she was buried in. About ten years before, a picture taken on Easter Sunday on our way to church shows her turned out in a white dress with short sleeves and tucked-in waist she'd outlined with grosgrain ribbon. She'd bought herself white gloves, a small white hat that rested fetchingly on her curls, and if we could see them in the picture, white pumps.

Easter Sundays ensured new outfits for each of us children sewn by my mother. One family picture taken right before leaving for church shows me at about nine wearing a new dress with puffed sleeves, a wide collar trimmed with lace, and a little bow at my throat. An Easter hat with a perky brim and new black patent shoes over white socks completed my ensemble. My older sister Judy is similarly attired, and Steve, my little brother, appears as a smaller version of my father who stands next to him, both dressed in white shirts, ties, black pants, and black jackets. My father's mouth is a straight line. He stares at the camera, giving off an air of self-pity, as if the world has affronted him somehow. Mama must have taken the picture, as she is not in it. My sister stands on the front step above the three of us. Judy's eyes are cast down toward my father. One corner of her upper lip is raised in a sneer.

I was not a wanted child. By the time I was conceived, Judy, graced with blond curls and quick learning, had already won my mother's heart. My father had already lost it. Under the circumstances, a second baby was not in my mother's plans. Finding herself pregnant with me, I'm sure she hoped at least to produce a boy. Perhaps my skinflint father was also unenthusiastic about welcoming a second child, as my parents decided on a home birth instead of the expensive hospital birth they'd chosen for Judy. Lacking an attending doctor to carry out the needed episiotomy, my large head tore Mama. I was born with jaundice, so my skin and eyes must have appeared an unappealing yellow. I was also born with pyloric stenosis, which causes projectile vomiting. My mother spent my first six weeks attempting to get milk down me and mopping up everywhere. By the time I was six weeks old, I had lost four ounces of my birth weight. I was dehydrated, weak, and lethargic. My parents decided to consult a doctor.

The Sherman physician assured my parents he could save me, and I was put under the knife for repair. At that time, there was a prevailing view that infants did not feel pain and that anesthesia and painkillers should be used sparingly. Instead, drugs inducing only light anesthesia were used, which produced unconsciousness but did not prevent pain. I was tied to my crib to keep me from struggling or kicking. Perhaps this early ordeal helps explain why I jump like a jack-in-the-box at the slightest unexpected noise or interruption.

A year and a half after my birth, my brother, Steve, was born. Finally, a boy! My brother completed our family. I enjoyed playing "cowboys and Indians" with Steve and stood compliant, a captured Indian, while he tied me to the light post planted in the Bermuda grass at the edge of our gravel driveway. Steve and I constructed towns in the dirt and drove his little metal cars along their roads. Though I loved playing nurse with my dolls, shredding their rubbery arms with needle injections from the large safety pins I found in Mama's sewing box, I soon concluded it would have been an advantage to be the boy my parents had wanted rather than the middle child, a girl at that. The inherent rewards enjoyed by my brother only increased as we became teens. Steve received a larger allowance because, Mama told me, "He has to pay for girls on dates." Steve was given a car because "He has to drive girls on dates."

When my mother met my father, he was employed as a bank clerk in town. She'd assumed he'd continue dressing in a suit and tie to go to work. His later decision to take up the farming he'd been raised with was a grave disappointment to her, though she did not openly complain. But though she didn't challenge my father, she also demonstrated no fondness for him. I can see her in the passenger seat of our pink Plymouth, pulling away from my father's attempt to put his arm around her. My father was shunned. On observing my mother petting one of our cats, I once heard him comment, "You pay more attention to that cat than you do to me."

He was right, but he coped with his loneliness by repressed anger he released in explosive rages. Meanwhile, Mama carried on all her duties, silently going from task to task, wielding a dust cloth, pushing a broom, washing up after meals. I rarely saw the smile I longed for on her face, though I never doubted her devotion to me and my siblings. She was the center of our home and of my sense of family.

When I was five or six, I was passing her in the hall when Mama bent down to ask me a question.

"Linda, do you think I should leave Daddy?" she asked.

Something serious must have happened. "Yes," I said.

The next few days, I watched for signs we might be leaving. Walking barefoot through the pastures, I gazed with a lightened feeling in my chest at the skittish cattle, our muddy cattle pond, and the drifting clouds in the sky. Days passed. Daddy came in from the fields looking glum as always. Mama took care of tasks with her usual resigned air.

Years later, I learned that she had asked Judy and Steve the same question. They'd both told her no.

Even then, I was the different one. I was a klutzy kid. My mother told me I leaned too far into our pigs' slop bucket and toppled in upside down as a toddler until she righted and rescued me. How I must have stunk from the rotting table scraps.

Once I accidentally punched my fist through a pane of our dining room French doors and then the story goes that I repeated the action on purpose, which earned me an understandable spanking from my father. Another time, he pretended to step on me as I lay on the floor and I complained loudly. Unlike my siblings, I developed a mouthy response to his provocations, even rare playful ones. My rebellious nature marked me as difficult, though my outspokenness was superficial, marking my differentness. I was easily wounded by my siblings' taunting that I was adopted. I learned to retreat into silence, deciding the cloak of invisibility was the best option.

When I was about five, Mama surprised me with a trip to a neighbor's house. The lady of the house brought out a cardboard box with four meowing kittens struggling to climb out. "Choose whichever one you want," Mama told me. Thrilled, I selected an orange one. Lazy B, short for Lazy Bum, became my best friend, putting up with multiple indignities as I dressed her in my doll clothes, carried her upside down, and sat on our front stoop telling her my troubles. I held Lazy B against my ear and felt comforted by her purring. I spent many hours searching for the kittens she gave birth to in our hay barn and chicken house, but I never learned how to protect them from Daddy, who drowned new litters in our stock tank. I did not forgive Daddy for his approach to feline population control, though perhaps many farm fathers did the same then. Veterinarians' services were reserved for valuable livestock, not for spaying pets.

15
DETERMINATION

We are never so vulnerable as when we love.

—Sigmund Freud

1950s

When I was in first or second grade, an event occurred which had a terrible and lasting effect on me. One Sunday, two Japanese ministers visited our church. Their yellow faces and slanted eyes marked them as exotic in our conservative white rural community. My mother had always longed to travel to distant cultures. No doubt, to her, the two men brought a sophistication absent in our community. She must have convinced my father to have them visit as rare guests.

We'd finished our lunch, which we called "supper," and most likely consisted of fried chicken, mashed potatoes, and cream gravy. Tired of the adult conversation, I went to the bedroom to play dolls or maybe read one of my Little Golden Books. Soon, I wandered back toward the living room, circling through the hall door into the kitchen area. A half wall separated me from the living room where my mother, father, and the two Japanese visitors sat. Just as I was about to enter, I heard one of the visitors comment, "Linda is so cute."

Then I heard Mama's reply. "Yes, Linda is cute, but Judy is beautiful. Linda is smart, but Judy is brilliant. Linda is good, but Judy is perfect."

I felt a sudden drop in my core, as if I'd been thrown from a precipice. I stood transfixed, momentarily paralyzed.

At last, I breathed again and entered the living room. I had the impression the Japanese men stared at me in discomfort, realizing what I might have overheard. I looked toward my mother, attempting to discover whether her expression would give anything away, but she maintained a wooden expression, as if I had not heard. But of course, I had.

My mother's judgment widened my already distant relationship with my sister, perhaps because Judy's favored position had already separated me from her. Mama's words also left me with a determination to surpass my sister, who, of course, bore no fault for this injury. Yet an injury it was, a deep and terrible wound that haunted me. I kept my profound love and an intense need for my mother. I did not openly turn away from her. Instead, I determined to outperform my sister in Mama's eyes. I acquired a competitiveness that became a powerful motivator to achieve.

When Judy was a teen, Mama sent her to spend a week in Tennessee with our aunt and uncle. Judy brought back pictures of the Allegheny Mountains covered with gorgeous blue flowers. "You'll go next year," Mama promised. Next year, she sent Steve. Mama told me I needed to be more responsible. Yet, I was a straight A student. I completed my numerous chores at home. In fact, I was a goody-two-shoes everywhere. I never understood why I was overlooked. On my fourteenth birthday, that same summer of 1958, my mother wrapped my single gift, a fountain pen, in an old hand towel and gave it to me without ceremony. What had I done wrong? I remember the way my stomach lurched when she handed it to me.

Mama was not an affectionate woman. I have no memories of her hugging me. Instead, she showed her love through service, arranging church camp, sewing my clothes and my doll's clothes, listening to my reports of school and complaints of loneliness. I wanted her to touch me. Once I fell asleep in the car coming home late from somewhere and she carried me into the house. I pretended not to awaken, enchanted by the unaccustomed warmth of my body curled into hers and wanting to extend the feeling of her arms encircling me.

When I was fifteen, I developed an acute case of appendicitis while she was on a rare visit alone to my grandmother. Finding me bent over in the bathroom in the middle of the night, my sister prevailed on my father to take me to the hospital. Emergency surgery revealed my appendix near to bursting. Judy may well have saved my life. My father phoned my mother and she and my aunt drove five hours to the hospital.

When Mama pushed open the hospital door, overwhelming relief washed over me. We caught eyes and I saw her impulse to dash across the room to throw her arms around me. Then she hesitated, stopped, like a mechanism whose spindle caught on a knot. The moment passed. She stepped formally toward me and asked how I was. My heart sank. We spoke as if we were two acquaintances.

In the ninth grade, a popular football star asked me to go to a party. He was a catch; his hulking shoulders and thick dark hair, along with his football player status, suggested he was second only to God in Texas.

When I asked to go to the party, Mama frowned. "Will there be alcohol there?" she asked.

"There'll be beer there," I admitted, knowing my classmates knew how to obtain contraband beer in nearby Denison, a "wet city." Besides, the thought of hanging out with the popular set at a party felt so intimidating that I didn't challenge her.

That weekend, I stayed home and missed my chance to join, even briefly, the favored in group. A couple of weeks later, I discovered my sister, Judy, was dating my football hero. Her victory was short-lived, though, lasting for only a few dates. I was glad, but I never dared confront her.

My mother, coming of age during the depression, was denied a college education, a lifelong sorrow for her. She scrimped and saved to make sure we three kids would attend college. She transferred us from Tom Bean to Sherman High School ten miles away to receive better college preparatory classes. She arranged for my sister to move in with an old friend of Mama's in Sherman, which proved to be an unhappy one for my sister. I felt relieved to be the remaining girl at home. Maybe I could become equally special to my mother.

In 1958 in the Bible Belt of Texas, women's liberation, feminism, and the sexual revolution, changes that would soon transform the world beyond our borders, were barely imagined. A girl's virginity was her greatest asset. Marriage was her highest goal.

One morning, I came into the kitchen to see my mother's head drooping and her face despondent. When I probed, Mama revealed she had read my sister's diary.

"She's been intimate with boys," Mama said.

"Oh, Mama, that's not so bad."

She trained anguished eyes on me. "No nice man will marry her now," she pronounced.

My sister developed insomnia. On weekends, she came home and laid awake at all hours. Next to her in my twin bed, I slept through her tortuous insomnia, but in the mornings, my mother would caution me, "Sh-h-h; don't wake Judy. She was up all night."

I tiptoed around, observing the worry lines etching deep into Mama's forehead, thinking unkind thoughts about my favored sister.

One day when Judy was back in school, my mother asked me to help her with her permanent. The kitchen reeked of ammonium and hydrogen peroxide used to induce tight curls.

Mama sat down in the wooden kitchen chair, a bowl of pink foam rollers and little white tissue papers next to her on the table. "I need you to roll them for me," she said.

I usually would have looked forward to these tasks, but that day my stomach tightened, and I dragged my feet to the table. Sure enough, as I combed a small section of her light brown hair and began to wrap it over the paper and onto the roller, she began her litany about Judy. Even though I stood behind her, I could almost see the worry lines gathering.

"Do you think Judy is doing any better?"

"I don't know, Mama."

"I don't understand it," Mama continued. "She was always so good."

I heard *perfect*. I picked up another section of hair, then another, rolling them tightly and clicking down the black plastic rods to hold them in place.

Mama kept up her recounting of concerns about Judy.

My neck and shoulders tightened. I grabbed the next section of damp hair and pulled.

"Ouch!" Mama exclaimed.

"Oh, sorry!" but I wasn't.

A few days later, overwhelmed by my role as my mother's confidante, I dashed out of the house and ran screaming down our gravel driveway. Mama pursued and grabbed me. I recall her hands on my shoulders as she turned me around.

"Oh, no, Linda. Not you, too!" she cried.

I felt at least she saw then that I had problems, too, not only Judy. I wanted her to ask me about them, but she didn't.

When I was fifteen, on our annual visit to see my maternal grandmother, we went to the family cemetery plot. While my mother and grandmother weeded and tended to my grandfather's grave, I wandered among the old tombstones, tipped crazily, their cracked concrete heads overgrown with yellowish-green mold, stopping at one.

Miriam Teller
Born May 6, 1920.
Died March 22, 1937.

Shock and fascination held me with that sense of immortality that life allows only the very young. What happened that a girl only one year older than me lay in the cold ground beneath my feet? Next to the headstone leaned a once-gilded cup with faded, fake chrysanthemums poking out of it. I suppose my mother must have known Miriam Teller in her school years.

"She killed herself," my mother told me in a flat, unemotional voice.

"Why?" I asked, my voice high and tight.

"She had to." My mother turned her face away and focused on the grass she was pulling. Her unaccustomed coldness warned me not to ask more. I knew why poor Miriam Teller 'had to.' She had found herself pregnant and knew she had only one way out.

Would my beloved mother have wanted me to take Miriam Teller's route? I can't believe that. I know she loved me. She sat up late at night and sewed a whole wardrobe on her old Singer machine for my Toni doll when I was eleven. A bright blue circle skirt with a tiny black button at the waist and a stitched zigzag buttonhole, little pique green and pink two-piece pajamas, a yellow ruffled shirt, a pink taffeta ball gown. She made sure I got to go to church youth camp every summer, taught me how to make devil's food and pineapple upside down cake and puffy golden biscuits.

She gave me a party once when I complained about having no friends. Paul Anka crooned "Put Your Head on My Shoulder" on our record player and I did put my head on my tall classmate's shoulder while we danced cheek to cheek in our living room. Afterwards, all of us girls and boys burst out of the front door and ran all over the large front grass lawn chasing fireflies and each other.

My mother would have been devastated by suicide and when my period didn't come in February 1964, she had already left us. She was only forty-three years of age. We buried her in West Hills Cemetery.

Conservative in her views, my mother many times warned me, "Never let a man touch you below the neck or above the knees" Mostly I didn't, those nights parking with boys on lonely country roads where the loudest sounds were the frogs calling from the stock tank pond down the field. Still, if my mother had been alive, she would have been horrified and deeply disappointed in me. She also would have seen to it that my equally guilty boyfriend stood with me at the front of the First Methodist Church in the country town of Howe as Reverend Sweeney pronounced us "man and wife." Back in those days, a girl could be redeemed by a shotgun wedding.

In the unlikely event that shotgun wedding failed, she would have required I pay for my sins with the same merciless sacrifice of my firstborn I had inflicted on myself. It wouldn't have occurred to my mother to rebel against society's insistence that no woman could be a mother without a wedding ring. I'm thankful she at least never suffered that shame.

When I recall my mother now, the woman I never knew as an adult, I realize she had no one else in whom to confide. My father was not equipped. The culture in Texas did not allow intimate discussions of problems. "What will the neighbors think?" people said.

Our church required us to put our best foot forward. What went on at home was never to be shared. Divorce constituted a major stigma, not only for the divorcee but also for her children. The wholesome TV shows were superficial comedies and did not speak to emotional needs and neither did the women's magazines I read. Women were to cook nourishing meals for their families, clean, and make a nice home. If the home wasn't a happy one, it was the woman's fault. Most women did not work outside the home and those who did were limited to the female-dominated fields, the same secretarial, teaching, and nursing jobs my mother recommended for me. Though my mother wanted to work, my father forbade it until we were teenagers and then she came straight home to do household duties, not even stopping to have coffee with a friendly co-worker.

I hate to think how lonely my mother's isolated existence was. I know she tried her best. Now I think of her with a lump in my throat and wish she'd lived long enough to see her way to leaving my father, renting a little house in town, coming to visit me and my brother and sister, and getting to know her grandchildren.

It's tragic, how she lived and how she died.

16

SUMMER FROM HELL

Hell is empty and all the devils are here.

—William Shakespeare

1963

We spent the summer at home with Daddy. Steve had just finished his junior year in high school. Judy came home from the University of Texas at Austin. I returned from East Texas State. Shock robbed us of the capacity to make other plans. Grief drained our energies. Besides, my father sounded so desolate and weak on the phone, I couldn't ignore his plea.

Daddy picked me up and helped me load two heavy suitcases filled with clothes and the detritus of my first year in college.

"I saw the Beatles on Ed Sullivan the other night," he commented on the drive home.

"Really?" I asked, surprised he was making conversation. "Did you like them?"

"They're all right, I guess. They need haircuts." We never made small talk. Now we were trying to talk about anything but the horror of Mama's death.

Entering our faded white asbestos-shingled house, I expected Mama to be standing in the kitchen doorway. Her absence felt like a hole in the ground, a sinkhole big enough to swallow me and our entire family.

Nothing that used to seem important held any interest for me anymore. How could I care about seeing "The Virginian" on TV or the clothing sale at J.C. Penney? My mother was dead. I cycled between disbelief and the certainty of irreversible disaster.

The early corn was already a foot high and it was time to plow the rich, black dirt for the second crop. My mother should have been driving the Ford pickup down to the fields where Daddy was. Stilling the motor of his John Deere tractor, he'd have clambered down from his black, plastic seat, wiping the sweat from his face with a cotton handkerchief. My mother would have handed him an aluminum pie tin with fried pork chops, pinto beans, and mashed potatoes covered in aluminum foil. He'd have washed it down with iced tea.

Without Mama, my father took no interest in farming. All night, a small air conditioner poured chilled air over the double bed my father hunched in alone now.

My sister and I made do on our matching twin beds in the next room. A tiny rotating fan blew hot air over our sweating bodies. I woke and stared through the thin faded yellow curtains to the forlorn mulberry tree in the dry yard. Formerly, I'd have heard the roar of the tractor as my father headed out to the bottom fields to plant the fertile bottomland in maize. There a small plot was saved to grow the huge, red tomatoes my mother and I tended. I'd spot the thick-bodied, horned green tomato worms that hid on the plant stems. "There one is!" I'd call out. My mother, her nose drawn up in disgust, would tug at the rows of sucker-like green feet that the "horny worms" used to crawl up the stem. I'd use the rusting clippers to snip the wriggling worm in half. We'd watch the green ooze before dropping the worm segments to the ground.

"It's a good thing you can see these," she'd compliment me. Her rare praise made me enjoy this activity with her.

Now each morning, instead of driving the pickup into the pastures, carrying salt blocks out to the Hereford cattle, and coming back to report on the birth of a new calf, Daddy set up residence on the embossed couch in the living room. He spent his days pacing back and forth. His slippers wore tracks in the beige carpet. He bypassed the aging yellow recliner to pivot before the 12-inch TV, then circle back to the sofa and pitch himself down. Each time Daddy threw his heavy body onto the hot, sticky vinyl, his bare legs in his boxer shorts stuck to it. A few minutes later, he'd leap up to make another round of our small living room. His calves pulled away, making a zipping noise, his flesh pink like an under-cooked steak.

Steve had taken over handling the cattle and pigs. He banged the porch door behind him on his way to check on the water level in the cattle tanks and put out the huge salt blocks for the cattle. Daddy stirred himself to look out the small window to the side of the couch whenever he heard a car passing by on the narrow road between our farmhouse and the pasture. Otherwise, he lay prone, his left forearm across his face, as if to shut out the world until one of us walked by.

"Where's Steve?" he'd ask.

"I don't know, Daddy. Out in the fields, I guess."

"What's he doing?"

"I don't know, Daddy. He didn't say. He just left."

After the accident, Steve was only able to open his wired jaw enough to insert a straw to suck up milkshakes Judy and I blended with milk from the milking barn. Big round cartons of Blue Bonnet peach and vanilla ice cream were stored in the white freezer chest on the porch. As Steve took the milkshakes, he'd make the motion he'd do ever after, rotating his neck like he needed to unwind it.

Judy and I plunged corn-on-the-cob from the field straight into salted, boiling water. We boiled beets and carrots from the garden and slathered them in butter. We sifted flour and made baking powder biscuits, spreading them with the peach and plum jams Mama had canned up last year from our orchard harvest.

Perhaps preachers in Texas are inspired to predict the tortures of eternal hellfire by the summer's brutal heat and humidity. The summer after Mama's death, my sister and I stuck our heads deep down into the old, low freezer on the porch and inhaled the chill, letting it wash over our foreheads like melting ice. We took our time pulling out white paper-wrapped steaks, chicken pieces, and pork chops, all from animals we raised and slaughtered ourselves. We pressed the hard, cold packages to our flushed cheeks, longing to cool the summer's tortures, too.

At night, I set five plates at our round maple table, then realized with a start that we only needed four. I ate without tasting. I buried my face in books I could barely comprehend anymore. My sister escaped into binges on pancakes drenched in artificial maple syrup. I found her sticky plates under her bed, remnants of the light-brown crust stuck in streaks of dried syrup.

One day I discovered a small brown bottle among the vanilla, baking soda, and corn meal in the kitchen cabinet. Valium for my father, the prescription read. I slipped one of the scored white tablets into my mouth and discovered amazing relief when my clenched jaw relaxed, and my tight neck loosened. The pill made my mother's absence seem not quite so devastating. I returned now and then to that little bottle. My father never seemed to notice. It wouldn't have mattered to me if he had. I needed them too much to care.

Riven by anxiety and distress, Daddy flung himself from one meaningless activity to the next. His clinical diagnosis I learned later of "agitated depression" fails to convey the torment he displayed.

"Louise always wanted to travel," my father confessed to my aunt once when she came to visit. "I should have taken her on that trip to Tennessee." Brows drawn, his face worn, and eyes hollow and pleading, he begged for absolution.

One day, a man came to the house. Daddy pulled himself off the couch and went outside to talk to him. "He says Jerald's parents don't have any money or insurance. It seems like there's no point in suing," Daddy told us. His face had that timid look he got when he had to deal with the world outside his little fiefdom.

"I guess there's nothing to do then," I replied, feeling helpless. Steve and Judy agreed. It would be decades before I'd learn there were laws to punish drivers who committed "negligent homicide" or "vehicular manslaughter." Then I'd wish my father had insisted the sheriff arrest both the racing boys. But Daddy always kept his rages at home, blowing up only at us, his screams reverberating through the house, accusing and sick with self-pity. He was incapable of battling the small-town negligence then that wanted to call it "just an accident," "too bad," "so sorry."

When the man left, I retreated to my bedroom. I laid down on my twin bed and closed my eyes.

17
BIBLE BELT OF TEXAS

"... whoever blasphemes against the Holy Spirit never has forgiveness but is guilty of an eternal sin."

—Mark 3: 29-30

1944 - 1962

I know the effects of being raised to be "religious."

East Texas is known as The Bible Belt of Texas. Each Sunday at 9 a.m. and 7 p.m. and Wednesday at 7 p.m., Daddy steered our latest Plymouth or Chevrolet up and down the hilly two-lane seven-mile road to Howe to attend the First United Methodist Church my mother had chosen. Topped with a high steeple and wrapped in white clapboard, the church stood tall next to the two-lane highway to the Grayson County seat of Sherman and rested on a wide expanse of grass, which I recall as always green, unlike the usual yellow Bermuda grass in summer. Out on the highway, the traditional announcement board warned passing motorists of salvation or damnation with exhortations such as "The devil loves a sinner" or "It's HELL without Jesus!"

The church enriched our isolated rural lives, and, without it, we would have been far more impoverished. It was the center of our meager social activities and gave us a needed community to belong to. Stories of Christians serving as missionaries in darkest Africa and other distant places exposed me to a wider world, even if the people there appeared primitive. Teachings about love, compassion, kindness, generosity, and wisdom instilled in me the importance of universal virtues. Our Sunday and mid-week services prevented us from being available for even more farm work, though sometimes my father herded us out to the yard to chop the hated white blossom weeds between Sunday services.

Inside our church, sunlight streamed through stained-glass windows and illuminated Jesus wearing a cream-colored robe, his light-brown hair long and curled on his white skin. Small children and a few furry lambs gathered about his seat. Above hovered winged angels strumming golden harps. Though I knew Jesus told his followers to "suffer the little children to come to me and forbid them not, for of such is the kingdom of Heaven," I found it difficult to trust his gentle scripture. It contrasted so with my daily experience at home with the father I had learned to avoid.

Our ministers regaled us with visions of heaven awaiting us, though in order to enter this realm of angels and harps, we had to accept God's Son, Jesus, as our Lord and Savior. They also stressed the constant risk that our multitude of sins might cause God to deny us heaven. Their elevated voices carried such fervor that I imagined the flames of hell licking my ankles and a horned and long-tailed devil tending the eternal fires and brimstone, God's never-ending punishment for the wicked.

Sometimes we children filed in to stand on the dais and sing "Jesus Loves Me" for the congregation. I searched for my mother's proud face, next to my father's stern one. It appeared the Holy Father and my father were similarly harsh and unpredictable.

I was six or seven when my parents instituted a new ritual. We gathered five chairs in a circle in the kitchen after supper and opened our Bible. "We're going to take turns reading," my parents announced. I sat tensely, my feet dangling from my chair, watching my father and mother read, then my sister. Judy passed the Bible to me and I read:

"Truly I say to you, all sins will be forgiven the children of man, and whatever blasphemies they utter; but whoever blasphemes against the Holy Spirit never has forgiveness but is guilty of an eternal sin." Mark 3: 28-30.

As I read, a terrifying thought came to me. "Curse God!" I thought. I knew I had blasphemed against the Holy Spirit, committed the unforgiveable sin, and was damned to eternal burning. No one could help me. For the next several months, while the rest of my family watched Ed Sullivan in the dim living room, I snuck into my room and fell onto my knees. "Please forgive me, God! I didn't mean it!" I never considered telling anyone my panic, nor did anyone ever ask.

"You are forgiven," one night I felt the silent message washing over me like a warm bath. My body softened. My terrible terror drained away.

As a pre-teen, I became aware that millions of people followed other religions. One Sunday, I screwed up my courage and asked my Sunday School teacher what happened to these people when they died.

"Mrs. Peabody, surely God doesn't condemn all the Jews and Hindus and Muslims and Buddhists to hell; does he?"

Mrs. Peabody looked down at me, her face contracted into a mask of pious sorrow.

"Well, they had their chance. They could have accepted Jesus as their Savior."

I dropped my head in silent dismay. Why would I want to go to heaven with a God that mean?

Fear of becoming one of the condemned promoted my "goody-two-shoes" persona. I followed my mother's expectations to study hard, be responsible and proper in all things, wear white gloves, hot nylon stockings, and high heels to church, turn down the date with the cute Hispanic boy and date only white boys, resist all but deep tongue kisses, and prepare for a college education.

In elementary school, teachers sent home report cards commenting to my pleased parents, "Linda is unusually mature." I presented these report cards with a mixture of pride and the stiff rigidity required of a child performing beyond her age level.

My high school graduating 1962 Athenian yearbook picture shows me smiling eagerly, credited as the President of Dance Club, 60; Choir, 61,; Student Council, 61; Homeroom President, 61;

Athenian Business Staff, 61; Hi-Talk Editorial Staff, 61; National Honor Society, 61, 62; Reporter, 62; Variety Show, 61; Mu Alpha Theta, 62; Ready Writing, 60, 61, 62.

I wrack my brain now to kindle even one memory from these busy undertakings. They seem to have been the doings of someone else, a perky, sunny someone I wore as a disguise; a false self who protected me.

"I'm no good; I'm worthless." These thoughts tortured me. I hid them under a cover of achievements and compliance.

As a teen in our church production, I played a persecuted Christian on my way to the Roman Coliseum to be eaten by lions. Belting out my lines appealed to my need for noble sacrifice. Self-sacrifice and service to others, even at the cost of myself, seemed to be our church's message. To avoid Daddy's rage at home, we all walked on eggshells. At church, we learned to "turn the other cheek." Nowhere did I hear encouragement to stand up for myself. The word, "want," which would become an essential part of my therapist's vocabulary, was unknown.

18
RETURN TO COLLEGE

Shared joys make a friend, not shared sufferings.

—Friedrich Nietzsche

FALL, 1963

I dragged my suitcase upstairs into the dorm room Ellen and I shared our freshman year. Ellen was already there, unpacking her stuff into the small dresser on her side. I glanced towards the bunk beds and saw she'd already made up the top bunk. She'd given me the bottom again this year.

"Hi," I said, venturing a smile.

"Welcome back," Ellen greeted me. "How was your summer?" She averted her eyes.

I wanted to tell her the truth, but my answers wouldn't have been what she wanted to hear. "Okay, I guess. How about you? Did you have a good summer?"

"Yeah, great!" she said.

I felt a chasm between myself and Ellen now; a chasm I had no idea how to cross. My throat felt numb, frozen. My voice seemed to come from a faraway distance. A few minutes later, Ellen slipped across the hall to Karen's room. I could hear their muffled voices through the closed door. Were they talking about me?

I knocked on Karen's door. "Hi." A few more mumbled words and silence fell. My presence felt like a shroud covering their chatting and giggles, their relating summer secrets, their excited plans. I wanted to join in. Yet, none of it really mattered anymore. The classes, the instructors, the assignments, the dates –it all seemed irrelevant. Ellen and Karen turned away; or was it me? It wasn't long before Ellen started spending her free hours across the hall studying with Karen. I didn't follow along. It was easier to be alone.

Instead, I threw myself into studying. T*hink, don't feel.* I hurried to class, the faster the better, compulsively plucking at shrubs lining the paths, breaking off twigs along the way, ripping leaves from the Cotoneaster bushes and tossing them to the dry gravel.

I tapped a crazy drumbeat to the professor's voice with my pencil until other students stared in annoyance. I had no word for the anxiety that throbbed through my limbs.

Periodically waves of grief made my knees buckle. Faster, faster, run, there must be a way to outrun the unbearable fact that Mama is dead. She's never coming back. Forever.

19

I HAVE TO KNOW

When you have seen as much of life as I have, you will not underestimate the power of obsessive love.

—J.K. Rowling

MAY 2000

In an email, Cathy Bowman, the post-adoption social worker, encourages me to stay in touch with Marilyn, the first/birth mother I'd met at Gladney. She also tells me my son asked if he could write me through Cathy. She assured him she'll forward anything he sent for me. Cathy encourages me to call during my difficult waiting period. She is trying to help.

But having her as the go-between for me, a fifty-five-year old mother and my son, now thirty-five, strikes me as an unreasonable block and kindles my rebellion. Though I need her emotional support, I won't accept it. I resent the fact Cathy knows who and where my son is, while I don't. Yet, I fear alienating her by allowing my anger to show; so, I can't open my heart to her.

Meanwhile, Marilyn sends me a friendly email, telling me of her work as a volunteer searcher. She wants to help me in any way she can. I write Marilyn my great news about my son.

Marilyn writes back the same day with prophetic words:

"I want you to realize that this is the biggest roller coaster you will ever ride. You are going to be scared, excited, joyful, just every emotion and sometimes they all hit within a minute or so."

My son has become real to me, no longer as if dead, no longer missing-in-action. My original hope to reconnect with him has caught fire and now threatens to take over my life. I begin living in minute-to-minute scenarios of possibilities, bombarding Dave with questions he can't answer.

Out back under our fig tree, we nurse glasses of Gallo Hearty Burgundy at the end of long workdays. Crows chase and complain to each other across the dimming sky. Our two cats, Girlie and Bouvier, weave between our legs as I reach to pet them.

"You could hear from him any time," Dave encourages me. His willingness to listen is my lifeline to sanity. Yet, I lurch from hope to despair, haunting my email and hurrying to grab the snail mail as it falls through the slot in our front door. No word.

A good Samaritan emails me. Ruthanne found me on the adoption registry, TxCARE. Ruthanne asks if anyone has looked in the old Texas birth index to see if my son might be listed under my name. She tells me I can download the names of all the baby boys born on his birthdate in his birth county.

Ruthanne's email electrifies me. A hidden world exists in which women unraveled for each other the secrets hidden by adoption agencies and laws! My stomach tightening, almost holding my breath, I rush to follow her instructions. When my efforts fail, I type out a request to this generous unknown new friend.

"I can't seem to do it. Can you help me?"

The next day, I receive another message from Ruthanne with a list of all the males born in Tarrant County on Oct. 30, 1964.

I vacillate. What good would it do even if I could figure out this baffling list? I write back to thank Ruthanne and learn when she responds that she is neither an adoptee nor a birth mother. She and her husband had adopted a daughter. Twenty years later, they helped their adopted daughter find her original mother. How amazing! I didn't know there were adoptive parents like this! Could my son's parents be anything like this open-minded adoptive mother?

The roller coaster Marilyn warned me about has dips as well as peaks. That weekend I begin to have mysterious crying episodes. I didn't expect this to surface so much grief. I decide to slow down. I can't sleep or eat and am crying a lot.

I can really see how my son might be very reluctant. The whole thing is very destabilizing to our normal view of how our lives and selves are. If I feel that way, how much more must he?

Marilyn writes, confirming my feelings, feelings she says we never dealt with because we stayed in hiding. She tells me she could take the list and find my son's adoptive name.

"Information is power," I tell my clients. The need to grab back the power I gave away pushes me to uncover Gladney's secrets.

I send Marilyn the list.

That same day, Marilyn emails back.

"Robert Lee Yates is your son."

His name and address appear like a magic carpet. My son is in New Orleans, a place I visited with Peter, my then boyfriend who became Chad's father. We had eaten bread and cheese on a stoop in the French Quarter while I wondered out loud about my lost baby. Now I knew. I could call my son. I could write him directly. I could show up at his home, ring the doorbell, and maybe he'd invite me in.

But I can't. My son may already have my anonymous letter sent by Cathy. I imagine him reading that letter from Cathy, hunched over a mint julep, throwing nervous glimpses at his window in case I am outside. I know he needs time. Maybe he's never even wondered who his first mother was or if he had another family somewhere. If he knew I'd learned his name, he'd probably be alarmed, shocked.

Having his contact information feels like having a stick of dynamite in my pocket. It's lit, but I can't throw it; not for a long time.

Besides, I feel afraid. I sit at my piano and attempt to play my slow rendition of Debussy's *Clair De Lune*, only to find myself peering toward my living room window. I imagine the doorbell ringing, Robert Lee standing on our porch hidden by the sheer curtains that screen our large front window. A shiver goes through me. What would I say to him?

I've taught relaxation to hundreds of clients. Now I just have to do it for myself. I let my shoulders and trunk sag. I tell my arms and thighs and calves to relax. I feel them go warm and heavy. I feel good, but I can already tell it isn't going to last.

We'll be celebrating Terra's seventh birthday together in a month. I tell Chad we'll celebrate this new development, too. Chad says his partner, Marcia, wants help to find her daughter, who would also be in the Texas Birth Index. When I call my search angel, Marilyn, she assures me she'll help.

Next month, Dave and I, Chad, Marcia, Jared, and Terra, sit in the warm June dusk listening to crickets and enjoying Terra's birthday cake and ice cream.

Marcia, who has been very quiet during dinner, says, holding back tears, "Linda, Marilyn got my daughter's name and I called her. I was so excited. Her name is Delilah and she told me she grew up in a Lutheran minister's family near Dallas, Texas. She just had her first baby; a boy. I told Delilah I'd like to send a gift for the baby, my only grandchild. I thought the conversation went well, but I got a letter from her a week later." Marcia wipes away tears with her napkin.

"What did she say?" I ask, dreading the answer.

"She told me she'd prayed about it and God told her not to have anything to do with me. She told me on the phone she didn't want to know anything about her origins, because she said she always knew it was bad." Marcia's voice chokes with sobs.

"So much for God is love," Chad interjects.

"Yeah," Jared agrees. "That's terrible."

"I'm so sorry," I say. "That's devastating." My heart aches for Marcia.

"Her daughter is foolish," Chad says, his voice tight. "She's passing up her opportunity to learn her heritage and to connect with her original family."

"Yes," I say. But maybe next week my son, Robert Lee, will write something similar. Or maybe he'll never answer my letter at all. I promise myself I won't call him.

20

WAKING UP

When truth is buried underground it grows, it chokes, it gathers such an explosive force that on the day it bursts out, it blows up everything with it.

—Emile Zola

2000

Weeks drag on. I search Amazon for books on adoption and reunions. Marilyn emails that there will be about six first/birth mothers in a room of one hundred women about my age.

Six first mothers out of a hundred? The number staggers me. Yet Marilyn's statistics confirm what I am reading. A term I have never heard becomes part of my new lingo, The Baby Scoop Era. Somewhere between four to six million girls and young women gave up their babies to adoption from the end of WWII to 1973. At least two million of us went along with adoption for our babies during the 1960s alone. [8]

8 Karen Wilson-Buterbaugh, *The Baby Scoop Era: Unwed Mothers, Infant Adoption, Forced Surrender*, Karen Wilson-Buterbaugh, 2017, p. 35.

Rickie Solinger in *Wake Up Little Susie: Single Pregnancy and Race before Roe v. Wade* writes, "The availability of white illegitimate babies met an overwhelming demand from white childless couples who wanted to create normative American families" by adoption.[9] "In post-war America, there was only one public intention for white unwed mothers and their babies: separate them."[10] She quotes Leontine Young, a consultant about unmarried mothers, citing "the tendency to regard [white] unmarried mothers as breeding machines, means to an end."[11]

Psychological experts then defined young white mothers as neurotic and disturbed, while also prescribing a method for their rehabilitation – giving up their babies for adoption. This relieved the stigma and shame of post-war white families who strained to move up in the social strata and worried about what the neighbors would think. Most followed the social workers' and society's advice to require their daughters to dispose of their guilt in unwed mothers' homes. Afterwards, girls could pursue marriage and future parenting.[12]

After the war ended, a period of upward mobility began, creating an unprecedented expansion of the middle class. Those who prosecuted the war against fascism came home eager to move up economically and begin families; that is, nuclear families defined as two parents with one or more children. Those children, born between 1946 and 1964, became known as the "baby boomers" and constituted an essential part of the so-called "normal" family. Infertile white couples who could not produce their own babies became a ready market for the millions of white babies born to unwed mothers like me.[13] They paid thousands of dollars to obtain them, making them into valuable commodities.[14] As one social scientist put it, illegitimate babies were

---

9 Rickie Solinger, Author, Elaine Tyler-May, Foreword, *Wake Up Little Susie: Single Pregnancy and Race Before Roe v. Wade*, Routledge, 1992, p. 154

10 Ibid, p.187

11 Ibid, p.28.

12 Ibid, p.153-4.

13 Ibid, p.155.

14 Ibid, p.154.

"the silver lining in a dark cloud" since there were not enough white babies available to satisfy the desires of infertile couples.[15]

Alternatively, Solinger explained how unmarried black girls were expected to keep their babies, especially since white families did not want them.[16]Interestingly, a Children's Bureau report in the mid-1940s contained a statement: "...Negro families care for Negro children when something happens to their parents and that the neighborliness and kindliness of Negro relatives far exceed[s] that of white relatives."[17] Ironically, white officials used this statement to justify not providing services to black unwed mothers.

My white baby—well, white if you didn't know about my Choctaw Indian great-grandfather--constituted a *commodity*. I look up the word in the dictionary:

> "Commodity: an economic good, something useful or valued, one that is subject to ready exchange or exploitation within a market."[18]

If I had thought to mention my baby's Native American DNA, his life prospects likely would have diminished substantially.

This was what I had participated in! My hands jerk as I turn the pages. I lie sleepless most nights imagining my son's face, yearning to meet my tiny granddaughters, watching the numbers on my clock flip the minutes away, and arising most mornings with heavy limbs and stinging eyes.

Reading Solinger's book in bed only increases my tension, but I can't put it down. I turn towards Dave, nearly asleep next to me, and exclaim, "Listen to this! I was a breeder!"

Dave groans and mumbles.

I get up to make a snack, hoping it will help me sleep, and bash my arm on the dresser leaving our bedroom. I picture my brother's

---

15 Ibid, p.154.

16 Ibid, p.196.

17 Ibid, p.190.

18 *Merriam-Webster's Collegiate Dictionary*, 11th Edition, Merriam-Webster, Incorporated, Springfield, Mass., 2014

bull out in his pasture in Texas. He helps create commodities for Steve to sell.

Marilyn doesn't seem to have the anger I'm falling into. Or maybe she's channeling it into her work as a searcher. She writes me how wonderful it is to see the healing that comes from the reunions she helps occur. In Marilyn's descriptions of her volunteer work with birth parents and adoptees, I see myself reflected. I'm beginning to feel stronger. At the same time, learning about how I was a victim of a giant adoption experiment shocks me. How can I regain the power I lost when they took my baby?

The next morning, summer air wafts through the open window, reminding me of East Texas heat. To calm myself, I sit down at my piano to practice one of my favorites, "Summertime" from *Porgy and Bess*. Reading the lyrics of "Summertime," I wonder how life has been for my southern son. How were his Mama and Daddy? A heavy weight oppresses me. I always told my clients, "The only way out of grief is through it." I let my fingers lie on the piano keys, the music forgotten, while my head droops and tears roll down my cheeks.

21

SECRETS AND LIES

Secrets are so hard to live with.

—Marilyn

2000

Yes, Marilyn, my search angel, put her finger on it. Keeping my secret requires me to live a lie. Living a lie requires a lot of separation. Separation is lonely. Keeping a big secret requires a lot of energy. I often tell my psychotherapy patients, "The one who carries the secret also carries the shame."

When my obstetrician-gynecologists for my next two pregnancies asked how many children I'd already had, I mentioned my first pregnancy but never revealed that I wasn't raising that child. When I applied for my Master's in 1973, I disclosed giving up my first baby in the required bio, with comments that I believed I'd made the right decision, which was true then and probably helped me be admitted to the competitive graduate school, where the social work admittance panel likely approved. I told my brother and sister at the time I was pregnant. I told my serious partners through the years, and certainly, my husbands. Otherwise, even though I became a therapist and developed skills to help other people with their deepest pain, I kept my secret. I never told any of my own therapists; not even my best therapist, Ron.

In 1992, Ron's office in Ventura was in the same building where I had my private practice. What began as clinical supervision with Ron metamorphosed into intensive psychotherapy. Each week, I locked the door to my office and stepped across the hall into his. "You were a child," Ron said, "trapped, helpless to receive the nurturing every child desperately needs. When you were emotionally abandoned, you concluded there must be something wrong with you." Ron was right. Even with all my clinical training and work, I still felt a need to hide from other people, expecting them to find something wrong with me. "You tried everything to find a way to please your parents, to be valued, to find some way to get the approval you had to have."

Ron's words rang true. I'd become the over-achiever, the super-independent one, always trying to prove myself. While that pushed me to work hard and to accomplish a lot, it didn't free me. The feeling I wasn't good enough required getting up every day and proving myself all over again. It was exhausting.

My self-sufficient shell cracked open. "A child can't understand why Mommy and Daddy don't respond to their needs," Ron said. "They know they're there to take care of them and when they don't, they can't make sense of it. They assume something bad inside them must be the problem. That's the tragedy."

I'd done what all children do. If I'd really grasped how helpless, how powerlessness I was to fix my parents' inability to nurture, especially my father's, I'd have been face-to-face with the knowledge that I was trapped, that nothing I did would help. That would have been unbearable. Like all children, I had to have hope to be able to grow up.

My therapy brought up intense pain, anguish, and release. By the end of that deep work, my memories lost their power to bring me suffering and confidence that I was worth loving replaced them. Somehow though, I managed never to share the loss of my first child.

I 'd learned to live in the loneliness of being different, ashamed, and stigmatized, even while no one else knew. I couldn't do that without carrying anger along with the pain. If I'd smashed my thumb with a hammer, I'd have known where my few choice curse words came from. But in the case of my deep, secret loss, making the connection wasn't clear. I tried hard, not always successfully, to keep my hurt and anger buried. But again, as we say in therapy, "What we don't work on, works on us."

Baby showers were especially difficult. My young Kaiser co-worker, Margie, sat among our employee group like a princess, full of joy, rich with promise, wearing a tight jersey top over her bursting round belly, her long dark hair pulled back from her radiant face. I admired her. Except for the happiness she exuded, she looked little different from the girls at my unwed mothers' home.

The fragrance of Orange Tang Tea in dainty china cups drifted like clouds over a tropical island through the room. We passed the gifts around the circle, oohing and aahing - a tiny stretch jersey emblazoned with yellow butterflies, a blue plush baby blanket, an adorable brown and white stuffed monkey. I wanted to cuddle the monkey.

Marianne, sitting next to me, leaned over and said, "I heard she's having a boy."

"That's great," I replied, forcing a smile. Inside, my heart clenched up like a fist.

"I'd love to have a boy," Marianne continued. "I've only got girls."

My stomach tightening, I held my breath, managed another vacuous smile, and turned away before she could ask, "How about you, Linda? Do you have boys? How many?"

Althea cut the vanilla cake. "Whoever gets the piece with the rattle will be the next new mother," she trilled. The cake stuck in my throat. The sweet chocolate frosting tasted bitter like the secret I was keeping.

Thirty-five years I kept that secret. It choked me the whole time and the worst thing is I didn't even know it.

22
CODE PHRASES

Sunlight is the best disinfectant, both in government and in our personal lives.

http://www.aquarianadoptee.com/secrets-and-lies/?utm_source=hootsuite

2000

I know Cathy is eager to help me. Yet, as both a first/birth mother and a social worker myself, I begrudge Cathy's continuing to work at Gladney, who still promotes adoptions. "How can you keep doing this?" I ask her.

"I don't believe in abortion," she answered. "I'm a Baptist."

I protest the prevailing practice that adoption records remain closed even into the adoptee's adulthood. Surely, everyone deserves to know who their first parents are.

"I'm just not a political person," she volunteers, leaving me vexed, aggravated, and glad she can't see me through the phone shaking my head back and forth.

I don't challenge her further. My fears of lifetime sterility or bleeding to death from a botched abortion kept me from seeking an illegal abortion in 1964. My religious background also ruled out my considering abortion then. Yet, I couldn't wish the agony of losing a full-term baby on any other woman. I support the rights of women to legal abortions now. I'd read that most women who'd had legal abortions since Roe v. Wade passed in 1973 didn't report long-term grief.[19] They apparently didn't fall into fits of weeping while practicing the piano.

In any case, adoption is not an alternative to abortion. It is an alternative to parenting. Why not help mothers raise their own children? Then I read that the average adoptive parents pay $28,000 for an American infant.[20] Who would pay that to help a mother keep her child? I thought of the saying, "Follow the money." More head shaking.

Now I risk abandoning the hard-earned confidence I've gained through years of therapy and my professional training and experience. Gladney holds the power and I don't dare challenge them. Cathy holds the "keys to the kingdom," while I approach like the supplicant at the gate of the castle.

I finally dial Cathy's number.

"Hello," she answers on the second ring.

"Hi, Cathy."

She recognizes my voice. "How are you?"

"I've learned my son's name," I tell her. "Some searchers found it and sent it to me."

"What name did they give you?" Cathy inquires.

"Robert Lee Yates," I answer, holding my breath.

"Well," Cathy says. "I have a lot of faith in the searchers. They're very good."

When I hang up, I flop back with a loud yelp in my chair before I jump up to run and tell Dave. Cathy has used the art of obscure replies to convey what the law doesn't allow her to say directly. With her code phrases, she offers all the support she can.

---

19 Kirsten Black, "Some women feel grief after an abortion, but there's no evidence of serious mental health issues," *The Conversation*, April 25, 2018, http://the conversation-com/some-women-feel-grief-after-an-abortion-but-theres-no-evidence-of-serious-mental-health-issues-95519..

20 Dawn Davenport, "How Much Does Adoption Really Cost?", *Creating a Family*, https://creatingafamily.org/adoption-category/how-much-does-it-really-cost-to-adopt/, Accessed Feb. 22, 2019.

October 30, 2000. I know my son's name and location. He has had my letter for six months. Today, he's turning thirty-six. I've never been able to wish him a happy birthday. I still can't this year, but I write this poem.

Uprooted, the baby ejected, lost
Caught, arms reaching, holding, loving, raising

Becoming, man with roots divided
Torn, bandaged, made whole?

Sought, rediscovered by the mother stranger
Yearning for the one she lost

What answer he, with no recall,
Nor memory, nor need
To be uprooted one more time?

She waits, he now rebirthed,
She longing to see unknown face,
Eyes on distant place.

Wiping my eyes, I close my notebook. I pick up Girlie to take to bed, where her purring next to my ear will comfort me.

23

REACH MY OWN MOON

Ignorance is the curse of God; knowledge is the wing wherewith we fly to heaven.

—William Shakespeare

2001

The year is a blur, a haze of clinical work. Individually and in groups, I see up to eighteen clients a day in Outpatient Psychiatry at Kaiser. My feet sound like rapid drumbeats as I walk up the bare clinic hallways to bring the next struggling patient back to my office, where I focus on their suffering instead of my own.

Underneath a thin veil of normalcy, a constant thrum of thwarted energy pulses in me, leading me forward to a dimly imagined future. I am like a prison inmate yearning for a reprieve, haunting the prison law library.

I obsess about how to promote a response from my first son. After work, I propel our big white Dodge van through the little town of Dixon, passing the old Milk Farm sign of the cow jumping over the moon that no longer lights up. I need to create my own light. I need to reach my own moon.

I wrack my brain for the right time to write Robert directly. Six months seems reasonable, but that would be near his birthday. I discard that idea, along with Thanksgiving and Christmas. I consider waiting nine months. The irony of a nine-month gestation between the letter he got from Gladney and the one I'd send appeals to me. Perhaps he wouldn't appreciate that. Besides, it would fall on New Year's.

I decide to wait a year. If Robert doesn't respond then, I imagine myself tumbling off a ledge into depression; for surely that would indicate he'll never answer.

I try to slake my thirst imagining this son with a Confederate general's name, Robert Lee. Is his adoptive mother a Daughter of the Confederacy? Does his adoptive father spend his free time reenacting Civil War battles with other die-hard Confederates? Since I left my home state of Texas for California, I would not find it easy to relate. Yet, I take perverse pleasure in knowing his adoptive parents gave him the same name I would have chosen, his birth father Bob's name.

Now I need to make sure I have the correct address. I begin to surf the net. A man named Robert Lee Yates was just arrested, accused as a serial killer! Reading on, this Robert Lee Yates lived and was arrested in Washington State. I thank my lucky stars that I know my son is in New Orleans.

I write Marilyn for more information. The list of Robert Yates expands. There are addresses for New Orleans and outlying areas. Perhaps my son uses his adoptive father's permanent address? How could there be so many Robert Yates?

The next day, I dial Cathy's number. "Hello," she answers.

"Hi, Cathy, this is Linda Franklin. Do you remember me?" I haven't called her in almost a year.

"Of course," she says, her voice sympathetic. "How are you?"

"Not bad, Cathy. I'm fine, but it's been a long year, and I haven't gotten any response from Robert. I really want to try writing directly to him, but I have several addresses. I know you can't tell me, but I'm hoping you can help," I say, trying not to drop the papers clutched in my hand.

I can almost hear Cathy sit up straighter. "What do you have?" she asks softly.

I read the first address.

"That's not the one I have," Cathy replies.

I read the next one.

"I wouldn't get attached to that address," she says.

I scan rapidly down my lists, looking for the ones that seem most likely and read those out. I hear Cathy's sharp intake of breath.

"I can't keep doing this!" she says. Perhaps her supervisor was there, overhearing our conversation.

I grasp my list with sweaty palms.

"Just one more. Please, Cathy," I beg. "Just one more!" I read out one more address.

"No, I don't recognize that one," she says in a firm voice, "Linda, I can't help you anymore. If you want me to send your letter through us, let me know. I can do that. Don't forget, I'd do the same for you if you didn't want your son to reach you directly."

Cathy's insistence on protecting privacy seems paternalistic and unwarranted. My chest tightens with unreasoning rage. I want to scream. Almost against my will, I blurt, "My son is grown now! We're both adults who should be able to protect ourselves. I don't want you to protect me!"

Cathy remains calm, obviously used to angry first/birth mothers. Her voice is pleasant as usual, reminding me my resistance is useless. I feel like a bratty child whose mother sends her to her room. When I hang up, I immediately regret my foolish outburst. The next day I call to apologize, but, really, I'm not sorry. I'm just afraid to alienate the one person with the information I need. I dislike myself for manipulating her with my questions, but I have to reach my son.

24

TRY AGAIN

If all you can do is crawl, start crawling.

—Rumi

2001

What to do next? I email Marilyn asking if she can find a credit address for a Robert Yates with my son's middle initial of "L." An hour later, Marilyn's email lights my computer screen. On two more credit databases, Marilyn had found six Robert Yates, three with the middle initial of "L."

Trying to keep the tremor out of my voice, I call Cathy again and read off the first address. "I'd try that one," she replies.

She really is trying to help me. I picture Cathy leaning back in her swivel desk chair with a sense of satisfaction. I wish I trusted her more. Unearthing my baby has made me question my decisions of long ago. How might my life might have been different if anyone at Gladney had asked, "Have you thought about raising your own child? You have your mother's inheritance, after all." How much pain I might have been saved had someone there questioned the conventional assumption that adoption was the only answer.

Now I can write my son directly. I dash into the kitchen and tug open the refrigerator freezer. I taste the cold little marshmallows and nuts in a carton of Rocky Road Ice Cream with a soup spoon before tossing the spoon into the sink. I head to the bedroom and grab my tennis shoes. Large blue scrub jays chatter in time to my racing mind as I walk rapidly around our neighborhood until returning home in a sweat, my face hot and red, my body fatigued and relieved.

25

NOTHING MORE TO LOSE

Your pain is the breaking of the shell that encloses your understanding.

—Kahlil Gibran

2001

I call Chad to suggest he may want to include a note with my planned letter. Chad could be more welcome as a family member than I, who Robert Lee may believe guilty of abandoning him. Chad had lost a parent, too.

There was only one time I'd told Jared and his older brother, Chad, about their brother, and that was twenty years ago. I'd just been hired as a brand-new social worker, case-managing sixty clients with developmental disabilities at Alta California Regional Center in Sacramento, California. The year before, I'd crossed the stage of California State University at Sacramento in my cap and gown to receive my Master's in Social Work diploma. In my graduate program, there'd been very little training on adoption and all of it had been positive. After all, social workers were the primary professionals handling adoption.

Our instructor assigned a small green book, *Beyond the Best Interests of the Child.* [21] Everything I read there seemed to confirm the benefits of adoption done at the earliest possible moment in cases like mine or for children in foster care. In class I kept my eyes focused on the manual, not wanting my classmates to suspect I was one of those unwed mothers who gave up my child, trying to ignore the ache in my heart.

That summer of 1980, I took Chad and Jared on a plane trip home to Texas. Right before we flew back to California, I stopped at the Gladney adoption agency, seeking to find out whatever I could about the infant I'd left there. I knew I wouldn't get any identifying information, but I hoped to learn how my child fared.

It was the day before that visit that I finally shared with my sons, then twelve and ten years old, that they had a brother. They listened silently the next day to the social worker. I saw the shock in their eyes, but the calcified place in my heart where I'd kept my long-buried secret prevented me from finding the words to help them understand what I didn't myself.

We accompanied the staid social worker across the grounds of the Gladney campus I'd traversed sixteen years before. I could feel Chad and Jared hanging onto the few words she shared, just like I was.

Chad, gangly in his Guess jeans and Keds sneakers he thought he needed to wear to fit in with other kids. Walking next to him, Jared, shorter, a little plump, was quiet, introverted, too withdrawn already. I looked at my two boys and wondered if their missing brother looked anything like either of them.

"The last contact we had with the adoptive parents was when they came back two years later and got a baby girl," the Gladney social worker told me. Another unmarried woman's baby is my baby boy's sister, I thought.

I learned nothing that day at Gladney about how my missing son was. I discovered nothing about where my then sixteen-year-old son might be. What name did he carry? What parents did he call mom

---

[21] Joseph Goldstein, Anna Freud, and Albert J. Solnit, *Beyond the Best Interests of the Child*, New York: The Free Press, (MacMillan Publishing Co.) 1973.

and dad? I left Gladney and let the lid close back over my unspoken guilt and sorrow. They'd promised letting him be adopted was an act of love.

It had been. Hadn't it?

I'd done the right thing. Hadn't I?

After leaving my baby at Gladney, I'd moved in with my sister, Judy, in Austin, preparing to transfer to the University of Texas at Austin for the Spring, 1965 semester. Judy had an upstairs apartment in an old house. Downstairs lived a couple with their baby. Each time I passed the mother carrying her infant, an ice pick of pain stabbed my heart. I got a job at Sears in the candy department. Mothers with toddlers pushing strollers came in the front entrance, following the excited squeals of their children to our glass-fronted candy case filled with the chocolate aroma of peanut clusters, macaroons, and creams. I filled little paper sacks with candy while taking furtive looks at babies in their strollers. Could that one with dark hair by mine? How old is that one wrapped in blue flannel?

In 1965, the Vietnam War was in full throttle, as was the protest movement against it in the United States. Emerging from my classes' registration, students manned tables inviting participation in sororities and fraternities, ROTC, music, dance, and other social clubs. Native Texan, Lyndon B. Johnson, was President of the United States and his daughter, Lynda Byrd Johnson, was reputed to be a student at UT and to belong to a popular sorority.

Arriving from my recent sojourn at Gladney, I couldn't imagine joining any of the happy activities. I passed up the clean-cut, cheerful students, attracted to a table with a sign, "Make Love, Not War." It was peopled by a small group of young men in tie-dyed t-shirts whose stringy hair appeared in need of a comb and young women dressed in loose flowery peasant tops and long skirts, both sexes wearing strands of beads around their necks, colorful headbands, and Birkenstocks. It was my first view of hippies. One of the rebellious-looking young students at the anti-war table offered me a brochure, "Resist Johnson's War." Other brochures cluttered the table along with announcements of planned sit-ins and protests.

With this anti-war group, I attended protests at the Texas State Capital when President Johnson came there, once getting hit in my head by a clashing pro-war protestor's cardboard sign. My new short-lived boyfriend dressed in all black and drove me to protests on his Harley Davidson where TV cameras filmed our roaring entrance. Another protest took our group on Easter Sunday to Lyndon Johnson family's church on a dirt road outside Austin. The day was hot, and I stood under a shade tree until a polite FBI agent asked me to step into the sun for a photograph, which I presume is still in some ancient file.

When not protesting, we partied, smoked marijuana, and dropped occasional hallucinogenic mescaline made from peyote cactus and obtained from the nearby farm of a Baptist deacon. A local law enforcement man usually attended our parties but never interfered. I felt he kept a protective eye out for me. Later, I learned the Austin police chief was working closely with the FBI. Was that him? What is in my file?

I soon became involved in the Civil Rights movement. My objections to the Vietnam war and racism were sincere, but our rebellious group also felt like a haven for outcasts like me. I wouldn't be rejected. I could rage against the war's injustice and racism's cruelty and no one needed to know about my hateful father, my dead mother, and my lost baby. One hippie couple had a baby. The mother carried him everywhere, well-wrapped, placid. Were they married? I didn't know. I didn't think so. I envied them. Why hadn't I kept my baby?

During the student break of 1966, I traveled to Alabama to explore helping register blacks to vote. On the way to speak at black churches, we were tailgated on dark country roads. I felt menaced by their bright headlights. When walking on the dirt roads in the black part of town where we stayed, we were forced to leap into ditches by teen drivers racing too close. I had grown up with "Whites Only" signs tacked next to drinking fountains and restrooms. I took seriously the Ku Klux Klan literature displayed on card tables at service stations on our way through Mississippi and Alabama where we stopped for gas. I feared being murdered, as student activists Chaney, Goodman, and Schwerner were in the civil rights struggle in 1964. I withdrew from planned voter registration that summer.

I became involved with Peter, a decent man, quiet and retiring. I wanted to love him. He felt safe. Peter considered himself a conscientious objector, though he had no religious background to be able to receive an official deferment. Peter was thinking of fleeing the country. We moved into an apartment over a garage just off the main street fronting the UT Campus, Guadalupe, which we called "the drag" and where we hung out with friends at bookstores and coffee shops. On August 1st, 1966, I walked across the campus to meet Peter for lunch where he worked. Five minutes after I passed under the University of Texas Tower, Charles Whitman opened fire from the college tower, killing sixteen people before law enforcement shot him. The first person he shot from the tower was my eighteen-year-old, eight months pregnant acquaintance, Claire. Her unborn baby was killed. She was in the hospital for months. I heard she could never have another baby because of internal injuries. Ruined, her baby stillborn. At least my baby lived, I thought.

On October 21 of 1966, Benjamin Spock, M.D., baby specialist and anti-war critic, called President Johnson "the enemy," speaking from the Lincoln Memorial at the beginning of a rally in Washington, DC where a hundred thousand people marched on the Pentagon. Violence broke out and nearly seven hundred people were arrested. In Austin, the anti-war protests gained strength. Black friends on the street told me of their suffering under racism. After Whitman, the campus felt like a war zone, too. Passing under the tower took courage.

After graduating in January of 1967, Peter and I rode Amtrak from San Antonio to Chicago and across the northern US, crossing into Vancouver and being admitted by immigration. After that, Peter was officially a "draft dodger" and couldn't enter the United States without being subject to immediate arrest. I knew my feelings for Peter would never be enough. Yet, with no mother to answer to and my baby gone, too, neediness drove me to go with him. On our way to Canada, I stared out the large train windows, feeling I might plummet into the endless open grasses of North Dakota, the landscape as bleak as I felt.

After my mother's death, I felt alone in the world, completely on my own. With the loss of my baby a year and a half later, that feeling intensified. I listened to Janis Joplin's rough voice singing "Me and

Bobby McGee," belting out her line about having nothing more to lose. The clacking of the wheels on the track resounded as if repeating her message. I felt I had nothing more to lose myself; that I had no one left to answer to. I had managed to convert my anguish at being alone into an intoxicating sense that I was free to do whatever I wanted. But that freedom robbed me of any sense of connection or stability. In a profound way, it no longer mattered what I did.

"Do you think they're married?" I heard the woman whisper behind me on the train. I'd already observed her with a man. No doubt *they* were married. He solid in a checked shirt, short sleeved, his waist wide from her good home cooking. She exuded security and comfort in her pastel dress and low-slung heels, her nails glowing a soft pink that set off her diamond ring as she rested her hand on his arm.

"They don't *look* married," I overheard her murmur.

I flinched, pretending not to hear. She was right, though. We *didn't* look married. I didn't *feel* like being married, either. I envied her.

Would feeling I had nothing else I could lose make me free? I wanted to believe that. Instead, one afternoon after we'd settled in Vancouver, Peter encouraged me not to bother with my diaphragm I'd gotten. I gave in. I became pregnant again. Even though I hadn't intended to get pregnant with Peter, I never considered giving up this second baby. When my doctor let me know he could arrange an abortion, though that was illegal in Canada also, I declined. I called my father in Texas and told him Peter and I had married.

Chad was born in Vancouver, Canada. The day after his birth, I developed a fever. The medical staff removed Chad for three days so he wouldn't contract my illness. I was inconsolable. I sobbed so continuously that a nurse came in my room and asked why I was so upset. When I revealed I'd given up my first baby, the nurse blanched, turned on her heels, and hastened out of my room without a word.

On a visit to Texas, I met Don. Childless no more, I soon left Peter back in Canada.

26

GO FOR IT

Run from what's comfortable. Forget safety. Live where you fear to live. Destroy your reputation. Be notorious. I have tried prudent planning long enough. From now on I'll be mad.

—Rumi

2001

This letter will be short, almost business-like; no emotional appeal this time. Robert will be surprised enough to receive a letter directly to his home.

I write Robert letting him know that I have known his name for almost a year while waiting and hoping he'd reply to the letter Cathy sent him from the Gladney Center last April.

All during my search for addresses, I'd read offers on my computer screen. "Just type in your credit card and click the blue circle with the word 'yes' inside it." For sixty dollars, I could receive criminal, bankruptcy, and arrest records. Each time, my fingers reached towards the blue circle, I pulled them back. I wouldn't spy on my son no matter how desperate I felt for information.

I told him I had always thought of him and wanted contact, but I didn't want to intrude. I assured him I understood his mother and father who raised him would always be his parents. I told him I don't want to take anything away from his relationships with them, but he always has been and always will be important to me. If he chooses to keep me out of his life, that will be agonizing, but I have to respect whatever decision he makes.

Chad sends me a thoughtful letter encouraging Robert to write back, Chad sharing his experience of being adopted by Jared's father, Don.

> "I'm your half-brother, Chad. I'm adding a short note in with my mom's, hoping you will contact one or both of us. I imagine you have a full family life and are probably busy. You may not feel you need to know this part of your life. I would like to know you at least a bit and so would the rest of my family, including my daughter."

I'm glad Chad is interested in meeting his brother and including his daughter, but will that brother answer this time? Chad writes more:

> "My birth father lived in Canada and I met him when I was a teenager. I never thought about him much, truthfully, and consider the man that adopted and raised me my dad. However, as I got older and matured, I decided I did want to at least talk to and get to know him a bit. That was about a year ago. When I called, I found out he had died two years prior of cancer. His wife said he did try to find me and couldn't."

Did Chad regret that he had awakened to awareness of Peter's importance to him too late? I've always regretted that Chad never really got to know his biological father. The few times Don and I traveled to Canada, we contacted Peter so he and Chad could meet. Because Peter could not return to the US, Don officially adopted Chad. Severing Peter's legal ties cut off his commitment to sending the little cards and fairy tale books he mailed during Chad's toddler years. Just as with my firstborn, the laws of adoption removed Peter's official significance and name from Chad's. No longer Chad's legitimate parent, Peter dropped out of Chad's life. No adoption papers, though, took away the feelings Chad expressed in his letter.

The next morning, I ask Dave to read the letters.

"They're good," he assures me.

"What if this doesn't work?" I ask.

"Well, if anybody can make this happen, you can."

Now there's nothing to do but wait and hope. As Cathy warned me:

"Now the part that can often be the hardest is about to start."

I fold the letters into a leftover Christmas envelope decorated with green holly leaves and red berries.

Our Vita-Mix roars, grinding my morning smoothies. Soy powder, a frozen overripe banana, a raw egg, ice, and the smooth aroma of vanilla. Like the Vita-Mix, I am all sharp edges spinning at high velocity and threatening to lose control. Every cell in my body pulsates, straining to reach my silent son. I might lift off the ground and whirl like a dervish. Or plummet from a low-flying plane like a sky-diver falling toward ground. But would my parachute open in time?

PART 2

Enjoying this book?
The best way to thank an author
is to post a review on Amazon.
Thank you!

27
TROUBLE AND KINDNESS

Whoever finds love beneath hurt and grief disappears into emptiness with a thousand new disguises.

—Rumi

FALL 1963

Aunt Jenna called me at college to say my grandmother died. She was discovered lying on the kitchen floor. This was the grandmother who gave me *café au lait* in delicate china cups when we visited. She brought out tattered, yellowing copies of 1900s Ladies' Home Journals and showed me sketches of the women in long dresses with bustles and hats. She introduced me to vivid Audubon prints of exotic birds and unrolled her prints of early Americana art for my education.

"It was a heart attack, probably brought on by the shock of losing your mother only six months ago," said my aunt. "She laid there for two days." I pictured my crippled, legally blind grandmother lying helpless on the floor in her small home, feeling sad for her and for me. "You don't need to come for the funeral, Linda," said Aunt Jenna. "Everyone will understand, after what you've been through."

I took Aunt Jenna's advice, mostly because I didn't want to make the six-hour drive with my father, trapped in his car. Instead, I went on a date that night, but I wasn't really interested in the boy. I couldn't recall him a week later. Afterwards, I wished I'd gone to the funeral. I wished I'd told my grandmother goodbye.

Without Grandmother, there was no adult left to take an interest in me, none left to love me. I felt doubly alone. Afterwards, I learned that my aunts took everything, not even leaving an old magazine or a teacup for me, my sister, or brother. Many years later, Aunt Marie offered old textbooks from Grandmother's school teaching years. Aunt Jenna stitched a delicate lace section from Grandmother's wedding dress to a square of black velvet and framed it for me. They didn't mean to hurt me. They were also grieving their sister and their mother. Nevertheless, the relationships with my aunts and cousins also became casualties of my mother's death. Decades later, I would reach out to them and they would welcome me, but that couldn't take the place of our separation during those long years before.

My brother, sister, and I tried to support each other as best we could, but we had all grown up in the home in which we each seemed to be marooned on a separate island, only connecting through hard work and a church culture that too often mirrored my father's harshness.

In the first month of sophomore biology, a look passed between me and a classmate at a nearby desk; just a glance, but I felt the attraction. There was a sensuous quality about Bob. He was a year ahead of me, a music major who played the clarinet. I liked his long fingers, the way they held his clarinet that made me want him to hold me, too. I liked his mouth, the way his lips circled the reed, the delicate fleshiness of his upper lip I wanted to hold just lightly between my teeth. I liked his dark slightly curvy hair that wanted to curl onto his forehead.

Bob took me to visit his large family in Dallas, where all his little brothers crowded around the small dinner-table with Bob's mother and stepfather. Like me, Bob had lost a parent, his father. Our parents' deaths, his father and my mother, were always in the background, but never discussed, like portraits hung over a mantel in a castle, large, imposing, and silent.

Bob and I left his crowded house, bought red-hot links, sardines, and crackers, and ate them greedily in the parked car. We necked in the car, our mouths greasy, while the chill gray sky turned winter dark.

On November 22, 1963, President Kennedy was assassinated. Our whole East Texas State campus seemed to go into some frozen time warp, everyone staring at the television replay, our handsome young president slumping over in the convertible motorcade. We watched Jackie, his beautiful young wife, attempting to climb out of the car or perhaps climb onto her husband to protect him. I didn't know which.

Two nights later while visiting in Dallas, Bob and I went to a bar and saw the accused killer, Lee Harvey Oswald, murdered on TV right in a line of policemen who wrestled his shooter, Jack Ruby, to the floor. We lowered our voices to whispers. Who knew who might be listening? While the whole country was grieving, our own college president had refused to lower the flag to half-mast. Why on earth had President Kennedy ridden in an open motorcade in Texas where he was so unpopular? How many people in the bar relished his death? I felt danger all around.

At Bob's parent's house, it was assumed that he and I would share a bed. Nothing like that would have happened at my home, where my father would have melted down in rage. The same openness was true at Bob's aunt's house in Greenville, where Bob lived while going to East Texas State and where we went regularly, driving under a banner stretched across the main street, *"Welcome to Greenville, home of the blackest land and the whitest people."* Though the streamer offended me and, I think, also Bob, the sentiment expressed then seemed commonplace.

I was surprised Bob's aunt never questioned when we closed his bedroom door during the daytime. Hidden, Bob probed the secret places that made me squirm with pleasure and inhibition. "Let me look at you," he said as I lay nude, feeling exposed and self-conscious. I wanted to throw off the repression inculcated by my family and church. Bob's touch was an antidote to the aloneness that plagued me, the emptiness that needed filling.

During the week, Bob took me to the one movie house in town and afterward he drove onto lonely roads and then parked to kiss, his tongue and hands probing deeper and deeper. I protested, knowing I'd be late for curfew and in trouble with the dorm mother, but he reassured me. "It's okay, just a little longer," and I'd give in.

Every night I was late, the dorm mother became angrier. I, the former goody-goody who feared authority and followed the rules, observed her stern face scowling at me and didn't care. "I'm sending you to the dean," she said finally. The dean, the very ring of the word, suggested the worst trouble. Yet, with Mama and Grandmother already gone, it rolled over me without a ripple. What else bad could happen?

The Dean of Women, seated behind her pecan wood desk cluttered with papers, pens, pencils, and erasers, was plump, middle-aged, and dressed in a skirt and cashmere sweater. Through the window behind her, I noticed a large pecan shade tree spreading its broad limbs. She invited me to sit down and gazed at me with patient eyes. "What seems to be the problem?" Her voice, calm and interested, invited my confidence.

"My mother was killed in a car accident last May," I told her. "My grandmother died last month."

The dean's brows drew together. "How difficult for you," she said. I felt her concern like a warm blanket.

"Yes." A faint hope rose in my chest.

"What about your father? Is he helping you?"

I hesitated. How could I explain? "My father's mean. He's always blowing up, except now he just paces and barely says anything."

The dean leaned forward, resting her round arms on her desk, emitting a warmth I'd never received before, even from my cherished mother.

"Perhaps you'd be happier living off campus," she suggested.

I took a deep breath. "Yes," I agreed, craving the kindliness of this woman.

No more trying to fit in. No more false laughter at the girls' stories I couldn't follow. I'd be able to stay out as late as I wanted. Yet, I'd also lose touch with the friends I barely connected with now.

"Check in the placement office," she told me. "You'll find listings of rooms in local homes."

"I will," I said, peering into her gray eyes.

"Good luck."

I closed the door behind me, wishing I had more reasons to visit the dean again.

28

TRYING TO DO THE RIGHT THING

Stupidity has a knack of getting its way.

—Albert Camus

FALL 1963

I moved into a room off campus. When I stayed out late, the only penalty was a look of mild disapproval, or maybe concern, that my gray-haired landlady gave the following morning. She didn't pry and even helped me make Shrimp Newburg one night for Bob. I felt she wanted to mother me. Yet accepting her attempts felt disloyal to my mother. I couldn't let another woman move into Mama's place in my heart.

Sometimes I sat in the yellow easy chair in the living room and pored over my Sociology 101 textbook. Low-grade anxiety buzzed through me like a swarm of bees. I comprehended almost nothing.

Bob took me to school concerts where he played jazz and I sat in the bleachers, trying to follow his complicated riffs. Once he and his band mates went on a road trip. I knew they were returning on a Sunday afternoon and wanted to go and greet him at the music department, but I didn't have the confidence to do so. Afterwards, Bob told me the other musicians' girlfriends came and he wished I had.

I went out of my way to seem independent, pretending not to really want Bob as much as I did to cover my neediness lurking just beneath the surface. How could Bob want someone as unimportant as me? I knew the rubbers Bob had weren't very reliable, but I continued taking the risk of becoming pregnant, because saying "no" would have led to the worse risk of being alone. Besides, despite severe prohibitions against having sex before marriage, all the "good" girls I knew were doing the same.

Birth control pills had become available recently, but they were restricted to married women. After Bob's rubber slipped off prematurely, leaving its slippery contents nearly inside me, I worried they weren't enough. I told Bob I thought I should pretend to be married and get a prescription.

I bought a cheap round circlet I hoped would pass as a plain gold ring and made an appointment with the only obstetrician-gynecologist in town. I entered the doctor's office under false pretenses, muttering my name to the receptionist. She pushed a clipboard and forms to complete across the counter. Her cool gaze unnerved me. I sat down in a row of three other women holding their Ladies' Home Journal magazines. I imagined they were planning tonight's dinners for their devoted husbands. I wrote "Mrs." before my name on the form. Could they sense the lie I'd inserted into their safe, honest worlds? I wished Bob had come with me, though I had not asked him. I'd assumed I would be on my own.

The door to the doctor's exam room opened. A middle-aged man with graying temples and a white coat called me in. Feeling my legs weaken, imagining the eyes of those proper, decent women boring into my retreating back, I followed him. The room contained a gray exam table, stirrups on the end, and a swivel stool nearby. A potted plant at the window curtained in gingham gave it a slightly homey quality, even with the cotton balls, Kleenex, alcohol, and syringes on the counter opposite.

"So, you want birth control pills?" the doctor inquired. I stared at the blue ink stain on his medical jacket pocket and nodded. Stern, perhaps in his fifties, spectacled, tired, he did not appear unkind.

"How long have you been married?"

I looked up into his eyes and hesitated, confused. His brows drew close, face tightening. The same sensation I felt when my father blew up at me surged like an electric shock down my spine.

"You're not married!" the doctor accused. He threw open his exam room door and yelled, "Get out of my office!"

I burst into tears, stumbling out the door past the other patients in the reception area, nearly tripping on a low stoop.

29

PARANOID SCHIZOPHRENIA

One of the greatest diseases is to be nobody to anybody.

—Mother Teresa

DECEMBER 1963

Christmas break arrived and Daddy pleaded, "Come on home now."

Steve cut a cedar tree from our pasture and Judy and I hung it with the colored lights and shiny glass balls Mama had stored away last year. Without Mama, Christmas felt empty.

One morning after Christmas, our party-line phone gave three short bursts. When Daddy answered, his face turned white and stricken.

John, my father's gentle brother, known to suffer from depression, had propped himself against a hay bale in his field and killed himself with his shotgun. But Uncle John and Aunt Martha were the relatives whose puppy Steve and Mama had gone to get that fatal day.

A few days later, it was early afternoon and Steve, Judy, and I were in the kitchen when the porch door banged. Daddy entered the kitchen wearing his blue bib overalls and worn leather work boots. He held the long barrel of our shotgun pointing toward his left ear. The three of us froze.

"No, Daddy, don't do it!" Steve yelled.

I echoed, "No, don't do it!"

Judy stood silent, watching. It was as if we'd all just spied a rattlesnake poised to strike. One false move and we'd be bitten.

Maybe he's going to shoot us, too, I thought.

"Daddy! Put the gun down!" Steve hollered. "Just put it down!"

Daddy's shoulders sagged as he lowered the gun, turned, and dragged his body out toward the tractor shed, where the rifles and shotguns hung on the plank walls.

While Judy and Steve acted as if nothing had happened the next morning, I convinced Daddy to get help. We three drove him to the small hospital in Sherman and waited in an empty waiting room where the only sound was the loud ticking from a wall clock. Finally, Dr. Higgins, the psychiatrist, came through the white double doors.

In beige slacks and an open-necked plaid shirt, Dr. Higgins towered over me as he gave us his verdict.

"Your father has paranoid schizophrenia," he pronounced. "I've spent an hour and a half talking with him and all he's talked about is the lawsuit he's had going for decades. He didn't even discuss your mother."

I pictured my father ranting in the doctor's office the way he did at home, leaping up from our kitchen table, pacing back and forth between the stove and the refrigerator. Whiny and agitated, his strident voice would fill the kitchen. "That fool judge oughta be thrown off the court. They oughta throw that no-account old woman in jail!"

Daddy carried on this legal battle during our entire childhoods, never convincing a judge. At least the psychiatrist recognized there was something seriously wrong with my father and there was a name for it. Paranoid schizophrenia.

Dr. Higgins told us he wanted to keep Daddy a few days. That night, with Daddy not home, Judy, Steve, and I drank homemade wine coolers from our hidden gallon jug of Chardonnay and 7-Up.

The next morning, Daddy's peremptory voice on the phone commanded, "Come get me!"

We learned afterward that another of Daddy's brothers known to be even crazier than Daddy had gone to the hospital and convinced Daddy there was nothing wrong with him.

"Hell! That asshole!" Steve exclaimed. "He's the last person who'd know!"

A week later, Christmas break ended. Judy returned to the University of Texas. I exhaled a sigh of relief driving my car back to East Texas State. Steve was left with Daddy.

30

EXPECTING

All hope abandon, ye who enter here!

—Dante Alighieri

FEBRUARY 1964

My period didn't come. Soon my breasts enlarged and became tender. I didn't need a doctor to know that the worst thing that could happen to an unmarried girl had happened to me.

When I told Bob, he reassured me my period was probably just late. I hoped he was right, but my body said otherwise. March came and again my "friend," as we girls said, didn't show up. The seriousness of my situation was evident. Yet Bob remained silent, never offering a solution, never speaking of marriage, which both of us knew was the only way to save me.

I visited my old dorm, confiding to my former friends. "Try Quinine," they suggested. A night spent doubled up over the toilet bowl didn't change my condition.

Did Bob and I discuss abortion? Strangely, I don't remember. I don't think so. Beyond my fears of a botched illegal abortion, my ministers had never wavered on The Ten Commandments. If I had asked their advice, I did not doubt that "Thou shalt not kill" would carry far more weight than my need for a way out of my desperate plight.

One somber, gray afternoon in late April, I walked to a nearby park, placed my hand over my lower abdomen, and felt for the first time the beginnings of another person. The conviction that this person wanted to live overtook me. I could no longer entertain any thoughts of ending that life.

Weeks passed and Bob seemed to ignore my obvious pregnancy. We continued dating as if there were no problem to face. Like a child hiding under the covers from the monster in her closet, I tried to banish my fears, waiting for Bob to speak. He's the man. Men are the ones in charge, I thought. But Bob remained silent. Finally, the two of sitting alone at our favorite outdoor barbecue place, I uttered the fateful words, "Well, I guess I could have it adopted."

I waited for Bob to say, "No, we'll get married." But, instead, his face relaxed with relief. "Yeah, you could go to Gladney! They have a home for unwed mothers in Fort Worth."

How did Bob know about the Gladney Home for Unwed Mothers? The eagerness in Bob's voice betrayed the fact that he was pleased. I'd just let him off the hook. I looked down. The hard dirt under our picnic bench looked as scraped bare as I felt.

Bob seemed to consider the matter settled. "You'll be able to finish this semester," he assured me. "After that, you can go to Gladney."

At the end of that sophomore year at East Texas State College, I visited my father. I was already four and a half months along. In the early June heat, my yellow cotton shorts were already too tight to button and a blousy ruffled top did a poor job of hiding my swelling breasts and abdomen. My father told me he had attended the Sherman High School graduation ceremony and talked to a woman whose daughter was graduating pregnant.

"I hope you never come home and tell me you're pregnant," he said, his eyes hardening into cold nuggets. With those casual words, he made certain he wouldn't be there for me. Because his explosive rages punctuated my childhood with fear, I never went to him with my problems anyway, but maybe he'd imagined I would in this crisis. The familiar shiver ran down my back to my buttocks as if he was going to spank me. My jaw, always sore from clenching, clamped down harder. I kept silent.

The last shred of hope I'd secretly harbored dropped in my stomach like a cold stone. I realized he'd abandoned me when he accepted my unlikely story of taking a semester off college and working in Fort Worth. He knew I was in trouble.

Once, when I'd been about seven, my father was waiting with me on the porch for the yellow school bus. Suddenly, he stared down, his penetrating eyes boring into me, and blurted, "You're on your own, Linda." Shock roiled through me, rooting my feet to the worn linoleum floor on the mud porch. I said nothing, but I felt petrified. I wasn't important. I didn't matter.

Bob drove me to the Edna Gladney Home for Unwed Mothers in Fort Worth. His show of taking responsibility for the new life he'd fathered seemed so much more thoughtful and caring than any I'd received from my own father that I felt abjectly grateful. On our two-hour drive, the silence in his car felt suffocating, but I had already submitted. Retreating inward had always been the safest route.

Bob pulled up in front of Gladney.

"Will you come see me?" I murmured.

He kissed me lightly, sliding to open the handle of my passenger door. "Sure, I'll be in touch."

"Do you still have Gladney's phone number?" I almost stammered, trying not to appear pleading.

"Yeah; I'll call you."

I stepped out onto the concrete curb. The sun glinted off the brown metal hood of his Ford sedan as I watched Bob pull away and disappear around the corner. He never even got out of the car.

31

HIDE YOUR IDENTITY

Out beyond ideas of wrongdoing and right doing there is a field.
I'll meet you there. When the soul lies down in that grass
the world is too full to talk about.

—Rumi

JUNE 1964

I turned to face the two-story sandstone building. The Texas summer sun beat on my back. Even though it was morning, the high pink-brown steps radiated heat. I trudged up the steps, my body pulling me down like lead on a fish line. Rivulets of sweat dripped between my swollen breasts.

Opening the heavy wooden door, a welcome blast of chilled air struck me. A receptionist wearing black horn-rimmed glasses and a rose pastel blouse greeted me from behind a polished wood panel. The clock behind her showed the time: 9:30 a.m.

"Hello; can I help you?" she asked with an encouraging smile.

I gave her my name. "I have an appointment with Mrs. Lewis," I added.

"Of course." She handed me some forms with a clipboard and fountain pen. After I completed the paperwork -- name, address, date of birth, date of last period, any medications taken since start of pregnancy – I sat down in a mustard-colored stuffed chair to wait.

Hours passed. The tiny clock on the receptionist's desk ticked in the somnolent hush. Occasionally, a door opened, admitting one woman or another, who glanced in my direction and hurried through the opposite door. No one asked for me. I sat and waited, feeling invisible, which didn't seem strange as I'd always felt invisible, except during my good freshman year of college.

I was getting hungry though and wondered if I should say something. The silence in the room made it seem impossible to speak, as if anything I said would hang like a curse word in the cool air. How could I possibly interrupt the nice lady clacking away at her typewriter who never looked in my direction?

At 1 p.m., a plump, middle aged woman in a belted, navy dress opened the door, stuck her head in and peered at me. "Are you Linda Franklin?"

"Yes."

"When did you get here? Oh, my goodness!" she exclaimed. Her pasty face registered surprise when I told her nine-thirty that morning. "Why didn't you say something?"

I could not reply. I followed her to her office. She sat down at her scratched metal desk, leaned back in her wooden office chair, and studied my papers. Then she took my medical history.

"You'll need to pay $450 a month for your room and board. There may be some way to work off part of that. Some of the girls help in the kitchen or do cleaning or other work." Because my mother had died without a will only the year before, my father had to give us three kids her half of their cash savings, so I had the money. I didn't question the payment. In fact, I was surprised the rate was so low.

"We'll take care of all your medical care and you'll live in a nice apartment with the other older girls," Mrs. Lewis said. We give IQ and some psychiatric assessment tests," she added. "You're a psychology minor, I see, so no doubt you're familiar with those."

Later that week when I took those tests, I scored in the 99thth percentile on verbal reasoning, 97th in language, and 95th in mathematical ability. "You're really smart," Mrs. Lewis told me, adding that I could earn part of my room and board by helping test the new girls.

"OK; let's take you over to the apartments," Mrs. Lewis concluded. "The older girls live in their own apartments and do their own cooking. You'll be responsible for your own cleaning, too."

This didn't sound bad. I'd been taught by my mother to prepare fresh meals. Our Saturday regimen of cleaning bathrooms, bedrooms, and doing laundry had prepared me well. As we walked across a grassy field, I noticed a line of girls about to enter a building, their dormitory, I supposed. They looked so young they could have been middle school girls waiting in line for a school event. But now they were all waiting to give birth, their t-shirts grotesquely stretched over their huge protruding bellies. Soon I'd look like them, just a little older, I thought. I turned my eyes away and tried not to stumble as my muscles went stiff.

Still, I found life at Gladney surprisingly pleasant. The demands were few. Groceries were delivered to our apartments, eggs and cheese for breakfast or maybe Rice Krispies with a banana and milk. We girls made ourselves baloney sandwiches for lunch and pork chops for dinner. We cleaned up after ourselves and no one ever hounded us about the place being a mess.

We each had our own small room with a twin bed. Looking through the small wood-framed window in my room, I saw a straggly hackberry tree struggling to survive in a patch of yellowing Bermuda grass. It reminded me of home.

I spent a day or two a week passing out tests and explaining them to girls in ponytails with tummy bumps and sad, scared faces. I learned I was a good tester. I also knew I wouldn't be putting this on my resume.

The stay at Gladney was short; usually less than five months. We were instructed to hide our identities, even from each other, and not expected to get close. After giving birth, we were not even permitted to return to the apartment to retrieve our personal possessions. Perhaps because of this, no cliques formed. I felt a comforting equality among us. Since no one was especially popular, I did not fear being different or excluded. We were all suspended in a temporary halt from our lives.

There were no campus tours or orientation at Gladney. We just did what we were told. The staff was uniformly pleasant and seemed kind and accepting. I was a motherless girl in a sea of mostly motherly social workers who never spoke harshly or demonstrated they believed we were the bad girls the culture claimed we were.

Many days, we sat around our maple dining table and played cards. One girl taught us the rules, snapping cards through her nimble fingers. Behind us, the Beach Boys "Fun, Fun, Fun" and the Beatles "I Want to Hold Your Hand" crooned from our plastic radio. But there was no laughter from us four circling the table, no stories of fun on the beach with boyfriends holding our hands.

The complexity of Bridge, a card game I'd never played before, was a welcome distraction from my gloom. "Bid, no trump," we called out. We amused ourselves by balancing cups of coffee on our bellies while our babies tumbled inside us. The cups never tipped over.

A Gladney staff drove us to a nearby knitting shop. I chose my high school colors of orange and black to make a garish sweater. One girl was knitting a square in fuzzy pink yarn. "What are you making?" I asked.

"I'm making a blanket for my baby."

Briefly, I considered doing the same. But then the thought flashed through me: I'm not worth making something for my baby. I abandoned the idea.

Gladney required us to wear fake wedding rings whenever we went out to the small store a few blocks away to buy cigarettes, Hershey bars, and my favorite, Butterfingers. Standing in the check-out line wearing my ring, I read the newspapers full of headlines about the presidential campaign in full swing with Barry Goldwater, the Republican nominee.

"How come Goldwater's so popular advocating nuclear bombs and we're considered so bad?" I wondered out loud. The girls snickered and other customers laughed at my smart-aleck remark. Our fake wedding rings weren't fooling them.

Every three weeks, and then weekly as our pregnancies advanced, we walked across the acre campus to our medical appointments. When it rained, the white metal awnings over the sidewalks sheltered us. Each of us got on the tall scale in a basement room with stark white walls. We watched with trepidation as the staff moved the heavy black weight. They didn't want us to gain more than twenty pounds.

"You only gained two pounds," a smiling nurse told me. Or was she a nurse? I didn't know. After the weighing and the tight blood pressure cuff slid off our arms, we were free to go.

Passing through the gate to our apartment buildings on my way back from a clinic appointment, Mrs. Thomas, our apartment social worker, called out, "How did your check-up go?" Her friendly eyes showed warmth and interest.

"I only gained two pounds." I held up my snack of a stem of green grapes.

"That's good," she encouraged, nodding toward the grapes. "You're watching your diet."

"Yes, only a hundred calories a cup," I assured her.

Mrs. Thomas smiled approvingly. These simple pleasures - being smiled at, talked to, noticed, and treated with kind interest and occasional praise - provided some shield from acknowledging that I no longer had, or ever would again have, my mother. A restful, secure sensation seduced me, allaying my apprehension about what would happen soon. I felt safe behind the fence and gate with its scrolled metal trim separating the four apartment buildings located in a grassy meadow a distance away from the administration buildings. I felt protected in our cozy apartment. My father couldn't come there. We girls were already established as "bad." I was no worse than the others. With eyes half-closed, I waited to sacrifice my firstborn.

It seemed I had found a place where I could finally relax. For the first time in my life, I almost felt at ease.

I remember only one of my short-term apartment mates, Rachel, small with short dark hair circling her sensitive face. I liked her immediately. She was quiet like me, an introvert, too. On the rare occasions we left our apartment, we hooked up to walk across the campus and compare notes on growing up, I on a farm in East Texas and Rachel in New York City.

"What's it like there?" I asked, envying her. I longed to have grown up in a place with skyscrapers and lots of places to go. There

I wouldn't have to worry about stepping on brown furry tarantulas or hidden water moccasins and rattlesnakes.

"Come see me afterwards, if you want to," Rachel said, looking down at our bulging fronts. She pulled a small black notebook from her pants' pocket. We both cast stealthy glances around to see if there were any staff watching. "Write down your real name and your phone number and address," she said. She wrote her information and tore off the page for me. I stuffed it in my pocket.

A year later, on my way to spend the summer in Europe after I'd returned for my junior year at the University of Texas at Austin, I took Rachel up on her invitation. I had a long layover in New York City, and we met at a coffee shop. We tried to be cheerful, neither of us saying a word about the babies we'd left behind. I looked across the table at Rachel's face and saw sorrow like a dark veil beneath the smile she pasted on. I knew she saw the same in me. I don't recall a single thing we talked about.

32

BASTARD

"To belittle, you have to be little."

—Kahlil Gibran

AUGUST 1964

My caseworker, Mrs. Harrison, always seemed to have just come from her hairdresser. Her reddish blond permanent curled into little corkscrews. She dressed in trim little jackets bordered in round peplum trim. Above the square neck of her silk blouse, sandy freckles dotted her pale chest.

From behind her desk, a pen in her right hand, Mrs. Harrison inquired, "How are things going?"

I gazed past her out the window at a yellow cat scampering across the scruffy brown Bermuda grass. The cat reminded me of Lazy B. I wished I could go pick it up. I missed my cats more than I did people.

I'd run into Mrs. Harrison the week before in the hallway scurrying somewhere important. Perhaps she was hurrying to meet the adoptive parents who'd been chosen for my baby, because with my high IQ test scores, I'd learned they'd be placing my baby with educated parents. She even said the parents-to-be were in the science field. She wouldn't say what kind of science, but she did say, "They're not the life of the party, but they'll make good parents."

All week, I'd thought about nothing else. "Mrs. Harrison," I asked, "Can't I know where my baby is going? Just who has him? Where he is?"

I thought I saw a shadow of sadness pass over Mrs. Harrison's face, like a cloud obscuring the sun. "No," she said. She cleared her throat. "Linda, you know your baby needs a mother *and* a father. You'd be selfish to keep your baby."

So, Mrs. Harrison knew I'd never be a good enough parent.

I wish she'd ask about my mother, I thought. Did she know Mama was killed a year ago? I told the admissions worker. Why doesn't anyone ever mention it? If she were alive, maybe she'd have made Bob marry me. But I'd be no good for my baby. I'd screw everything up. Only maybe not, if Mama helped me.

The main thing was to keep up the pretense. Telling the truth would drown me in shame. It was amazing how my bogus self could appear so grown up, so normal.

Perhaps I was too hard on myself. Mrs. Harrison was getting paid to help me do what I was at Gladney to do. We both must have believed all of that stuff about my baby needing two parents and me being selfish to keep him. It was the official line everywhere; at home, at school, at church, in town.

The kids might chase him and shout. "Bastard! Bastard!" I imagined their mouths wide open, spit flying out.

Parents might whisper, "She wasn't married." They'd tell their children, "Don't play with that boy." I didn't want a child of mine to suffer that.

Mrs. Harrison fidgeted, cleared her throat, and shifted her eyes. "How's your job going?" she asked.

"Good."

I liked passing out and instructing new girls on taking the IQ tests and the Minnesota Multiphasic Personality Inventory (MMPI).

"I hear you're doing well," reported Mrs. Harrison.

I raised my head. "Really?"

Why didn't they care about my MMPI scores, which measured personality traits? I felt certain my scores identified me as emotionally stunted, neurotic, and immature.

"Mrs. Warren said you're good at passing out the forms and helping the girls understand how to take the tests," explained Mrs. Harrison.

"Yeah, I like it." I sat up straighter at the idea I was good. Completing all my homework at the kitchen table while my mother cooked dinner, earning ropes of wooden Camp Fire Girls beads by sewing my own dresses, preparing creamy macaroni and cheese for my family, gluing labeled rocks and lichen into cigar boxes for the science bead, caring for baby chicks under infrared lights for the animal husbandry bead. Yes, I had dozens of examples to prove my capabilities.

No matter how hard I worked though, my father's voice never ceased hollering in my head. "Don't do that, Linda! What's wrong with you? You know better than that!"

Mrs. Harrison looked across her desk, "Do you have anything else you want to talk about?"

I cast wildly about, wishing I could break the silence, the same silence that pervaded our family at supper time.

"No, I don't guess so." I said, clearing my throat. I struggled up from her office chair, closed her door, and lugged my lopsided body down the empty hall. Outside, the sky threatened an afternoon cloudburst. My baby fired a hard kick into my abdomen. Sadness curled in on itself like dead leaves on a parched plant.

33

WATCH WHAT THEY DO

As I grow older, I pay less attention to what men say.
I just watch what they do.

—Andrew Carnegie

AUGUST 1964

Bob agreed to come visit me at Gladney late that summer. I must have written and asked him to keep his promise. Mrs. Harrison gave her permission, apparently not worried I might disappear with the father of my baby. I don't recall anyone else having visits from the boys who abandoned them. Some girls were prohibited from any contact by their parents who likely wanted their daughters to give birth with no chance to marry and then return to unstained educational futures. Mrs. Harrison even arranged a small room where Bob and I could visit in private.

"Hi," we greeted each other. He looked as I remembered; tall and slim. Bob's probing brown eyes took in my shape without comment. His conversation about registering for his senior year of college felt remote. After three months hidden away in an unwed mothers' home, I could hardly relate to choosing classes or standing in long lines with fellow students to register.

Our visit dissolved into joyless groping. At least I can't get pregnant this time, I thought. Would Bob tell me to flee with him and get married? We'd raise our baby together. Maybe even be happy. But Bob got up from the sagging couch and adjusted his checked shirt and khaki pants.

"Call me when the baby's born and tell me what you have."

"Okay."

He left the room. I stood at the doorway and watched him walk to his Ford. He drove away without looking back. I watched until his car was out of sight.

There'd be no reprieve.

Dr. Malone, the psychologist and the only man we girls ever dealt with at Gladney, regaled us during group therapy with how happily married he was. "Even just watching TV with my wife is special," he assured us as we sat in a circle on plastic chairs.

One day as the group ended, Dr. Malone pulled me aside. "Cathy was masturbating during the group," he confided.

I gaped at him. I hadn't seen anything, but then I'd been staring at the floor, which usually seemed like the best way to get through his sessions. I imagined Cathy squirming in her chair, twisting and gyrating her body into strange sexual positions. Why was Dr. Malone telling me this? A creepy sensation ran down my body, but I explained it away. Maybe he knows I'm a psychology minor. He knows I help the girls take psychological tests.

A few weeks after I'd delivered and was back at home visiting Daddy, Dr. Malone called me. "I'm in Sherman and thought you might like to come have dinner with me," he said. "I'm staying at the Holiday Inn."

Why was he inviting me for dinner? Why had this educated doctor come to the small town where I went to high school? How naïve I was not to question. I had dinner with him, feeling special, until he suggested we retire to his hotel room afterward.

My knees locked tightly together. I stood and pushed away from the table, feeling my cheeks on fire. I hurried home.

In 1980, when I visited Gladney, I told the social worker what Dr. Malone had done.

"Yeah, he tried that with a few of the girls," she answered nonchalantly.

34

HE'S BORN

And your body is the harp of your Soul, and it is yours to bring forth sweet music from it, or confused sounds.

—Kahlil Gibran

OCTOBER 1964

My bizarre sense of humor led me to hope my baby would be born on Halloween. Perhaps I imagined myself already in costume in my pleated maternity clothes draped over my huge belly. Perhaps going by a fake name at Gladney made me already a Halloween character.

My plans didn't work out. The morning of October 30th, I awoke to feel my stomach clenching down hard. I drew on my pink fuzzy robe and padded to the bathroom, the pressure exacerbating my urgent need to pee.

I felt relieved the squeezing across my pelvis and into my back wasn't very painful. The thought that these contractions portended my baby leaving me hurt more. I'd been trying to avoid facing that ever since arriving at Gladney. Often, I lay in bed with my hands on my belly, imagining I'd just get bigger and bigger and somehow nothing would happen. The other girls and I would go on playing bridge, going to knitting class and the drug store, wearing our fake rings, and pretending we were married women.

My groans must have alerted my housemates, for one girl dashed out to notify staff. Another began timing my contractions. Soon Mrs. Wilson bustled in, letting in the chilly autumn air.

"How close are the contractions?" she asked.

"Eight minutes when we last checked," I answered.

She was all efficiency, "When did you feel the first one?"

"Almost three hours ago now." I gasped, bent over, and clutched my stomach as another contraction hit.

"All right, let's get you over to the hospital," Mrs. Wilson said. "You don't need to get dressed. You need an extra nightgown if you have one and a toothbrush."

The other girls watched with a mixture of curiosity and dread. Mrs. Wilson's hurried orders interrupted whatever thoughts we might have had of saying goodbye.

I wobbled out of our apartment and down the steps. I didn't know that the hospital was on the grounds till Mrs. Wilson walked me over. When a contraction came, we halted while I bent over the frost-covered grass. As soon as we arrived, she left. I cast a forlorn look at her, but she didn't look back.

The bare-walled labor room was small and windowless. I lay on the thin mattress and longed for my mother. Silent hours passed with no sound except the occasional padded feet of nurses passing down the hall. Finally, an anonymous woman in white came in and injected my chilled arm. The clear liquid mercifully dulled my loneliness. Off and on, I slept.

Sometime later, I was tossing in tangled, sweated sheets when a dark shadow appeared at the foot of the narrow bed. "Roll over," commanded a male voice. "Open your legs." The flash of what looked like a long shiny knitting needle sparked into the man's shadow. I felt a quick cool sensation followed by warm wetness. "Thar she blows!" Dr. Shadow exclaimed, quoting the line from *Moby Dick's* story of a whale, then departing as quickly as he had appeared.

In the delivery room, the urgent voices of the doctor and nurses commanded with each new contraction, "Push! Push." I pushed one final effort and felt a vague sensation of release as the slippery baby, the baby I'd been hoping to keep hidden, slid from my exhausted body. A hollow place collapsed in me. I slumped onto the delivery table, straining to hear "It's a boy!" or "It's a girl!" Instead, silence reverberated from the end of the table where my legs were still propped in stirrups. Then my baby announced himself with a faint cry. I raised myself at the sound of the cry and glimpsed a nurse hastening out of the room, a small bundle in her arms. I pushed my elbows down hard on the table, straining without success to focus my eyes on my disappearing infant.

"What is it? A boy or a girl?" I croaked before collapsing back down.

"It's a boy," the nurse replied, without turning around. Then she was gone, her footsteps echoing down the hall like a beating metronome.

I felt a prick at my right forearm. "What are you doing? What's that for?" I slurred to another nurse with a needle.

"It's to dry up your milk."

That was the first moment I realized what all of these people already knew. This wasn't my baby at all. I had just grown him in my body, like a broodmare.

The records I got four decades later showed I was only dilated one centimeter when I was checked in at 8:30 a.m. Why? Perhaps they admitted us girls so early to keep us away from the others before we could alarm them with our intense labor pains.

They'd given me Seconal first and then Demerol at 10:30 a.m. Twice more, at 12:50 p.m. and at 3:15 p.m., they'd injected me with Nembutal. My baby was born at 4:01 p.m.

Even if my mother had been alive, she wouldn't have been there with me. None of us had anyone with us, as far as I know. We were to be picked up afterwards by our parents, if we had them. Some girls' parents never even asked what sex the baby was.

I never got to say goodbye to the girls I'd lived with for several months.

35

WHERE IS MY SON?

They are the sons and daughters of Life's longing for itself.

—Kahlil Gibran

OCTOBER 1964

The sound of the door opening woke me. Another woman wearing nursing garb padded in on white tennis shoes. She carried a round white plastic object with a hole in the middle that looked like a life preserver for a drowning person to catch.

"Where am I?" My mouth felt dry. "How did I get here?"

"Sit up," she instructed. "You're in the recovery room."

I struggled upright and leaned against the metal back railing of the hospital bed. A bag of clear liquid hung from an IV pole to the side, the tube inserted in my arm.

"It's time for you to get up," said the nurse, levering the rail down and grasping my sore arm, pulling me up.

"Ouch!"

The waxed linoleum floor was cold beneath my bare feet and I swayed.

She held up the life preserver. "I've brought you a donut. You run a few inches of very hot water into the tub and sit on it. It will help your bottom to heal."

"What time is it? Is it still light?"

"It's 7:20 at night. Come on and use the bathroom. I've brought you a fresh pad. After that, I'll bring you a tray with dinner."

The next day, I ran the hot water for a tub Sitz bath to soothe my episiotomy cut. I lowered my nether regions gingerly down and perched on the donut. Threadlike streaks of blood slithered down and through the hole into the bath water. Heavy silence absorbed every sound but the dripping of the tub faucet, which seemed to count out quarter notes.

Where-is-my-son-where-is-my-son?

I grasped the safety bar on the wall and pulled myself out of the tub. I dried off with the thin white towel and pulled my flannel nightgown over my wet, stringy hair. Where-is-my-son? I snuck to my door and peeked out. Down the white, stark hall, two heavy wooden double doors stood like sentinels guarding a vault. All was quiet.

Careful not to make any noise, I crept out my door and down the hall, tiptoeing so my blue fleece slippers barely clacked against the slick floor.

There were no windows. I must be in the basement where we always come for our medical appointments, I thought. Maybe they're keeping my baby behind those doors.

I tugged the wooden doors open. No one there. Mustn't make any noise. Another hall with the same white walls. No pictures, no windows. We are in the basement. We must be! Sh-h-h, please God, don't let anybody hear me. Don't let anybody…!

About twenty feet further, a door opened. "What are you doing here? You're not supposed to be here!" challenged the nurse. She strode toward me, mouth set.

"Come on. Let's get you back to your room."

"But, can't I look? Just for a minute? I just want to see..." My voice sounded plaintive, weak to me.

"No; you're not allowed in this area! Come on now."

I sagged and felt my arms go limp. A few drops of water from my wet hair dripped onto the pristine floor. Or maybe they were my tears. The woman gripped my arm and led me back to my room.

"Get back in bed. You're leaving tomorrow."

I folded the towel from my bath that I had draped on the end of the bed and placed it under my head. Lying down, I turned toward the bare white wall and heard the door close as the nurse left.

36

GOING THROUGH WITH IT

The best way to make your dreams come true is to wake up.

—Paul Valery

NOVEMBER 1964

I'd lost track of time. My room door swung open, admitting a new woman. This one wasn't wearing white. I remembered passing her in the hall when I went for counseling appointments. She was young and pretty, with auburn hair and a flawless complexion. She pulled away the tray over my bed. I noticed a gold circlet with a band of small diamonds on her left ring finger.

"How are you? You get to go home today! Isn't that great?" she said in a forced, cheery voice, crinkling her eyes.

I stared at her fake smile and the plastic bags she held. Where is *her* baby?

"Here are your things. Go ahead and get dressed and I'll walk you to the chapel. How about this nice yellow sweater?"

She pulled out a baggy knitted sweater. I nodded. That would probably fit over my pudgy tummy.

As we walked to the chapel, catty-cornered from the hospital under clouds heavy with rain ready to drench the field, I looked back toward my apartment in the distance. It had rained already since I'd left my apartment. The yellow Bermuda grass in the field was greening up on the tips. I'd walked across that field a hundred times. I wasn't ever going there again. I wondered what Rachel and the other girls were doing. I imagined them just stirring inside, the heater blasting warm air as they prepared their breakfasts.

We'll all go back to our lives and forget this ever happened. Right? That's what they said. It's true; isn't it?

The social worker led me into the building where the chapel was. My legs felt paralyzed. My thighs and calves were stiff, and I could barely lift my feet suspended like weighty anchors. I clutched my arms to my chest. This must be the way criminals feel being led to the electric chair. I wished the hall would go on forever. It was much shorter than the one in the hospital.

The chapel had polished warm brown pews and stained-glass windows through which sunlight streamed on sunny days. I was glad today wasn't sunny. A couple of wooden chairs were pulled up at the back. Dr. Malone, our psychologist, sat in one. "Hello, Linda," he said, getting up and pointing toward the other chair. "Have a seat." His eyes were cast downward, his brows drawn together, as if he were sad. I didn't believe him.

On the small table lay a couple of official-looking papers. Dr. Malone cleared his throat. "Linda, these are the legal adoption papers you'll be signing today. You understand, after this, you'll have no right to ever see your baby or be involved with the people who raise him; right?"

I couldn't answer.

"But before you sign, the social worker is going to bring in your baby. It's important that you see him," he continued.

"You need to know that this is real," he always said in group therapy. No one ever explained how this fit with the other messages that we'd forget all about having a baby and giving it away. I was excited, though. They were bringing my baby!

I'd have fifteen minutes. Fifteen minutes to say goodbye forever. "Your baby will have a mother and a father who can give him everything you can't," they'd promised.

I believed them.

"You'll finish college and get married and have other children," they told me.

I believed them.

I never questioned how any other child could replace the one I'd given away. I didn't know yet that one child can never replace another. In truth, I had no concept of what I was losing.

The chapel door swung open. A woman came in carrying a baby. *My* baby, a tiny bundle wrapped in a blue flannel blanket. She bent down and placed him in my arms. "Like this, see; you hold him like this." She showed me how to cradle my arms around him. He fit perfectly. His eyes were closed. "He's just been fed. He's sleepy," said the woman. She leaned over and rubbed my baby boy's plump cheek and he briefly opened his eyes.

> I want to look into his eyes. I have to memorize his face. His eyes are a deep blue I could drown in. He has my nose and his father's sensitive mouth. He has lots of dark hair, like me.

I had no idea he'd be this beautiful. My mind raced frantically, searching for another ending. It seemed way too late to change my mind. Hadn't they assured me I'd forget? I'd go on, walk down the aisle in a long white dress and pledge myself to my prince charming who would never know about my missing illegitimate child.

"You can't bring that baby home," my father's harsh voice boomed in my mind. "What would people say?" Then, I'm no good. I'm worthless.

"It's time to bring him back to the nursery now."

The woman leaned down and lifted my baby into her arms. It felt like tearing off skin, but I didn't resist. I had no idea how to change my mind. The chapel doors swung shut behind her. She was gone. My baby was gone.

Dr. Malone leaned and tried to put his arm around me. I shrank away. Men are cruel. My father is mean. My baby's father left me.

"Let's go over these," Dr. Malone said. He withdrew his arm and picked up the papers.

I didn't hear the words he read. My hand felt heavy, as if it were filled with lead. My fingers that grasped the pen he handed to me, my joints that bent to hold it, my palm that cupped it were all lifeless, without feeling, dead. It took me a long time. Slowly, very slowly, I wrote my signature on the adoption papers.

Chad

Jared

Lee

Five-year-old Terra

Dave

Dave and Madeleine on blanket

Dave holding Terra

Ellen and Gwendolyn

Ellen with Madeleine

Jared, Marcia, Terra, Chad, Linda – Christmas dinner 2005

Linda, Lee, Gwen, and Maddie

Linda and girls in park

Linda holding Gwen and Maddie

Linda with Terra

Marcia

Dave, Jared, Terra, Chad, Linda, and Lee – Brothers meeting

PART 3

37

CALLING ON MAMA

Certain thoughts are prayers. There are moments when, whatever be the attitude of the body, the soul is on its knees.

—Victor Hugo

FEBRUARY 2001

Most days at Kaiser Psychiatry, I quickly eat a sandwich at lunchtime while completing client notes. Then I make my way up to our employee gym. Forty minutes on the Nordic Track, the round calorie counter promising I've worked off three hundred calories, and I jump in the shower to arrive back at my office feeling energized for the rest of the day.

That noon, I ski the wooden slats extra hard, headphones blasting a tune I've forgotten, my mind on my mother and grandmother. Are you wondering what happened to your grandson, your great-grandson? You must want him back, too. Can you help me?

I close my eyes and suddenly I am eight years back in time on an acupuncture treatment table, my eyes shut, fine needles inserted under the space blanket the doctor covered me with. I have gone down a white tunnel where I see a vision of my mother and grandmother dressed in their church choir robes with the peplum collars that I recall from childhood. Their faces, tired and careworn in life, now radiate pure joy. They appear more alive than they ever did on Earth. "Why are you here?" I silently ask them.

"So you'll know you're not alone."

Relief suffuses me. My breathing slows. Ever since their deaths, I'd needed to hear that message. The impact of Jerald Smithson's racing car not only stole my mother's life, it tore the bottom out of my world and left me feeling as if I had no skin. The loss of my first baby the year after amplified my feeling of being separate and different. Young, dogged by a conviction of worthlessness and rootlessness, I pitched and yawed like a boat without a rudder, easily lurching from one mistake to the next. It took me a long time to stabilize.

I continue thrusting one leg, then the other, on the Nordic Track. My mother's and grandmother's luminous reappearances provide me a blanket of comfort and assurance of their presences. Now I call on them. "I know you're here. Can you help? It's been a year since he got my letter from Gladney. Maybe you can get through to Robert."

Exercise over, I strip off my gym shorts and t-shirt to step into the shower. Behind the black fabric curtain, warm water cascades onto my head. Steam swirls over me. I close my eyes. Gentle hands seem to stroke up and down, across my back, along the length of my arms and legs, light caresses glowing and warming me.

"I feel you, Mama. You're here. Thank you, Mama. Thank you, Grandmother. Thank you! Thank you!"

38

BROWN ENVELOPE

Love is everything it's cracked up to be. [...] It really is worth fighting for, being brave for, risking everything for.

—Erica Jong

APRIL 2001

It's Friday, the last day of a hard week at Kaiser where I'd seen my usual sixty patients. Vibrating with anxiety, I'd launched a second letter directly to the address Marilyn and Cathy had helped me discover. Ever since, a hurricane of fears buffeted me. Will Robert finally answer? Maybe he'll inform Cathy at Gladney that he doesn't want any contact. Now, driving home, I wish the weekend traffic to Tahoe would move faster. The jangling of my cell phone makes me jump. It's Jared.

"Mom, I have a flat tire! Can you come help me?"

I call Dave, already home from work, and tell him I'm going to meet Jared.

"No! Come home!" Dave blurts.

"Why? What's the matter?"

"There's a brown envelope in the mail. I think it's from your son!"

"Oh my God!" I push my foot down harder on the gas pedal. "Oh my God!"

I phone Jared to give him my AAA number and tell him he'll have to wait for me. A few minutes later, as I turn into our cul-de-sac, there's Dave smiling in the front yard, waving the envelope.

"Why would it be in a brown envelope?" I burst out. "It looks like a legal document."

Dave keeps smiling. "Open it!"

I tear open the seal and tug out a thick packet labeled Dante's Kitchen showing a logo of a cast iron skillet filled with orange flames. Pictures tumble out as I pull out the handwritten letter. Robert, wearing a deep red shirt buttoned over a generous belly, a round face, curly dark hair, a dark goatee, and mustache. He has his father's sensitive mouth. I'd memorized it by heart when he was three days old.

Next to him in the photo stands a beautiful woman wearing a black sweater and burgundy taffeta skirt, her dark hair pulled back from her face, her arms wrapped around my son, her cheek pressed close to his. This must be his wife, Ellen Kaye. I see love in her eyes.

The next picture makes me gasp. Here are the two little girls I'd imagined all year. A toddler, her long brown hair pressed against her pillow and her brown eyes shining. Next to her, her younger sister in pajamas decorated with little flying animals. Her pudgy fingers clasp her sippy cup under round cheeks, sparkling brown eyes, and short blond hair. Both girls have the high cheekbones of my Choctaw great-grandfather.

Another picture of Robert shows him in a tie and white shirt, holding his baby girl, kissing her. Finally, a picture of the entire family dressed for Mardi Gras, all in angel or maybe fairy costumes. A large sheer wing protrudes from my son's shoulder. His wife looks like a woodland nymph. They both wear circlets of twigs and small flowers woven into natural-appearing coronas on their heads. Robert holds my oldest granddaughter wearing a tiara, a sheer dress, and transparent wings matching his. His wife holds their baby, her little round face capped by a headband topped with frothy material. Something green is tucked under her chubby chin. Perhaps she and her mother are leprechauns and Robert and the oldest girl are angels?

I grab the pictures and rush to plop myself onto our couch to read.

"Dearest Linda,

How to start. A year ago, during a busy lunch in the restaurant where I was working, I got a call from my sister. At that moment, I knew something must be up because we don't have the kind of relationship where we casually call each other.... we are not extremely close. She said she had been trying to get information about her birth parents, as she was also adopted, and that the Gladney institute asked her to pass on a message to me. As of this writing, she has had no success."

I suck in my breath at "dearest," a term I haven't heard since leaving rural East Texas. His warm greeting feels like a caress. "Bless your heart!" I want to reply.

I remember how the social worker told me in 1980 that my son's parents had come back to Gladney two years after adopting him to adopt a baby girl. I wince. How did his sister feel calling my son to tell him *his* first mother was seeking contact?

Robert explains his reaction to his medical information in the letter I'd left with Cathy. He writes that learning my father was suffering from heart disease and that his half-brother and grandfather had some mental illness didn't faze him. He says:

"My gut response to this was that just about everyone in the restaurant business in New Orleans was a 'little bit touched' by some form of mental illness or another."

I let myself relax. My son takes a pretty casual attitude towards mental illness, though the effects in my family's lives have been anything but casual. It's reassuring that Robert won't easily be threatened by his brother's peculiarities. I read on. He tells me he waited two weeks for the letter from Cathy to arrive. When he saw the pictures of Chad and Jared, he says he was:

"a bit taken aback looking into the faces of blood brothers I had never imagined...I read the letter a few times and then I set it aside. I shared its contents with several friends and my wife,

> soliciting their opinions along the way. I kept waiting for some kind of inspiration, a sign if you like, which would give me some insight into how I should deal with this new dimension."

My showing up had to be a shock to my son. I hope he sees my letters as an opportunity. He goes on:

> "I had a happy family and adoption was just another fact of my life. I thought of it as you might imagine filling out a form which asked you to check a box for race, sex, religion, income level, or whatever statistic. Like there would be a box you would check if you were adopted."

Did the worthlessness I felt when I carried him in my body make me not matter to him? He never questioned his adoption. It's a good thing I searched for him. Curiosity or a sense of loss wouldn't have driven him to seek me out, as it must have his sister.

Still, I admitted that I too had thought little about him all these years until now. I'd had little conscious awareness of grief and chronic sorrow. Wasn't it easier not to think about it? It must have made his growing up simpler. Perhaps we both sealed the subject off for similar reasons, both unconscious, both playing it safe to protect ourselves. Yet, for a therapist like myself, my son's lack of concern about his origins could not but suggest a great capacity for the same denial and repression I had relied on to protect me until Jared's life-changing question a year ago.

Would giving up a girl have been different? I'd heard girls were more likely to search. His sister is thwarted in her own search. I wonder if she left a letter with medical information at Gladney, too.

My son goes on to tell me about his PhD educated, talented parents, the beautiful home they raised him in overlooking Audubon Park, the best school in New Orleans they sent him to, the encouragement and great support they offered him. He tells me about obtaining his BA in Economics and his MBA at Tulane, tuition-free because of his father's alumni position. He says he'd fallen in love with the New Orleans restaurant business and the food, music, fun, and art that New Orleans offers him. He describes Dante's Kitchen that he and an old friend opened in the fall. He tells me he has a passion for hospitality. My chest lightens. I might be the beneficiary of that passion.

His amusing style shows up as he describes his chef.

> "My task is to train him to be a businessman as well as a chef and that is not an easy task, as his degree from Rutgers was in botany."

Well, at least the chef will make sure no toxic greens get into the salad!

What a good life my son seems to have enjoyed! Mrs. Harrison, my Gladney caseworker, had promised me my baby would have the benefits of placement with educated parents. Perhaps giving him up had been the right thing; at least for him, if not for me.

Yet, as I read Robert's letter, I feel my confidence shrinking. My deep psychotherapy with Ron freed me of previous feelings of inadequacy and low self-esteem. Yet my son's description of his life sounds perfect; too perfect for me. Maybe because he'd had such a great childhood, he didn't feel compelled to search for his birth family. I admire his allegiance to the parents who nurtured him so well. But a secret, poisonous thought surfaces. Maybe I've found the son I'd always wanted, the one with an advanced college degree, the one I can brag about when co-workers describe their successful children. Neither of the sons I raised completed college educations as I did. No web pages extoll their accomplishments.

How would Chad and Jared feel if they knew I had these insidious thoughts? Now that I've struggled to find their brother and left no stone unturned, unwelcome feelings of my own failings and disappointments about the sons I raised arise. Chad, brilliant, ambitious, and hard-working, earns perks and recognition in his every sales job. He lightens any atmosphere with clever quips and devotes himself to his daughter, saving in a college fund for Terra to get the education he didn't. Jared attended and excelled in art classes at Ventura Community College and worked in their on-campus art studio, earning accolades for his artwork and reliability, all while desperately sick and waiting on effective anti-psychotic medications to be approved by the FDA and Medi-Cal. Both sons are respectful, decent, loving people, good to me and others. I'm proud of how well they've both done. But I have to admit hoping, and dreading, that this son might turn out to be my ideal one.

Yet, what right do I have to expect Robert to develop a relationship? What are the chances? What can I offer? At his stage of life, what time or interest does he have to consider the significance I might have for him or his children?

My heart sinks. Suddenly, I remember Jared stranded on Highway 80. I glance at the last line of my son's letter.

"P.S. I am called Lee because my father was also a Robert."

Lee; my son's name is Lee. Finally, I know his name. And he has signed his letter with the best words I could hope for:

"With love"

I call out to Dave, "I've got to run, Dave. I'll take the letter along to share with Jared. He'll be excited."

"It *is* exciting! It's wonderful." Dave replies.

"Yes, his letter is very articulate," I say, "and a little intimidating, too."

Dave reaches out to hug me. "You're a very impressive woman yourself. He's going to find you very interesting." Dave's rosy face beams with love and I cheer up.

"Yes! You're right! Tonight, we'll sit out on the patio and have a glass of wine."

Jared's gray Subaru sits stranded on the far right of Highway 80 in Sacramento. He's still waiting for AAA to arrive.

"I got a letter from your brother!" I cry, as Jared climbs into my passenger seat.

"That's great! What did he say?"

"He said he never thought much about being adopted. He was shocked to see your and Chad's pictures. He never imagined having brothers! His two little girls are named Madeleine and Gwendolyn. Aren't they pretty names? It turns out he goes by Lee, not Robert, because his adoptive father is named Robert."

"I hope I get to meet Lee soon," Jared says. "He sounds nice."

"Yeah, me too," I reply. "I really hope so." In my rear-view mirror, the yellow roadside vehicle pulls up behind us. A quick tire change and Jared is back on the road.

"Thanks, Mom; I love you."

"You're welcome. I love you, too."

We head back to our separate homes. I can't wait to read Lee's letter again!

39
GRANDCHILDREN

There's no love more intense than the love we have for our kids - and where there is intense love, there is also intense fear lurking beneath the surface.

—Arianna Huffington

April 2001

Back home, dusk is falling. Pots and pans clatter as Dave starts to make dinner. "Relax," he encourages me. "How does rice and tilapia sound?"

"Wonderful." I sit down to re-read my letter. This time I'll take my time.

> "Madeleine is three and a half. When my wife was pregnant and during the first year or so, I worked part-time and freelance, so that I could experience all that came with having a daughter. She is bright, funny, and creative and we are very close.
>
> Gwen was born on my thirty-fifth birthday and is also an angel. She is blessed with her mother's good looks and I am dedicating much of my energy to developing the close bond like I have with her elder sister."

Granddaughters! Two little girls I've fantasized about ever since learning of their existence a year ago. I pick up their pictures again, leaning in close as I stare, struck by our family resemblances -- round faces, wide high cheekbones, and high foreheads. Madeleine has my dark hair and eyes, Gwen Judy's lighter coloring. If they'd worn the little shorts and skirts my mother sewed for me and my sister from fifty-pound cotton flour sacks, they could have almost been Judy and me. A pang passes through my heart.

Will they grow up as he did, not knowing me, their grandmother? Surely, the fact my son sends pictures and writes about them means I might be able to meet them. But when? The precious, irretrievable years of Lee's infancy and childhood are already gone. I imagine his babies becoming my second-generation loss and hear myself moan.

Then I read his concern that it will raise issues of how his mother will feel to know he and I have been in contact. My stomach tightens. Lee feels protective toward his mother. He doesn't want to hurt her by telling her. I understand. Yet, if he closes me out to shield her, it will be like losing him all over again, only worse now that I realize what I've lost. My shoulders hunch over a heavy feeling in my chest. His adoptive mother has had him for three and half decades. Is it too much to ask her to spare a little for me now? Lee assures me his adoption has not caused him deep emotional problems as he always felt loved and wanted. My heart feels full for him, but I get lost thinking about my own worst-case scenarios, as he tells me his doubts.

> "Quiet reflective time is pretty much extinct at this point in my life, and thus you haven't heard from me. I am also a rather private person and must admit that I was somewhat shocked to get your letter today. I am not really afraid of anything, but rather I am really not sure that I have the ability to seriously engage in an emotionally complex relationship with someone I never really knew existed until April of last year…The fact that there is another family all the way across the country who want to meet me and that we are blood relatives is a bit overwhelming."

Reading further, though, I perk up. He is open to communication through snail-mail for now. He urges me to write and ask whatever I'd like to know about him. He is curious, asking about my father, mother, work, and more. He wants to know about his biological father and the fathers of my two sons, how they were raised, and what they are like. He doesn't want phone calls or emails and isn't ready for face-to-face visits yet, but he encourages me to write as often as I like and says he'll do his best to not let another year pass.

As often as I like might be daily, but I'll write quarterly. I don't want to bombard him. There are enough questions for many letters!

I jump up, eager to go tell Dave my good news. After we eat dinner, I go back to my letter one more time. Then, out of sight of Dave, I tuck it into my bra next to my beating heart. I keep it there, as if it were my baby in a sling against my heart.

40

COMING OUT

I was in a queer mood, thinking myself very old: but now I am a woman again - as I always am when I write.

—Virginia Woolf

MAY 2001

I sit at my desk and write, re-write, change words, remove whole pages, sometimes type, and then write in longhand. Once I mail my letters, I fidget and rub my face. How will Lee receive my letters?

I reassure him that I understand contact with me poses significant complications with his adoptive mother. I tell him his mother must be an impressive and giving woman and that I appreciate that she took her responsibilities seriously to inform him about his hidden origins. I commend her for the wonderful start she and his father gave him in life and express my gratitude. I assure Lee I don't want his mother to be hurt. I tell him I believe there's enough love to go around. I understand keeping secrets and his letter feels like it frees me now to open mine. I hope Lee won't live in secret too long. I know the destructive results of that.

Marilyn consoles me, writing that she took cigars to work when she found her daughter. Like a Jack in the Box, my secret begins to pop out everywhere. Dave and I attend Buddhist groups but also the Davis Unitarian Church. Next Sunday, I climb over Dave in the pew at the call to commemorate important events and make my way to the front of the church. Selecting a speckled brown and white pebble from a wooden bowl to symbolize sharing, I drop it into a bubbling fountain and address the congregation.

"Thirty-six years ago, I gave up my first son for adoption when I was pregnant and unmarried. I found him and wrote him, and Friday I received a wonderful letter from him. He has two adorable little girls, too; my new granddaughters!"

After the service, people hug and congratulate me. A woman at least seventy-five leans into my ear and whispers, "I suppose you can guess my story." She hurries away, but not before I get her phone number.

"Call me," I tell her.

When she doesn't call, I call her. "I gave up my daughter fifty-five years ago," she says. Her voice trembles.

"Well, maybe she'd like to hear from you," I suggest.

"Oh, no; I don't want to interrupt her life," she answers.

As we get off the phone, I know she won't want to talk with me again. I reflect on the familiar sorrow still locked inside her and my heart feels heavy.

Sharon and Grace, Dave and my lesbian couple friends, are at church also that morning. Sharon is a frustrated writer and poet, hoping to leave an unsatisfying contract teacher position at a city college and obtain her PhD. She too had grown up in Texas. The year before, just after I'd learned Cathy contacted my son, I was trimming the wisteria when she poked her head up to the fence between our properties. I couldn't resist telling her about rediscovering my son.

"Where did you give him up?" she asked.

"Gladney."

"Oh yeah; everybody goes to Gladney," she responded in her Texas drawl. Gladney, 130 years in existence, is widely known to Texans, I've learned.

That afternoon, she and Grace ring our doorbell. "Your story is so beautiful," Grace says. The next hour, we sit wiping tears away together.

After our friends leave, I pull out my new autoharp. It's easier and more mobile than my piano. I'm hoping singing and strumming along will relax me. That night, though, melancholy sets in. I strum and sing my newest Beatles' piece, "The Long and Winding Road." Would Lee ever lead me to his New Orleans door, I worry? Then, I sing "Let It Be," but Mother Mary does not answer.

The next day, I write my son about my family history and feel I am telling him about the alternative life he might have lived.

There was our French Chennault family who came to the colonies in about 1700. After Stephen F. Austin, known as the Founder of Texas, and another Stephen who fought for the Confederacy in the Civil War, Stephen became a family name given to my brother. There was our ancestor, the famous Claire Lee Chennault, whose work with Generalissimo Chiang Kai-Check and the Flying Tigers helped defeat the Japanese after Pearl Harbor. Another ancestor was born in a covered wagon fleeing from Santa Anna's army during the Texas Revolution. My maternal grandmother, Hattie, became a teacher by the age of sixteen and opened a Montessori preschool in the small Texas town of Comanche. Grandmother wrote to Maria Montessori, an Italian physician and educator acclaimed for her educational methods and purchased materials from her. My maternal grandfather was a one-time Texas state legislator. Dressed in his black suit and black string tie, he walked to his law office daily long after he'd retired. A picture of him still hung in the Texas Legislature.

On my father's side was my cousin, Benjamin Franklin, born many generations distant. As a child, I stared at pictures of this famous founding father and imagined myself mirrored in his high forehead. Then there was my great-grandfather, reputedly a full-blooded Choctaw Indian, though mostly recalled in whispers as an alcoholic who made my great-grandmother miserable.

In my letter, I enclose pictures of myself, my mother, and sister, juxtaposed with pictures of Madeleine and Gwendolyn to show the strong family resemblances.

I attend my Women's Altar group where the topic turns out to be "The Significant Men in Our Lives." I feel my face redden as I admit I gave up my son and have recently found him. Then another woman admits she'd gone through the same thing. I begin to realize there must be many women I've known who've given up babies, who share the same painful experience and the same secret shame.

Two and a half months later, hearing nothing from Lee, I send him a twelve-page letter, focusing on all the ways I hope we may be alike.

I end with a poem by a Japanese poet, Issa.

"In the cherry blossom's shade
there's no such thing
as a stranger."

41
SO MANY OTHERS

Out of suffering have emerged the strongest souls;
the most massive characters are seared with scars.

—Kahlil Gibran

2001

I attend a group therapy training conference and sign up for a Women's Group where the topic is to share something shameful that happened to you because you are a woman. Our trim group leader wears a matching pastel blue jacket and skirt with blue satin heels. Her blond hair curls and coifs around her sophisticated face. She exudes perfection. Ms. Perfect Therapist, I dub her.

"We'll pair off," she says.

I am left without a partner.

"I'll be your partner." she tells me.

I eyeball the room, hoping to discover another stray member, but all the others are already partnered up, pulling their chairs to face each other. "I don't know if I can do this," I choke. Ms. Perfect Therapist is the last person in the room I want to reveal myself to.

"Well, you either have to tell me or opt out of the group," she declares. Since childhood, my great fear was to be left out. After I spill my story, Ms. Perfect Therapist surprises me by exclaiming, "Oh, he's going to be so happy to know he has a high-functioning mother like you instead of some loser!"

Is this a compliment? Or a judgment? I don't see the girls at Gladney as losers.

After the training, another member reaches out to me, telling me of her several friends who gave up babies under the same pressure I'd felt then. "My friend, Joan, and her son hang out together every week now," she says. How enviable for her!

Why had I kept my secret so long? Maybe I was not so different from the too-perfect therapist. Hadn't I, too, protected my image? Was I more locked into my conservative upbringing and Bible Belt heritage than I wanted to believe?

I determined I would do that no longer. I will build my strength by seeking others who survived this. I will no longer hide behind this shame that poisoned my youth and defined my era. I am beginning to see that the strength in others is also in me.

Becoming obsessed with the topic of adoption makes me a lodestone for others. First mothers are drawn to me like iron filings to a horseshoe magnet.

June says her daughter she'd given up for adoption contacted her a few years before and then pushed her to meet her grandchildren, two little girls, three and five.

"I just couldn't," June's voice is tinged with a pain she doesn't put words to.

I picture June's granddaughters, imagining how much they might remind her of the child she lost.

"Are you still in touch with your daughter?" I ask.

"Once in a while, just a letter. She lives in Ohio. I haven't been to see her."

Reading between June's sparse lines, it feels as if she were tiptoeing from her bedroom at night, wary and suspicious that a stranger is lurking in the dark. That stranger has a name – grief. I know that grief. I also know not everyone has the strength to face it -- the heartache and anguish that roar like a tsunami out of unexplored loss from the past.

Then there is Beth, a nurse at Kaiser. When I tell Beth of my adopted son's discovery, the firm line of her mouth betrays a faint edge of tremulous anger. Then Beth surprises me.

"My son was born in Germany," she discloses. "Last year, I got a phone call in the middle of the night. He didn't even bother to ask about me, just started accusing me, telling me he'd had a terrible life. He was so angry. I finally hung up on him."

"How sad," I say.

By accusing his unknown mother, this son eliminated any chance of healing himself and exacerbated the suffering Beth already endured.

When I have lunch with Jean, she speaks of the despondency she felt when her parents insisted on sending her off to an unwed mothers' home.

"My father told me that even though I might feel my life was ending, I could still go on and have a good life. I felt so comforted," Jean said. "I went back to school afterwards, got my law degree, and successfully raised another daughter."

I try to imagine what having a father like Jean's would have been like, but I can't.

I signed up for Concerned United Birthparents' annual retreat at Asilomar, a retreat center bounded by the Pacific Ocean and thick with Monterey Pines and walking trails through sand dunes. Sitting with about a hundred women my age around tables covered in crisp white tablecloths and sipping wine from tall crystal stemware, we don't look like bad girls. We could be a gathering of the Soroptimists or the American Association of University Women or maybe even Planned Parenthood, I snicker to myself. Instead of watermelons for bellies, we're succumbing to middle-aged spread. We are drawn together by shame and our determination to emerge from it.

I allow my eyes to rove from table to table. Are we women wearing bright print blouses and lipstick, the flotsam and debris remaining from the era of the '50s, '60s, and early '70s when adoptions were closed, what they call the Baby Scoop Era? Aren't I?

Though weird, it's a relief to be at the retreat. We pass Kleenex boxes freely around and wipe our eyes at stories of loss and reunion. I stroll under coastal live oaks there with a woman who tells me she'd been raped. "I haven't told my son yet. I don't know how to tell him what his father did." Her blue eyes radiating gentleness, I feel her sadness. "Some people claim there are six million of us." Yes, four to six million of us, almost all from the closed adoption era. It feels overwhelming to comprehend.

The next time the CUB retreat is held at Asilomar, I convince Marcia to come with me. We share a room in a cabin. She attends a group of other birth mothers like herself who have children who have refused reunion with them. I hope knowing she's not alone helps her.

I learn of open adoption. That's what they call it now. Adoptable infants are in short supply. Cultural changes allow most unwed girls to keep their babies, so I hear only one to two percent agree to adoption now. Open adoption may be a marketing ploy to encourage pregnant girls to give up their children, implying they won't really lose their babies. On their website now, Gladney promises first mothers will be able to choose their child's parents. "It's that simple. You will have access to the profiles of all of our hopeful couples," they say.

I imagine myself back in 1964 propped in my narrow bed, my legs splayed to each side of my immense belly, leafing through a notebook of perfect looking happy couples. A mother-to-be with a perky pony tail and good teeth poses with her husband, his arm protectively around her shoulder, his brow a little furrowed to demonstrate what a responsible father he'd be. Would I have chosen them?

Would there have been a Unitarian couple? Since I'd left my fundamentalist religious upbringing, that might have appealed. Or someone who seemed to be psychologically attuned, like me; a psychologist maybe?

Perhaps I'd have left the choice up to my active fetus. I could have propped the notebook, one page opened to an affluent attorney and his stay-at-home wife, the other page an internist and his nurse wife. A swift kick to the left, and my baby might have grown up visiting the law library with his father. A fist struck to the right, and maybe he'd play with his father's stethoscope at night.

Never meeting the prospective parents, never talking to them, how could anyone choose from pictures and descriptions? How could it be "that simple?"

Still, a pang at the unfairness of my closed adoption era shoots through me. At least I'd have known my child's name. I'd have known who raised him. That would have been better than the black hole of secrecy.

Some first mothers refer to young women now as "drinking the Kool-Aid of open adoption." I see a video about a woman who gave up her twin boys only to have the adoptive mother close off her open visits when her sons were five years old. She tried to continue seeing her boys at school, until her twins told her, "Mommy doesn't want us to see you." Not wanting to put them in an impossible position, she stopped visiting.

Later, I met a few younger first mothers who had agreed to open adoptions but weren't informed of where the adoptive parents lived. One young California woman's baby was being raised on the East Coast, another in South America. Neither of these birth mothers had funds to travel to visit their children. Maybe that was never part of the plan anyway. Most open adoptions seemed limited to an annual letter and pictures.

I was excited to learn online of an organization called PACER, Post-Adoption Center for Education and Research, which has a support group at Sacramento's Trinity Episcopal Church, close to where I live. A woman with graying hair approached me my first night there.

"Can I help you?" she inquires, reminding me of the matronly church ladies of my childhood.

"No, it's okay," I stammer. Then I straighten my shoulders and look her in the eye. "I'm looking for the PACER meeting. Do you know where they meet?"

"Oh, I think they're back to the right, next to the AA meeting." The anonymous woman appears unfazed and I head right.

Twelve of us sit on folding chairs around a rectangular table with a Kleenex box prominently next to a glass jar for donations. Linda, a Hispanic woman who went by the name of "Mama O," reads out the rules. Five minutes each for personal sharing; no cross-talk allowed. We introduce ourselves and our place in what I've learned is called "the adoption triad."

Tonight, there are four adoptees; six first/birth mothers and one adoptive couple. "I'm Linda, a birth mother," I say.

Irene, the adoptive mother, speaks. "Our daughter-in-law told me our adopted son wanted to find his birth mother. When I learned how my son felt, I was upset at first. Maybe I hadn't been a good enough mother to him. Maybe he'd love her more. But then I realized I'd had him all these years and surely I could share him a little with her."

I wonder if Lee's parents might feel like this couple.

"There are so many lost years we can never recover," I share. "Now we're losing more years and my granddaughters are growing up and I'm losing them, too."

Tears begin running down the cheeks of the first/birth mother to my left. Mama O bows her face into her hands and grabs a Kleenex. She tells us how she's sent letters and cards to her son for years, but never received a single response. My heart breaks for her. I've received a letter after only a year. How fortunate that I've been able to have other children, too. Edie, a first/birth mother I meet that night will later introduce me to her friend who suffers from the secondary infertility that afflicts some first mothers, with up to twenty percent unable to conceive after their first child's loss.[22] Claudia Corrigan D'Arcy's blog, *Musings of the Lame*, cites claims that first mothers are forty to sixty percent more likely to experience secondary infertility than other mothers.[23] For these first mothers, the child they gave up turned out to be their only opportunity to parent. Adoption loss took not just one, but all of the children they might have had.

I learn of the American Adoption Congress and attend their annual conferences in Sacramento and San Francisco, hearing from many members of the adoption triad. I learn the numbers of adoptees, birthparents, and adoptive parents are legion. My own reactions are shared by many, many others. By unearthing my secret, I've discovered a whole new world I only now realize I belong to.

---

22 Isabel Andrews, "The Ghost Kingdom: Secondary Infertility and Birth Mothers. *Psychoanalytic Journal*, Vol. 30, 2009, https://doi.org/10.1080/073516903200184.

23 Claudia Corrigan D'Arcy, "Costs of Adoption: Increased Secondary Infertility Rates Infographic," *Musings of the Lame,* Oct.15, 2013,http://www.adoptionbirthmothers.com/musing- of-the-lame-an-adoption-blog.

42

TERROR AND JOY

If I held you any closer, I would be on the other side of you.

—Groucho Marx

2001

Early morning TV coverage on September 11, 2001 shows terrorists flying airplanes into New York's Twin Towers, destroying the World Trade Center and leaving the whole country reeling with shock. New Yorkers run in terror with handkerchiefs over their mouths and noses, huge plumes of white dust rising from the falling concrete behind them. I tear myself away from the news and dash to work to meet my 8 a.m. appointment. How strange that I have two clients with Middle Eastern connections today. A sense of group trauma hangs heavy in our clinic.

My young Muslim-American client wears no makeup and covers her hair with a scarf. My last patient of that day is an Afghani immigrant. She lost nearly all her family to the Russian invaders twenty years before, witnessing three thousand people buried alive in a pit by the Russians. She shakes in my office as she describes hiding and seeing the bulldozed earth move and shake as the people tried to escape.

I worry how this national tragedy will affect Lee. Arriving home from work a few days later, I spy a letter fallen through the mail slot into our front hall.

"Oh my God!" I shout, grasping the thick packet as if there were a million-dollar lottery check inside. No longer feeling exhausted, I tear open the envelope. Lee's letter is dated September 10th, 2001.

Lee tells me how nice it had been to receive my letters. He says more about his restaurant business, his chef's menus, and the struggles of competing in New Orleans. I fear tourism will likely decrease now, adding more stress. How can I help this son I barely know?

He goes on to reflect.

> "It sounds like your life has been most interesting and that you have been presented with many blessings and many challenges."

Indeed! Though I might not have objected to a less *interesting* life, this stranger son doesn't sound taken aback at the vagaries and peccadillos of my existence. I like his worldliness.

He writes that his life has been pretty easy, growing up in a grand old house where his parents still live. They sent him to a great private school where they had Rosh Hashana and Yom Kippur off, though I gather he may have felt some discomfort that his family was less well off than many of his classmates. His mother and father worked together for many years, she receiving little pay for grant work, but his father rising to the top of his field, becoming President of the American Association of Anatomists. His parents have traveled all over the world: Russia, China, Japan, and even Africa, including a week on safari.

I think back to what my Gladney caseworker had told me about my baby's parents-to-be, that they were serious, scientific-type people, both with PhDs. Gladney kept their word to place my son with educated parents. I feel glad my test scores had led to one good outcome for Lee. He describes his mother:

> "...a feisty firebrand from Kentucky whose father owned a lumberyard. She was quite footloose and fancy free in her youth. She is petite and has been rather deaf (can't hear thunder

> without her hearing aids). Her eyes prevent her from reading any longer (which was one of her great passions). But she is remarkably agile, upbeat, and light-hearted about it all."

He has never met either of his grandfathers. His grandmothers both died without much family contact. Remembering my grandmother's little china cups filled with pale warm café au lait, I wish he had the benefit of more extended adoptive family.

But he has done well, studying seven years tuition-free at Tulane where he got a BA in economics and an MBA. He got started in the restaurant business during college and is now in his twentieth year in the business. He tells me:

> "I am hoping to get a few successful operations together and then do more traveling and consulting, but this is a 'young man's game.' I spent the first four years delivering, cooking, and managing a pizza place near my home. I worked as a waiter in the best restaurant in the city during graduate school. After college I worked for two years supervising eight Domino's Pizza stores but could not deal with the corporate mentality."

I like his colorful, relaxed descriptions. I'm happy to hear that he pursued his interests and dreams. It seems my son is not a "button-down" type. His newsy, warm-hearted letter reveals a sharp-witted, creative, determined, inventive, and funny person.

I smooth his eight-page letter tenderly. A Bible verse not remembered for decades pops up.

"This is my beloved son in whom I am well pleased."

I'm overjoyed I can finally honor my son's thirty-seventh birthday. As Oct. 30th approaches, I search the birthday card racks. A standard card won't do. "Since the day you came home from the hospital, you've been our special son" reads one card. No, that won't do. "You gave your mother gray hairs, but you've grown into a fine man, son." No, definitely not that one.

Then I find a blank card with a picture of a naked baby boy in water, two hands about to lift him. Inside I write:

"Sweet baby
Birthed and separated
Lifted by loving hands
Kept in safety
Raised to manhood
Lost and now found at last
Sweet celebration"

This year, I can send a poem written just for him. I imagine Lee's reaction on receiving his card.

Two weeks later, his card is returned undamaged. A white tape with mysterious codes is pasted onto the bottom of the envelope. Is it a casualty of the post-9/11 events? I put the card into a brown envelope and mail it again. Lee must have thought I'd forgotten his birthday. Maybe he'd wondered if I was his true mother after all.

43

LONGING

The course of true love never did run smooth.

—William Shakespeare

2001

When Dave and I visit his family in Southern California, I take advantage of this irresistible opportunity to tell my exciting story. Julia, my sister-in-law, listens raptly. "We should Google Lee's name," she suggests.

I type his name into the computer menu bar. Up pops an article Lee wrote, "Music: Cats in Class," a New Orleans' Gambit Weekly publication, 11/10/97.

My son could write and write well!

Next, Julia and I click on Lee's Dante's Kitchen website. There is his signature logo sign with the cast iron skillet and flames and a photo of the old white house he'd converted for his restaurant, with a front porch swing ready to sit in. I imagine swinging on that porch, sitting next to him, the two of us sipping chilled buttery Chardonnay, swaying gently in the warm evening air, and trading stories of our histories.

Online, my son looks like something of a celebrity; a restaurant owner in Uptown, the best part of New Orleans, a published writer, a creative businessman, a Masters-in-Business-Administration. Maybe I really have found the son I always wanted, I think, guilt like bile in my throat.

Viewing my son's writings and restaurant photos reminds me our connection is one-way, though. Dante's site advertises, "Lee Yates and Eman [his chef] invite you to stop by for sandwiches and salads at Dante's or simply a glass of wine on their front porch swing. They will be waiting."

The invitation calls to me like Bali Hai in the musical *South Pacific*. Anyone else seeing his Dante's Kitchen website could call up and make a dinner reservation; but not me. Briefly, I imagine showing up in a blond wig, a floppy hat, and rose-tinted sunglasses.

I long to sprint to the next flight to New Orleans, but it would be ruinous to just show up. I have to wait for him to invite me. The raw truth tastes bitter in my mouth.

44

COOKIES

So long as you have food in your mouth, you have solved all questions for the time being.

—Franz Kafka

DECEMBER 2001

I pull down my beater from the kitchen cabinet to find it still caked with the mashed potatoes I whipped for Thanksgiving dinner. I scrape off the dried crust and pull out a whole pound of butter from the refrigerator to soften. What holiday cookies should I make this year? Definitely the Southern pecan balls Chad loves so much and the frosted nutmeg logs Jared favors. My Aunt Martha's butter cookie recipe with my mother's butterscotch frosting thick with caramelized butter, cream, and powdered sugar. Terra loves those and Dave adores them all.

A sensation of equal parts longing and apprehension runs through my heart. What about sending cookies to my new family members in New Orleans? I picture Madeleine's and Gwendolyn's faces if they received a package wrapped in red cellophane tied with candy canes on top.

But what if their father didn't like my cookies? Since he was a "foodie" like me, he could be picky. What if he found it presumptuous for me to send cookies at all?

I strew the kitchen counters with Corning Glass mixing bowls, measuring spoons, and cookie sheets, then tie on my flowered purple bib apron. Under the dull sheen left from years of wiping my greasy hands on my apron, the decorative orange zinnias and red roses are barely visible. I'm listening to NPR's Morning Edition on the kitchen radio, reporting on the latest anthrax mailings to news media offices and prominent senators. Five people are dead. The senators could have opened their packages and inhaled the anthrax spores inside of a highly refined white powder. I glance at the blue and white plastic bag of Sunny Select powdered sugar that the Pecan Balls would be rolled in. Maybe I should leave it off this year.

Last week, I'd told my friends, "Maybe he'll be afraid to eat my cookies. Everybody's afraid anyway since 9/11. What if he thinks I'm trying to poison him? They haven't caught the perpetrator."

My friends looked at me as if I might be crazy. "He'll be thrilled," they assured me.

They couldn't grasp my fear bred from thirty-six years of poisonous secrecy, toxic as the white powder filling the news. Even though my letters to Lee have been as loving as I could be, how could he be sure of my intentions? I could understand his being afraid because I'm afraid. If he were to show up now at my door, I imagine myself cowering behind the curtain, shrinking out of his sight. My friends think my fears are crazy. I think so myself. They don't know about the tears that roll unbidden down my cheeks whenever I'm alone.

Even though I've obsessed about Lee since hearing from him, I want Chad and Jared to know how much I love them. I have to make pecan balls. They have to be coated with powdered sugar to satisfy Chad's sweet tooth. Jared loves the finger-long cookie logs spread with vanilla buttercream. The sprinkling of nutmeg on them wouldn't look like anthrax, would it? Could the orangey-brown nutmeg speckles possibly resemble anthrax?

Washing my hands in my new stainless-steel sink, I gaze out the kitchen window. In the front yard, a few russet, tangerine, and lemon-yellow leaves still cling to the branches of the elm tree. I can already smell the vanilla fragrance of the butter cookies. Everything appears normal. But nothing is normal. Nothing has been normal for the year and a half since I finally found my firstborn son.

I take out Lee's letters and sit down in my dining room chair. Maybe re-reading them will help me decide. The cream-colored papers flutter in my hands like magical butterflies. "Linda, you understand that by signing these papers, you'll never have any further contact with your son, right?" the psychologist had told me thirty-seven years ago. The very fact that I could worry about sending cookies must surely be a miracle.

I gaze at the picture of Maddie, a toddler still in bright blue overalls, a pink ribbon circling her light brown hair. She is slumped behind her younger sister, Gwennie, who wears green overalls, a green barrette clasping her fine blond hair. Gwennie's two baby teeth gleam white just above her lower lip. Eyes and lips shining, both girls smile broadly.

They look so much like me and my sister at their ages. Maybe they'll never know I exist. Maybe I'll never meet them. I can't send toys or little outfits to them. They might chatter to their other grandmother. Probably my son hasn't yet told her of me. Maybe he never will. I've already lost his childhood. I may lose theirs.

The whiff of burning cookies stops my dire imaginings. I rush to the oven and pull out the blackened cookies. Opening the window to let out the acrid smoke wrenches me from my pointless self-pity.

If I send cookies to my son, the charming little girls are bound to see them. He can tell them a friend sent them. They'll love them.

Lee will appreciate the excitement in his girls' big eyes if I send cookies. He'll hear them clamoring over their favorites. He'll see the crumbs rolling down their chubby cheeks. I imagine the little girls' delight in the magic of cookies frosted in red, green, yellow, and blue, sprinkled with colored sugar and decors. I'll make pink peppermint meringues, butterscotch frosted cookies, and, yes, the nutmeg logs. I'll speak to Lee and the little girls in the wordless language of butter, sugar, spices, and "everything nice."

Both my other sons love my cookies. Chad told me they were better than any from the bakery. Why wouldn't Lee?

I won't give up! I sit up straight and raise my shoulders. Where's my recipe for rolled out sugar cookies?

But this year, I'll save the pecan balls for Chad.

45

REVISITING THE PAST

We can easily forgive a child who is afraid of the dark;
the real tragedy of life is when men are afraid of the light.

—Plato

MID-JANUARY 2002

Dark comes early. I've heard nothing from Lee. Staring out my kitchen window, I watch the last drooping stubborn elm leaf fall and drift slowly to rest on the wet ground.

With my Christmas cookies, I'd sent a Lee a letter suggesting I might attend the American Group Psychotherapy Association holding its 2002 annual conference in New Orleans in two months. Would Lee be willing to meet, even for coffee or lunch, I wrote?

Did my suggestion to meet pressure him? Catastrophic thinking overtakes me. Perhaps even sending cookies was unwelcome. I get out my Bic pen and write Lee, telling him I've reconsidered. I tell him I don't want to risk making either of us uncomfortable by showing up in his hometown without his full agreement.

I can't imagine being in New Orleans without seeing him or the little girls. I've heard birth mothers sometimes did "drive-bys," so desperate for connection they'd drive past their grown child's home and slump down low in the car to avoid being seen. I feel if I came to

New Orleans without being able to see my son and granddaughters, I'd be tempted to lurk outside their home or school, desperate to get a glimpse of them. My urgent need feels scary.

I decide to settle for writing a letter, something Lee has agreed to. I fill him in on information about his birth father and our relationship, hoping to get back in his good graces. I tell Lee his father was a nice, intelligent, sensitive, artistic, well-spoken, and decent young man who he can feel proud to have as one of his parents.

I tell him only good things about his father and assure him that Bob and I loved each other, that his existence wasn't due to a one-night stand. I tell him about going to jazz and classical concerts where Bob played his clarinet, about visiting his aunt in the little town of Greenville, about his mother and stepfather in Dallas where we all crowded around the dining table with Bob's little brothers.

Then I dare to speculate on how we both would have had different lives if two teenagers hadn't killed my mother the year before in what Dave, my attorney husband, says would now probably be considered negligent vehicular homicide. My mother would have made sure Bob married me. I hope Lee won't be put-off by my imagined life he and I might have had with Bob.

I don't want him to have any impression that I gave him up lightly. I explain that it seemed to me I was moving inexorably toward a conclusion which was extremely painful and somehow inescapable. When I called Bob after my departure from Gladney and told him I'd had a boy, our conversation had felt both sad and final.

> "Our relationship could not survive the devastation of losing you; even if it was apparently by our own choices."

My shoulders droop like the leaves outside. Sorrow from decades ago washes over me. I remember calling Bob not long after my 1980 visit to Gladney. In some strange synchrony, we were both flying into Dallas/Fort Worth Airport on the same day, within an hour of each other. We met then to talk about our past, and, for me, assess whether it might be possible to rekindle our relationship since by then, Don and I were divorcing. Bob told me he'd gotten an East Texas State cheerleader pregnant the year after me. Explaining "I couldn't do it again," Bob said he'd married her, been unhappy, and now they were divorcing. They'd had two children. Bob told me he'd welcome our son if he ever showed up. After our meeting, in which I felt we still had mutual attraction, I wrote Bob. He didn't answer and I gathered he was already in a new relationship.

I tell Lee now that he has two other half-siblings; a brother who studied dance and a sister. How will Lee feel about learning he has even more family? I've lost Bob's address and phone number, but I offer to help Lee find him if he wants to. The adoptees I know by now did their own searches. Still, I'll do what I can to make sure Lee can get to know his father and family.

Years later, in 2009, Lee will ask me to find Bob, and I will. Seeing records then of Bob's second son, born only fourteen months after I'd left our first one at Gladney, made my teeth grit. My heart clenched picturing him and his wife carrying their baby home wrapped in a blue flannel blanket. How quickly Bob had abandoned any thought of me, I felt.

Then Bob told me on the phone he'd come looking for me in 1986 wanting to see if there was still anything there, he said. But he didn't feel guilty about abandoning me and our baby, he claimed. I realized then that the young woman who'd let him walk away no longer existed in me.

The woman I'd become would never have reconciled with him. I feel taller and stronger.

46

DISTINGUISHED ADOPTIVE COUPLE

Life is the continuous adjustment of internal relations to external relations.

—Herbert Spencer

2002

A month later, another letter! I grab the now-familiar looking envelope and pitch myself onto our living room couch to read it.

I'd imagined Lee and his family having a great Christmas, one I longed to be part of and wasn't, but I was wrong. His February letter tells me he enjoyed the cookies, but not so much the holidays. He reminds me that the holidays are tumultuous and says the pressures of work and struggles with getting his restaurant to break even are weighing on him.

I can see Lee rushing home from work, arriving late to face wailing kids and harried wife, losing sleep over disappointing profit margins. I recall how Dave and I, each with our own private practices in Southern California, came to feel our townhouse was a mere pitstop as we struggled with long hours, many clients, running our businesses, and Jared's needs. I'm concerned when Lee writes:

> "My wife and I find ourselves at odds a bit lately because of the demands of owning a small business and the lack of time and energy it leaves you for anything else."

Intimations of marital problems? I know about those, too, mine and so many clients. Recently, Dave and I have benefitted from couples therapy for issues stemming from our childhoods and my complicated family, where Dave rightly refers to Lee as "the other man." Will Lee and his beautiful wife make it through the pressures of business and family? Maybe I could help in some way. I'd babysit. Yes, Lee and Ellen could go for relationship restorative date nights while I feed and bathe their adorable, but elusive, children! A thrill runs through me. Then I read on.

> "It is just not a very opportune time for the introduction of a second or third family into my life, as I don't have enough time for my own at the moment. It is not anything I am against but don't want to short shrift it when the decision to jump is made."

I'm not going to see him or them anytime soon.

I try to understand. I try to remember my professional perspective and cultivate patience. I can see this isn't all about me. Given Lee and Ellen's stage of life, their family responsibilities, and limited extended family, it would be hard to welcome a new family. They lack the experience I, a grandmother already, have to grasp how quickly their toddlers will transform into teens. I read on and learn that my son had a Gladney Christmas party at his restaurant for the local auxiliary. He was asked by friends who are currently trying to adopt.

My stomach knots up at learning my son may be building a relationship with Gladney's auxiliary in New Orleans, which I didn't know existed. He writes:

> "I also met a woman who, with her distinguished winemaker husband, had recently adopted. How different the process has become. The price is still high, but now the adoptive parents have absolutely no control over the process. They are told to

> compile a dossier and it is distributed to prospective birth mothers who then choose who they wish to get their child. Many agencies have long periods where the birth parents may change their mind well after the birth of the child and are given the right to see the child and be in their life as they grow up. How confusing this must be for the child. How hard for the adoptive parents. I find the whole climate rather disturbing."

I flinch, wanting to argue. Why shouldn't a girl parting from her baby have a choice about who'd be raising it? Shouldn't birth parents have some time to change their minds?

I Google "adoption revocation period" and find out that in most states, the time for changing consent is limited to a few days, if not hours. Otherwise, mothers must prove fraud, duress, or coercion. What young girl, flooded with new mother hormones, screaming for her missing baby, would be up to handling a complicated court process? What was the probability of her proving fraud or coercion?

In 1964, the pressure to give up our babies was like a poisonous chemical in the air, invisible, smelling of guilt, and cloaking us girls in shame. No one revealed there was any revocation period then. The system thrived on our ignorance.

If adoptions really allowed the birth parents to stay involved, couldn't a child adapt to the idea of having more than two parents? Children adapted all the time to having stepparents. Besides, I'd learned that adoptive parents could and did sometimes close off birth parents after promising them involvement.[24]

Back in the '60s and '70s, there were landmark cases where biological parents attempted to take back their children when they were already toddlers. I'd seen a picture in the Sacramento Bee of one of those children clinging to the adoptive mother's neck, screaming while being ripped away. I didn't agree with that, either.

It must be true, too, that having both adoptive and birth parents share the child would be complicated. I know the hazards of stepparent families. I live in one. Chad and Jared have siblings in Don's

---

[24] Lorraine Dusky, *hole in my heart: a memoir and report from the fault lines of adoption* (Sag Harbor, New York: Leto Media, 2015) p.132

new family. It can get confusing. It takes mature people to make it work. But aren't adoptive parents assessed for maturity?

The main thing I realize is that my son feels loyal to the parents who raised him. I admire his loyalty and, at the same time, am disappointed that he appears to lack empathy for the birth mother's position – my position. His sympathies are with the "distinguished winemaker" adoptive couple he met. We girls giving up babies at Gladney were mostly "distinguished" by our youth, abandonment, and desperation.

I read on, feeling criticized, as I did by my father and family growing up. Lee writes:

> "It seems as if you have yet to come to terms with your tumultuous time, as I have with my first two loves. How many times you must have pondered the results of your decision. You should take comfort in that it seems to have worked out well for everyone and thoughts of what might have been cannot be productive nor give you any real insight into the meaning of your or my life. What was, was and what is, is.... Once the page has been torn off on the calendar, there is no more practical use for it."

A flush of shame burns my cheeks. I sit down and cup my forehead in my hand. I feel foolish for suggesting things could have been different had my mother lived and for sharing my pain about losing him. It appears that is only about my need, not his. A few days later, I write back and say:

> "I can see that it would take extraordinarily mature people to make such an arrangement work. I imagine it is kind of like shared child custody in divorce cases. The concept often sounds better than the reality. For you, it appears it would have been a detriment. Perhaps, on the other hand, it would have prevented some of the difficulties your sister has evidently experienced. I doubt if there could be a one-size-fits-all approach in such a delicate situation."

I tell Lee I couldn't have done as good a job as his parents did. I think I even mean it. But in my secret heart of hearts, I am competing with them. I *want* to be this son's real mother. I *need* to return to the past and rewrite history. A part of me *wants* to wipe out his adoptive mother's contributions and convince him that I'm the real thing. I'm not proud of it, but it's the truth.

47

THE BODY KEEPS THE SCORE

There are only two mistakes one can make along the road to truth: Not going all the way, and not starting.

—Gautama Buddha

2002

I email Cathy Bowman asking for copies of my Gladney records. A few weeks later, they arrive. I expected notes from the rare counseling sessions with Mrs. Harrison or perhaps from our group therapist, Dr. Malone, describing his suspicions of oversexed girls squirming in hard-backed chairs. But aside from my Differential Aptitude Tests showing superior test scores, there is only the medical history completed by Mrs. Lewis on June 4, 1964. The shock is that Cathy also sent my baby's birth and nursery records. He was born at Duncan Memorial Hospital. Jarvis Franklin, his record says. Jarvis?

My shoulders and stomach tighten. No one asked me what I wanted to call him, of course. How many nurses offered a bottle to my baby, calling him by that name I dislike?

"Born: Friday, October 30, 1964, at 4:01p.m., in Fort Worth, Texas, male; nine months' gestation; spontaneous delivery. Measurements at Birth: Weight: 7 lb., ½ oz, Length: 20 inches,

> Head: 13 ½, Chest: 12 ½. No complications during labor or delivery, spontaneous primary respiration, bulb suction used, no resuscitator needed, good cry. Apgar Rating: 1 minute – 10; 5 minutes -10.

I open my pantry door. Inside sits a five-pound bag of Gold Medal flour. I pick it up and cradle it. He didn't weigh much more than this. I rock the bag gently before replacing it on the shelf and dusting the white powder off my blouse. I return to the records:

> First Feeding: 10/31/64 4:10 p.m. Kind: Caetose Amount: 1 ½ oz.; First Formula: 10/31/64 12:25 p.m. Kind: Enf 1-2; Amount: 1 oz.

As I read, my body sends a spontaneous rush surging through my breasts, making them warm and tingling. It's the same sensation of milk let-down I experienced nursing Chad and Jared. I feel my nipples now, checking for moisture, almost surprised to find none. But my fifty-eight-year-old body hasn't forgotten. It still wants to nurse my long-gone baby I never fed.

As a therapist, I've learned that whether we consciously think about our trauma or not, it is stored in our bodies. I completed a training course with Bessel Van Der Kolk, M.D. based on his book, *The Body Keeps the Score: Brain, Mind, and Body in the Healing of Trauma*.[25] Yes, my body had kept the score.

In Ann Fessler's book, *The Girls Who Went Away: The Hidden History of Women Who Surrendered Children for Adoption in the Decades Before Roe v. Wade*.[26], the interviewees told Fessler how they were never the same, feeling pain, shame, guilt, loss, isolation, and having problems with loss of confidence, turning to alcohol and other

---

25 Bessel Van Der Kolk, M.D., *The Body Keeps the Score: Brain, Mind, and Body in the Healing of Trauma*, Penguin Books, 2015.

26 Ann Fessler, *The Girls Who Went Away: The Hidden History of Women Who Surrendered Children for Adoption in the Decades Before Roe v. Wade*, Penguin Press HC, 2006.

substances for relief, and suffering from intimacy issues. This is not a comprehensive list, but I find myself in it.

Later on, I ask a nurse acquaintance about my baby's record.

"An Apgar Rating of 10?" she exclaims. "Even at one minute and then at five minutes? That's really unusual."

"Unusual? Good unusual? Or bad?"

"That's a great Apgar rating! Your baby came into the world very strong and healthy."

I let out my breath and feel a moment of pride.

48

TIME DRAGS

Time destroys the speculation of men, but it confirms nature.

—Cicero

2002 - 2003

Nine months pass with no word from Lee. I write him in February 2002 and again later in May. All summer, I wait. A blanket of thirty-eight-year-old grief descends upon me. The hot California Gold Country sun bears down on my summer of sorrow, while I listen to Joan Baez singing Bob Dylan's "Simple Twist of Fate." Is it really a sin to know and feel too much, as the song warns? I don't think so.

That summer, I meet an adoptive mother, Lucy, with a daughter nine years old. She'd been in the birthing room when her daughter was born to a fifteen-year-old girl, Mary Lou, who selected Lucy and her husband to adopt her baby. Mary Lou wanted her daughter to have the two-parent family she couldn't provide. Lucy tells me she writes Mary Lou an annual letter with pictures. That's what their open adoption agreement consists of.

Lucy and her husband divorced five years ago. Lucy has neglected for five years to mention this to Mary Lou, claiming she doesn't want to disturb Mary Lou by telling her. She knows Mary Lou is now married and could give her daughter the two-parent family she wanted her to have. Even nine years later, it seems a threat may still exist if the truth of Lucy's divorce were now revealed.

I reflect. How would it have been for me to receive an annual letter and pictures of my son? Reassuring? Yes, but every word, every image would have torn me apart, feeling how distant he was, so untouchable. I'd know him just enough to feel the anguish of his absence.

In the summer, I buy a humorous card, one of those, "What's new with you?" cards and send it to Lee, afraid that, if I do nothing, we may go for years with an annual, increasingly superficial correspondence, like Lucy's to Mary Lou.

October chills the air and stores begin displaying pumpkins and skeletons in their windows. I go searching for a birthday card, this one in plenty of time to reach Lee by October 30th. I long to send a separate card to Gwen, born on his birthday. I almost carry two cards to the cashier, the second with a fairy dressed in a diaphanous gown sprinkled with glitter. Then I find one that might serve for both Lee and Gwen. On the front is a picture of a little girl four or five years old. She has her arms outstretched and is dancing on a grassy lawn, her dress blown up by the wind, revealing her white cotton underpants. The verse reads:

> "Sing like there's nobody listening
> Love like you'll never be hurt
> Dance like there's nobody watching
> Live like it's heaven on earth."

Two weeks later, a thin letter from Lee arrives written on one lined piece of paper probably grabbed on the fly from his daughters' school supplies. He thanks me for the card, saying he and Gwen had fun birthdays together. He apologizes for not writing sooner, explaining things have been hectic and his time flies by without the time to accomplish so many of the things he'd like to. Both girls are enjoying school, he writes. The restaurant is doing well enough, though not making as much money as he wishes.

Lee includes pictures of Maddie and Gwen. Madeleine, with her broad face and high cheekbones and forehead, gazes out like a noble Indian princess. Gwendolyn, with her bone structure much the same but topped off with the froth of her reddish-blond curls, appears part fairy and part angel.

The best thing about Lee's letter is his casual, relaxed friendliness. He sounds comfortable and unthreatened.

"Each letter I receive is shorter," I half joke to Dave. "I'm like a starving castaway on an island who receives a constantly diminishing meal from afar every few months. It's enough to keep my hope alive and never enough to satisfy my hunger."

Since Lee said to write as often as I want, I compose five letters in 2003, trying to keep my mailings newsy and colorful. I assure Lee that whenever he feels ready to meet, I don't have to be identified as his first mother. I could be identified as his friend, associate, consultant, or whatever would be most comfortable and uncomplicated for him. At least I wouldn't need a wig or silly hat!

From one Christmas cookie package to the next year's package, no word arrives. That 2003 holiday, I begin baking just as the aging sewer pipe from the front of our home to the street fails. From my kitchen window, I watch Dave and Jared sinking into the four-foot-deep trench they dig. With no running water, I fill large tubs and pots with water to wash my hands and implements. I bake and frost nutmeg logs, lebkuchen, little apricot pies, and sugar cookies.

In my letter, I decide not to mention the sewer failure. This year, I do send the pecan balls rolled in powdered sugar, though.

49

JARED WRITES HIS BROTHER

Don't judge each day by the harvest that you reap but by the seeds that you plant.

—Robert Louis Stevenson

2003

Jared comes over to do some housecleaning for pin money, though weighed down with the extra hundred pounds his anti-psychotic medications help pack onto his 5'9" frame, he can't do too much physical labor. The meds he takes every day to control the voices and delusions that threaten to control him also make him sluggish.

He dusts, sweeps the kitchen and hall floors, vacuums, and heads into the bathrooms to polish the sinks and tubs. Then, sweat beading his flushed face, his wet burgundy shirt sticking to his copious belly after sluicing the bathtub, he pants, "I'm exhausted, Mom. I've gotta take a break."

Although Jared's illness means he can never quite inhabit the same world, he always reads the letters Lee writes. He exits to our joint study and TV room. Half an hour later, he approaches, smiling and waving a white sheet of paper.

"Here, Mom, I wrote Lee a letter," he says, and hands it to me.

> "Dear Lee, I have read your letters while at my mom's house. I own a mobile home in Sacramento and work for my dad at Papa John's Pizza, putting new stores together. My dad is married to Mona and I have a 10-year-old sister, a 19-year-old brother, and a 15-year-old brother. I just had a Dish Network satellite installed. The plumber I work with is putting a used dishwasher in from his rental house to mine. My 19-year-old brother goes to Sac State College to be a doctor. My mom's old cat was born with a walking and sight problem and now lives under my house. I went to Junior College at Ventura and paint sometimes. I do clerical work some. Hi, from Jared Schott."

"This is great, Jared. I'll include it in the letter I'm writing now."

I wonder what Lee will make of Jared's letter. Most people who meet Jared come to recognize and value his gentle vulnerability, his artless naivete. My boss, for whom Jared paints brightly colored flowers, jungles, and giraffes calls Jared an "angel." Will his new brother, who seems so ideal, have the capacity to look past his own apparent advantages and appreciate Jared's kind heart? In the long run, I won't be able to accept him if he doesn't, no matter how educated and successful he seems to be.

I tuck Jared's letter into the envelope with mine and send them both off together. I hope Jared gets an answer. It would mean so much.

PART 4

50
THE CLINCHER

Ever has it been that love knows not its own depth
until the hour of separation.

—Khalil Gibran

CHRISTMAS EVE 2003

Outside, Dave stands on a ladder stringing the last of the outdoor lights. Garlic and herbs simmer in bubbling tomato sauce on my kitchen range. Tomorrow I'll add piles of shellfish and chunks of whitefish to complete this Christmas Day's cioppino, prepared especially to please Chad.

But the piney fragrance and shimmering tree lights in the living room don't raise my spirits. Last night while Bing Crosby sang "I'll Be Home for Christmas," I'd gone from room to room lighting tall white candles in the windows while whispering with my voice breaking "come home, come home" to Lee and my granddaughters.

The mail slot clacks open at the front door. A long envelope with familiar block printing appears on the hardwood floor. This letter feels bulky, substantial, swollen with news. This is not a single sheet of children's lined paper! I tear it open and throw myself onto the living room couch. All my letters and cookies weren't in vain!

Lee begins by mentioning his pleasure in receiving my Christmas cookies. Then he goes into education concerns, affording Gwen's Montessori school and Madeleine starting kindergarten with a great teacher who is a wonderful aging hippie. I imagine their teachers bending to hug them good morning and feel a pang of longing. So many chances to know them have already passed.

Lee writes that his restaurant is thriving and the building he refinanced has appreciated. He and his chef are no longer working such brutal schedules, and they're finally making some profit. But his next comments suggest the day to day grind is wearing on his and his chef's relationship.

> "I'm beginning to think we might need a bit of group therapy, as I fear he tires of my passive aggressive, yet well-mannered rantings and ravings."

My shoulders tighten. A picture surfaces of my father, pacing up and down, his voice rising in a crescendo of rage. Could Lee have inherited that? Back in the sixties, many experts still believed babies were what John Locke originally described as "blank slates" or "tabula rasas." [27]Adoptive parents were encouraged to think that raising their children as their own would be just as if they'd given birth to them. Now experts know this is far from true.

Then Lee tells me:

> "My day was spent shopping with my mom and then the kids after 3 p.m. We put many miles on a new (used) Ford F-150 that I just got when my wife snuck away to France for 'skin care training' for 11 days."

My therapist-trained mind can't help but wonder, reading between his few lines. I hope he and his wife are getting along. Imagining the long hours and divided roles they deal with, I can see how it could be easy for conflict to arise.

---

[27] *St John of the Cross*, Translated by David Lewis, "The Dark Night of the Soul," *The Works of St John of the Cross*, Thomas Baker, London, MCMVIII.

Lee writes his dad retired at seventy-four, then experienced dizziness and memory problems, was diagnosed with a brain tumor which MD Anderson in Houston removed, and following radiation, has become especially loving and affectionate, as I've heard can happen. Follow-up doctor visits showed no trace of any resurgence.

No wonder Lee hadn't written till now! Sandwiched between his business, marriage, rearing his own progeny, and watching his father almost die, he's been overwhelmed himself.

But now, the clincher!

> "We may be out west this summer for a wedding. I'll let you know."

"Oh my God, Dave!" I jump up and run outside where Dave is still stringing Christmas lights. I lean into the growing dusk, waving the letter.

"Lee says they might be coming out for a wedding this summer!"

Dave smiles from his ladder. "That's wonderful!"

Suddenly this chilly Christmas Eve feels warmer. The baby grapefruits beginning to bulge on our huge tree glow like yellow lights among the dark green leaves. Mockingbirds flying to roost in the grapefruit tree call out their medley. "Birdie, birdie, tweet, tweet, tweet." I circle the patio, flapping the letter's pages like wings of mockingbirds and call out my own song.

"Hooray, hooray, hooray!"

After dinner, I practice the songs Dave and I will play tomorrow for the family, Dave on his violin and me on my autoharp. We'll play "The First Noel" and "Silent Night" and hope everyone will sing along to these beautiful Christmas songs. I imagine a future Christmas when my new son might join us and his two little girls may carol with us. Tonight, my heart sings.

51
DAYDREAMING

For my part, I know nothing with any certainty, but the sight of the stars makes me dream.

—Vincent Van Gogh

2004

Dave and I love hiking and camping. Out in the woods, we read and discuss spiritual books, *Living Buddha, Living Christ* by Thich Nhat Hanh, *The Power of Now*, by Eckart Tolle, and other spiritual books. Dave instructs me on the dense teachings of Ramana Maharshi, which I never manage to plow through. Somehow talking about the mystical perspectives of these and other authors surrounded by pines, cottonwoods, and junipers makes me feel connected to all being; as if all of nature, and even the trees, are awake.

Many warm mornings we've put on heavy hiking boots and trekked up the dirt trails, passing through dense forests interspersed with meadows, ferny patches, and the occasional stream we step carefully over on our way to a viewpoint where the trees show blue in the distance. We finish by swimming in mountain lakes surrounded by chaparral and icy from melting snows. The magic of our hikes is the way in which everything normally so important drops away, fading more and more with every mile of exertion. My thoughts take on fantastical imaginings. Our hikes have become my favorite opportunity to dream and allow free range to my longings for Lee and my granddaughters. On the trails, I concoct dramatic fantasies about how to win the undying devotion of my son; the son whose voice I've never heard and whose email address I still don't know.

In my favorite superheroine daydream, I save my little granddaughters from a burning building. It begins when I take them to an old-fashioned English tea where we eat little sandwiches and crumpets. Just as they are spitting out the cucumbers from their sandwiches, a violent fire breaks out in the building. Since it's an old wooden structure, in no time we are engulfed in a conflagration and gulping through thick smoke. Little Madeleine's face goes white with terror and Gwendolyn screams in horror. While all the other hapless diners around us collapse under falling beams, I grab the two girls. I already lost their father's childhood. I cannot lose them, the second generation. It's up to me to save them and I refuse to fail.

Struggling mightily, we emerge from the incinerated building blackened with soot, eyes red, and faces smudged almost beyond recognition. I am dragging and yanking terrified Madeleine after me and carrying the littlest girl, Gwendolyn, whimpering on my back. I, Super Grandma, am oblivious to the damage to my raw knees as I heroically propel us clear of cinders and beams plummeting from the ceiling. Emerging victorious, I see my son gaping at me with undisguised relief and admiration. I have guaranteed myself a lasting place in his heart.

I have replayed variations of this daydream over and over, substituting imaginary reunions for the real thing. Now that I can add real prospects to my fantasies, apprehension, and what in psychology is referred to as 'anticipatory anxiety,' or the idea that the anxiety ahead of time will be worse than the actual event, overcomes me. My professional knowledge doesn't stop my worrying. My chronic infatuation, the fanaticism that overtook and possessed me since the beginning, worsens. Exhilaration, eagerness, and apprehension turn me into a spinning top.

When spring comes, Dave and I sit at our back patio nursing glasses of Merlot. I gaze up at the first stars emerging overhead, dreaming out loud.

"Do you think he'll really come? I can't believe he suggested it at Christmas and now he hasn't said another word!" I twist in our plastic lawn chair and sigh.

"He seems to travel a lot and be a sociable kind of person. I'm sure he'll want to make it to his friends' wedding," says Dave.

"Yeah," I answer, appreciating Dave's reassurance, "but maybe the wedding was called off." I sigh again. "I've written twice to ask him. I just wish he'd say *something.*"

I hear Dave sigh, too, as I give more evidence of my obsessive fixation on my son Dave has christened "the other man" in my life. Eventually, I will realize my unfairness; but at that time, I felt like I was in love. As lovers do, I filled his absence with daydreams.

52

WE MAKE A PLAN

All you need is the plan, the road map, and the courage to press on to your destination.

—Earl Nightingale

MAY 2004

Warmth radiates all through me as I read Lee's first-ever email, all lower-case:

> "dear linda, thanks for the letter. I plan to visit some santa barbara area wineries and then head up to sonoma for thursday and friday and do the same. I would like to see you. let me know where this might work for you and we can take it from there. will have a better itinerary by about june 20th so I'll give you an update as it goes. Lee"

I laugh, enjoying his informal style, and hurry to respond. After several back and forth emails, we tie down a date for our meeting.

I show Dave Lee's latest email. "He's picking me up on July 8th!"

Dave hesitates, eyes darkening with concern.

"What's the matter?!"

"Nothing; nothing really."

"Really. I can see it in your eyes, Dave. What is it?"

"Well, I just hope he really comes. I just don't want you to be disappointed; that's all."

Until now, it hadn't occurred to me that my son might stand me up.

"He'll be there," I assure Dave. "We just have to get there. He'll show up."

Dave reaches out and pulls me to him. I lean into his embrace as this new fear grips me.

Would Lee revenge himself by not showing up? How can it be true that adoption never bothered him? What if he wants to pay me back for abandoning him?

"Don't worry; he's coming. He told you so. I shouldn't have said anything." Dave's pure blue eyes shine with kindness. "I'm just always trying to keep you from being hurt; that's all."

Well, it's too late for that, I think. "He'll be there. We just need to go," I assure him.

"Don't worry. I'll get you there," he promises, beaming at me as his lips curve into that familiar smile.

How lucky I am!

I breathe a sigh of relief. Now if I can just keep my expectations as low as Lee's lower-case email, it will all work out.

I make a reservation at the Geyserville Inn in Sonoma County, not too far from home.

53

THE REUNION HOLE

Youth has no age.

—Pablo Picasso

JULY 2004

Dave maneuvers the green Highlander along Highway 29 into the Sonoma wine country while I gaze out the passenger window at the wired rows of the vineyards marching in formation up and down the fields into the sun-hazed distance. Fat purple clusters of grapes peek from beneath broad green leaves drying to umber in the mid-summer heat. In the distance, a hot-air balloon lifts into azure space. Its little straw-colored basket hangs like a miniature toy beneath the swollen balloon, dangling barely visible passengers. They may be more grounded than I am.

My dark-haired baby, his black hair spiked in every direction from his sweet-smelling scalp, his rosebud ear smelling of the dried milk spilled from the bottle they gave him before allowing me to hold him just this once. This innocent, this blameless infant. Memorize him now. He will be gone tomorrow to a good home.

A peculiar experience has overtaken me since I stepped off the solid ground of my familiar life into this mysterious reunion with Lee. To outward appearances, I am still a middle-aged woman. But with each new juncture, like Alice in Wonderland, I feel myself shrinking; not in size, but in years.

I recognize in my experience the same occurrence that happens to many of my traumatized clients and that we call "emotional regression." Opening this buried trauma unlocked the door to my nineteen-year-old-self who I'd ignored all these years. It was she who studied each black pen mark in Lee's first letters like a mother who finds every move of her baby fascinating. She looks through my eyes now as Dave and I travel to meet my son.

This is what it means to fall down the reunion hole.

All week, one thought has repeated like a mantra over and over in my mind: My baby's coming home, my baby's coming home, my baby's coming home. I am a new mother about to unwrap my baby's blanket and count his tiny perfect fingers and toes. At the same time, sorrow makes my throat choke. I am caught in a second adolescence of wildly-swinging emotions young girls are famous for. Even as I thrill with ecstatic anticipation, I break into tears.

With every passing mile Dave and I travel, another year of hard-won maturity drops from me. A lot of people claim they want to return to their youth. This is not the way to do it.

The Geyserville Inn is a two-story wooden building painted sky blue with a blue-gray gabled roof. Its romantic ambiance is lost on me as Dave and I pass under the portico. To the right of the lobby, I glance into a small restaurant, step inside, and peruse the leather menu on the check-in counter. The Hoffman House, it reads.

This is where we'll have breakfast together; our first ever breakfast. Maybe waffles, maybe eggs Benedict, I think, but the thought seems unreal.

We reach the second floor and Dave slides our room key through the slot, opening the door to cream-colored walls, a fake-stone fireplace with a mantle, and a queen-sized bed with a red paisley coverlet.

"Do you want to lie down for a while?" he asks.

"Sure." Dave's shoulders slump and his face shows the strain of trying to support me while keeping a lid on his own worries at the same time. My obsession with Lee is taking its toll on him.

He stretches out under crisp white sheets, while I prop up pillows and open a book. The words blur, meaningless. I close the book and tiptoe into the bathroom, gently securing the door behind me. Dave's snores penetrate through the wood and reassure me I'm not alone. I turn on the water.

Hoping to relax my tight back and shoulder muscles, I sink into steaming water in a white tub deeply inset between sheets of mottled brown marble tile.

The nurse brought me the rubber donut the day after I gave birth and instructed me to sit on it in the tub. "It will help to heal your bottom," she'd advised.

Despite the hot steam, a shiver travels up me. I look down into the clear water, almost expecting to see heavy menstrual blood leaking as it had then. My body feels too leaden to ever arise from this tub of doom. Tears leak from my eyes. Hearing me whimper, Dave opens the door. Through the mist his forehead looks furrowed, his eyes full of concern. He squats beside me.

"What's the matter, sweetheart?"

"It's like I'm in the Sitz bath after Lee was born and I want to go find him again, but I know he's not there anymore." I hear my voice wobble.

"It's okay," Dave soothes me, handing me a terry-cloth robe. "It's okay. Let's get you out of the tub."

On the balcony, Dave pours two glasses of Syrah and hands me one. We stand by the red railing, the low Vaca Mountains in the distance patchy with blue vegetation under the fading light. A field crop has been planted behind the row of leafy trees behind the hotel. I take deep breaths and try to focus on my feet solidly planted on the concrete balcony.

"It's like I'm there again. I feel like that girl again. I didn't know what to do then and I don't know what to do now."

"You'll know," Dave assures me. "I know you. You're going to handle this just fine. Trust me."

I realize I'm experiencing a flashback, a symptom of post-traumatic stress disorder. My body remembers, even when I'd forgotten.[28]

"If I'm feeling like that lost girl of 1964, what must my son be feeling?" I wonder out loud. "He didn't even have words. He was just a baby. How old is he tonight? I hope he's not as confused as I am."

Tomorrow morning, I'll dress in my gauzy black skirt with the thin chiffon overlay and my silky rose-colored blouse and put on sheer black stockings and low black pumps. I'll add a carefree-looking light jacket I've brought with me. I want to look my best to go down to meet my son. I want to look composed and calm. It wouldn't be right to burden him with my emotional distress.

Tonight though, I'll swallow five milligrams of Valium and hope to wake up tomorrow feeling my real age.

---

28 Bessel Van Der Kolk, M.D., *The Body Keeps the Score: Brain, Mind, and Body in the Healing of Trauma*, Penguin Books, 2015.

54

I RECOGNIZE YOU

There is always some madness in love.
But there is also always some reason in madness.

—Friedrich Nietzsche

JULY 8, 2004

The phone rings promptly at 9 a.m. This son is punctual; not like me. This morning, I powder my nose early and finish applying the last coat of plum colored lipstick to match the silky shell I wear under my sheer, ruffled jacket.

I make my way slowly down the curved stairway, holding the handrail, being careful not to trip in my low heels. Lee stands in the foyer wearing a white Hawaiian shirt decorated with tropical green leaves and rose-colored flowers. He is wide and plump with a small beard just the width of his mouth, leaving the rest of his chin clean-shaven. He stands straight and is maybe eight inches taller than me. His round face is circled by wavy brown hair. He has a slightly flattened nasal bridge and high cheekbones -- all familiar to me.

Smiling, I step toward him. Lee gives me a light hug, his face serious, unsmiling. "I recognize you," I say. My father, Jared, myself, all there in Lee's face in our family mirror.

Lee doesn't reply. Instead, he places a light hand on my back and steers me into the restaurant. The host seats us across from each other at a small square table near the center of the room and hands us menus. Lee makes a rapid decision, then lays down his closed menu. I make a snap decision, too. "I'll have waffles," I tell the white-shirted waiter.

I look across at my son. "When do you need to be at your first appointment?" I ask. He'd emailed me that he'll be exploring different wineries today to increase his New Orleans restaurant wine menu options.

"11 o'clock. Fritz Underground Winery, a little winery that's just coming into the New Orleans' market. It's in the northernmost part of Dry Creek Valley."

"Sounds like it's kind of far away. How long does it take to get there?"

"About an hour."

This feels nothing like the reunions I've seen on TV, aging mother and thrilled son advancing toward each other in the airport, grabbing each other for dear life.

When my waffles arrive, I concentrate on chewing the doughy breadstuff quickly. It sticks in my mouth, while I try to prevent any stray syrupy morsels from dropping onto my blouse. I wish the large, solemn man across from me, my son, would say something. I wish he would smile.

Lee leans forward. "Is Terra your only grandchild?" he asks.

Does he know I already think of Madeleine and Gwendolyn as my grandchildren? Would he think me overfamiliar?

I cast about for the right answer and decide to play it safe. "Yes," I reply.

It seems only a few minutes later when we finish eating and leave. Lee steers the sleek black rental car one-handed on the curving two-lane roads of the Wine Country. I steal surreptitious glances in his direction.

Everything I can think of saying seems too risky. Despite his letters, my son is a stranger. He keeps his eyes on the road ahead.

Finally, I venture, "How's your wife?"

"We separated a month ago," he says, his expression impassive.

Oh, God! Worse, much worse.

His wife, the woman with her hair pulled back and her arms circling his full waist in the photo he sent, looking at him with a face full of love! What happened? I search for the right response but come up with nothing. Anything I say might be interpreted as intrusive. Or worse, insensitive. Finally, I manage, "I'm sorry to hear that."

I stare out my passenger window as we wend silently through fields of grass dotted with oak trees. A red-tailed hawk soars into the cloudless sky, floating on thermal waves looking for prey. I imagine a mouse cowering in the grass below.

We arrive at Fritz Underground Winery. The angular building emerges out of lush green shrubs and small trees covering the hill in rich emerald shades. White concrete retaining walls edge the winery, half-buried in the mountainside. Tall oval wooden doors frame an elegant entrance.

The cool air inside is a welcome relief from the July heat. Polished hardwood floors lead to an expansive bar. Mr. Fritz stretches his hand from behind the bar to clasp Lee's.

"So, you own a restaurant in New Orleans?" he asks. "It's pretty competitive there, I'm sure?"

"Well, we're hanging in there. I'm hoping to bring in some new wines. I understand you might be able to help us expand our selections a bit."

"Sounds good. I've got a few options we can start with." Mr. Fritz lines bottles of cabernet sauvignon, Russian River Pinot Noir, and Fritz Malbec in front of us.

"But let's begin with our white selections; a few of the more affordable choices. Vino Valpredo Bianca Mia. This is a nice wine." He pours two fingers of pale amber liquid into two slim glasses.

"Mmm, nice," I murmur.

Mr. Fritz looks at me. "It's got undertones of orange and tangerine and sweet pea flowers," he says. Is he curious about who I am, why I'm here?

I nod, trying to look knowledgeable. Sweet pea flowers? I imagine the little white petals, bees hovering in their honey depths. *Yes, this wine is delicious.* Already, I feel its magic spreading through my tight muscles.

Mr. Fritz introduces us to a tall slim young woman, Emma, who escorts Lee and I downstairs into a wide cool cave of stainless-steel wine barrels.

"This is last year's Reserve Chardonnay," Emma tells us. "It's on the citrusy side, light and fruity."

Buttery liquefied gold trickles into my glass from the spigot protruding from the barrel.

"Mmm, delicious," I say, wishing I had a more impressive wine-taster's vocabulary.

"Some tasters spit out the wine after they've swirled and sniffed and tasted it," Lee tells me. "It's a waste of good wine, as far as I'm concerned."

Yes, we've found a point of agreement, and I am suddenly enjoying this gourmet wine-tasting excursion. Each sample warms me more than the last.

Lee goes off to the men's room, and Mr. Fritz, his voice studiedly casual, asks, "How do you two know each other?"

What would Lee want me to say? Should I lie?

"Oh, we knew each other a long time ago."

Before we leave, Mr. Fritz offers a few bottles to Lee to bring home to New Orleans. Lee invites me to help choose. We depart with two expensive bottles with names suggestive of Italian villages, a deep red Morcinaia and a Sangiovese.

Following this first business visit, Lee expertly steers us through country lanes to a blurry lunch affair in a local restaurant where the chef must have received a large supply of local corn. There's Corn Soup with Prosciutto, Corn Fritters, and Penne with Zucchini, Corn, and Bacon on the menu.

Raising my eyebrows, I stare at the glass of white wine Lee is drinking, while I'm trying to sober up on black coffee. By this time, I wonder out loud, "How do you do that?"

Lee shrugs and pushes his plate of corn galette toward me. We trade plates and alternate dipping into the bowl of corn soup. He likes to trade meals back and forth, too! Could this be genetic?

We set off for the second winery, Lee expertly driving the narrow, winding route. More rows of staked grape vines stretch to our left and right. Inside Alexander Valley Vineyards, I make a visit to the ladies' room.

We are the only guests at the gleaming wooden bar. A dark-haired woman named Anita greets us warmly.

"We've been expecting you," she says. "How has your visit been so far?"

"It's going well." Lee seems reluctant to encourage any small talk, but of course he is on a business trip. "What do you have for us to try today?"

Anita presents a slim bottle of pink-tinged rosé. I imagine a fresh young girl tiptoeing into adulthood.

Sipping the delicate rosé, I become aware of a tugging sensation behind me. I reach my hand back and discover that my long black silky skirt with a slit up the middle is tucked into my panty hose. Only the sheer chiffon second layer conceals my bottom.

"Excuse me," I say with as much dignity as I can muster, as I set off to the ladies' room again. Feeling the rosy glow of fine wines, I'm contemplating that at least my rear has always been one of my best features.

When I return, Lee and I sample the five reds. I practice gently rotating the graceful bowl of my wine glass and peering into its depths to evaluate each sample's clarity and color intensity. *Beautiful.*

Lee's face softens and his reserve begins to drop away. He reaches out with delicate touches to my shoulder. He turns now and again toward me, his cheeks rosy, and casts light glances in my direction. I stretch my hand toward him, brushing his forearm and feeling the light hairs there. I sense our mutual hesitation, our uncertainty about how to reconnect. How can we find our way back from a past cut off before it could begin? It's too late for me to carry, wash, feed, or dress the baby who no longer exists. Anita might interpret our tentative affection today as romantic. Does she wonder if I am a "cougar" with a younger lover?

"How do you two know each other?" she asks.

I hesitate, and Lee turns to me.

"You can tell her," he says.

"He's my birth son from 1964," I tell her. "I gave him up for adoption and we are just finally meeting again."

"You just met today?" Her voice holds wonder.

"Yes," Lee replies. "She lives in California, so this seemed like a good time."

"Well, I was looking at you and thinking..." She trails off. "Would you like me to take a few pictures of you?"

"Sure," we both agree. She snaps a picture of us inside the winery and then two more outside. In each photo, Lee stands to my left, his right arm protectively wrapped around my shoulder. I circle my arm around his generous waist. In the afternoon sun, his Hawaiian shirt matches my rose blouse and our equally pink cheeks and noses.

My favorite snapshot shows Lee in the winery with his head tilted, a small close-mouthed smile over his dark goatee. His eyes are open, and he appears relaxed. His hair curling over his high forehead and ears looks very much the same as mine. We fit together, like two puzzle pieces.

When Lee pulls up to my hotel, we lean toward each other and brush the air between us in an almost kiss. I step out of the car and almost float up to our hotel room where Dave waits anxiously. He will join us for dinner.

In the bathroom mirror, I wash my flushed face. The person who looks back at me smiles. Her eyes sparkle, despite exhaustion. We've gotten over the hump. Tonight, we'll have dinner with Dave. I'll relax, leave most of the effort to the two men I love. They'll have a chance to get acquainted.

That night, Dave orders one, then another, ruby-colored bottle of Syrah, as he utters words of concern and sympathy about Lee's marital break-up. I watch Lee's broad shoulders and face relax as he listens, comforted by Dave's blue eyes and caring smile.

I wish I felt as able to converse with Lee as Dave seems to, carrying the conversation with such apparent ease. Once I lay my hand on Dave's knee and give a warning squeeze, but I don't remember what Dave had said to alarm me. My fears of uttering a fatal faux pas intimidate me. When will I stop worrying about losing my son again?

The next morning, we meet Lee at his hotel lobby. He wears another colorful Hawaiian shirt. The two men shake hands. He and I give each other a light hug. His whisker stubble and fuzzy goatee brush my face as we kiss each other on the cheek.

"You're welcome to come to New Orleans anytime," Lee offers. I feel a sudden release of tension.

Lee's words send me floating back home in a giddy haze, almost enjoying the disordered confusion of my hangover, a mishmash of thoughts, feelings, and words like confetti blowing in a celebration.

"Congratulations," Dave says. "You did well!"

"Well, thank you so much," I answer. "I couldn't have done it without you."

"No, it's not me," Dave replies. "You're the one who did it. You've persisted all these years and now the door is open." He reaches over, placing his hand on my knee, and squeezes it gently while I gaze out at the passing wine country in a blissful haze.

I turn to Dave. "Yeah, and now all I have to do is not fuck it up."

55

WHAT I SHOULD HAVE SAID

Love is the answer, and you know that for sure;
Love is a flower, you've got to let it grow.

—John Lennon

2004

Home from Geyserville, I think of everything I might have said and didn't. I write Lee right away, revealing that Dave and I have started couples therapy. Maybe Lee would like to know that we have struggles too. Maybe he'll even decide to try it himself. I don't mention that a good bit of what took us into couples therapy was my fixation on him, "the other man." I think back though to his reticence, the silences in the rental car, how he'd described himself in his letter as a private person. It doesn't seem likely he'd take the risk.

That week while searching my wallet for a credit card, I discover unexpected snapshots of two little girls. I peer at the pictures. Why do I have pictures in my wallet of two cute little girls I don't know? Then I realize these are my granddaughters, Madeleine and Gwendolyn. I remember Lee passing the pictures to me as we drove back from the wineries. More than half-lit, I'd tucked them into my wallet. Seeing them now, I realize he understood his daughters mattered to me. I wish I'd dared to tell him so.

Lee final words, "You're welcome to come to New Orleans anytime," reverberate in my mind. Anytime? That word gleams for me like a jeweled amulet. I write to him in October:

> "I was thinking of maybe making a trip to New Orleans in March or April sometime. Would that work out for you? I saw some packages of hotel and airfare on the net. Any ideas?"

Hoping I don't sound too motherly, I write him that I can't help but wonder how he's doing while undergoing a marital separation. I send good wishes to him and the girls and assure him I'm confident he's doing everything in his power to help them through this. I spend $72 to overnight a homemade cake to New Orleans on his birthday. It's my mother's recipe, studded with canned fruit cocktail and topped with coconut, pecans, and sweetened condensed milk. In November, I receive Lee's block-print letter:

> "The cake was enjoyed by many, as it went with me to a party some friends were having. My fortieth and Gwen's fifth were fun, although the latter more so than the former. In tandem with the long Halloween weekend, it was quite a blow-out. I guess I'll try to focus on slowing down a bit and pacing myself."

He liked the cake and shared it with friends. But what about the blow-out? He hints at the need to slow down in future. What kind of lifestyle is jeopardizing his health? When Chad and Jared were getting into trouble as teens, I sought help for me and them and insisted they cooperate. Their destructive behaviors turned around. Even now, when they are adults, I can at least give them information, make suggestions, and encourage them to consider my thoughts when they have problems. With this son, I feel I have no say. He has a mother. What credibility could I have now?

Lee's last paragraph perks me up:

> "If you'd like to come out in the Spring, March is better than April and weekdays better than weekends. Let me know what you envision."

Hurrah! My mind races with thoughts of another visit with my son. Maybe this time I'll meet those little girls whose pictures are in my wallet.

56

GRIEF HITS HARD

Be absolutely present in grief and sorrow will turn to something else.

—Rumi

2004

Despite my joy in Lee's pleasure in his birthday cake and my anticipated spring visit to New Orleans, I find myself spending most of my weekends closeted in my bedroom, weeping. Forty years after I buried the grief of losing my baby, it threatens to deluge me. For me, the baby I'd given up for adoption had died. I'd sealed his tiny hidden body in a coffin and, like the pain-killing drugs they gave me at his birth, administered my own anesthesia, numbed my loss, and carried it into the present, barely aware of its crippling weight.

Social worker and relinquishing mother Evelyn Burns Robinson wrote in *Adoption and Loss: The Hidden Grief,* that a first/birth mother's or, her term, natural mother's, grief was disenfranchised in that it could not be openly acknowledged due to the secrecy and stigma associated with unwed motherhood. She said that without community recognition, support, or rituals to enable grieving our babies' losses, we natural mothers could not process our grief. [29] In her second book, *Adoption and Recovery: Solving the mystery of reunion*, Robinson posits that the need to resolve our disenfranchised grief becomes our unconscious impetus for reunion.[30]

My tears prove her right.

I tell my patients: "A new grief always brings up past griefs, especially the ones we didn't know how to or didn't allow ourselves to experience in full." I also tell them that the only way out of grief is through it.

"I'm afraid if I let myself cry, I'll never stop," some clients worry. I assure them that isn't true. Grief comes in waves, rolling us over and over, almost drowning us, until it tosses us onto the beach, where we discover we can stand, brush off the sand, and walk again.

I allow myself to go through it. I feel certain that allowing my waves of suffering will in time reduce them to ripples. In bed, weeping into my pillow, sobs wrack my body while I yearn for the impossible, to retrieve my baby. At the same time, mourning his passing causes me to relive the anguish of my mother's death the year before I lost my baby. Behind the closed bedroom door, I carry on pleading conversations.

"Mommy, come back," I beg my long-dead mother, though I'd never called my mother "Mommy." It's the toddler, the little girl I'd regressed to who names her that now.

I flip into my young adult twenty-year-old self. "Baby, don't leave," I plead.

It would have been a relief to be reborn into one of those cultures where women can keen and bawl, wail, weep, sob, and cry in public without shame. Hearing my futile entreaties, some would wonder about my sanity. I recognize the social unacceptability of succumbing to this illogical regression, but my decades of grief require release and convince me mourning is necessary. I know the reality that repressed

---

[29] Evelyn Burns Robinson, *Adoption and Loss: The Hidden Grief*, Christies Beach, South Australia: Clova Publications, 2000, pp.128-9

[30] Evelyn Burns Robinson, *Adoption and Recovery: Solving the mystery of reunion,* Christies Beach, South Australia: Clova Publications, 2000, Revised Edition 2003, p. 41.

grief often turns into chronic depression, especially in a culture like ours that views grieving as weakness.

Dave carried on with his reading, music, and studies, taking over the preparation of dinner most nights. He knew I was grieving, never interfered, and was always available for a hug whenever I ventured out of our bedroom.

My dear friend and colleague, Sarah, used to say that all good therapists have gone through St. John of the Cross' "Dark Night of the Soul." I feel myself purging the "dark night" from my own spirit as I open the door to my heart. Monday mornings, I get up and arrive at Kaiser ready to work with my clients, feeling myself more able to enter with them into their dark nights as well.

Some nights, I pull out my autoharp, set up my music stand, and escape into my favorite African-American spirituals, "Nobody Knows the Trouble I've Seen" and "Sometimes I Feel Like a Motherless Child." I'd come to love this music as a teen, picking cotton with black pickers in East Texas. A few summers I worked for a neighbor cotton farmer, dragging a heavy canvas sack behind me and picking puffy white balls from the dry bolls with points that pricked my fingers. It was hard, grueling work under a blazing sun with the humidity often as high as the temperature. By day's end, I was exhausted, longing for relief from my dirt-streaked sweat, sore shoulders, and shaking out grasshoppers who jumped down my old white shirt.

In Texas, sunset brings only a few degrees of cooling, but as we pulled our bags down the last row toward the setting sun, the black cotton pickers would begin to sing. Their drawn-out melancholy stanzas of "Swing Low, Sweet Chariot" floated toward the setting sun streaking purple and orange across the wide horizon, making me wish I could be closer to them, though I realized the culture of that time wouldn't allow it. The work also taught me a lesson in social justice. I knew I was supplementing my college fund while my fellow-pickers did this brutal work for survival.

Now, I play my autoharp, allowing my singing and strumming to soothe me. In these mournful stanzas, I can feel the spirit of the people who created them in the hope of relief from their own suffering.

57
CAN THIS MARRIAGE SURVIVE?

One should believe in marriage as in the immortality of the soul.

—Honore de Balzac

2004

As I write Lee, Dave and I have started marital therapy. As with many marriages, decades of stress have taken their toll, with Jared's special needs eating up our energy, dollars, and emotional availability. Dave and I had already gone through the early years when Chad and Jared received the lion's share of my attention. Too often their needs relegated Dave to the background. Now my grief threatens to bury Dave and me in its lava of pain. Dave is right that I'm obsessed over Lee, "the other man," and my new unmet granddaughters. Little wonder tensions build between us and simmering resentments turn to infrequent yet traumatic verbal arguments.

As a therapist myself, I am more hesitant than Dave to put my mental and emotional health in someone else's hands. I've seen some good, some bad, and, rarely, a few excellent therapists. Diagnoses can be dangerous things. Spending whole weekends crying might be boiled down to a label of Major Depression. Or worse. Would all my weeping be seen as histrionic by a therapist who'd never had to contend with major loss? The stakes are high when some well-meaning, but sometimes formulaic, professional observes and assesses your traits and patterns of behavior, especially when they start overlaying diagnostic labels.

Now I have another son and two more granddaughters. Like the prodigal son in the Bible, Lee occupies center stage and receives star status. A primal need to retrieve the lost connection with Lee has overtaken me and Dave has been pushed into the background.

It is a good thing that Dave and I decide to seek outside help.

58

GRIEF HITS HARDER

The wound is the place where the Light enters you.

—Rumi

2004

Dave and I are home in our little back sitting room on the daybed that serves as a couch. That day in our weekly therapy session, we explored my marathon grieving sessions. Warm sun streams in from the back window onto our blue and yellow cornflower daybed, but my body feels tethered by heavy weights. Gloom grips me. Sensing this, Dave wants to offer comfort.

"It's okay," he tells me, his arm around my shoulder. "We'll get through this. Let's take a hot bath together." We have a long habit of soaking together, steam rising in a hazy cloud around us until we emerge pink as boiled shrimp.

Dave gets up to run the bath. Heavy sadness transfixes me to the daybed. Without warning, my belly begins to convulse and my abdominal muscles to press down. Maybe it is the sound of running water, like water breaking before birth, maybe sitting in a Sitz bath after birth. I don't know. I feel my baby travel down the birth canal with only pressure; no pain this time. The nurses exhort, "Push, push," as they'd done at his birth. Just like then, the second he emerges, they grab him. They won't let me hold him. I sob and sob.

"Please," I beg. "Don't take him! Let me hold him!" No matter how much I cry and stretch my arms out to reach him, they leave with him. Sobs wrack my body and the scene replays like a scratched record. Finally, I realize the nurses are gone and nothing will make them bring him back.

Suddenly, as if a curtain is pushed aside, I can see the young woman I'd been. She is utterly bereft. Her exhausted body slumps in abject despondency. Losing her mother and then her baby, all hope is stripped from her. Yet, instead of compassion, a murderous rage arises in me against her. I slam her against the wall, shaking her violently, and screaming, "You let them take our baby! How could you?" I pummel her senseless. She is silent. Sorrow weighs her down. Bereavement sculpts suffering onto her pale face, making dark circles under her hollow eyes.

Her profound sense of hopelessness touches me. How young she looks, empty, abandoned, lost. For long minutes, I sit with her, feeling sorrow and dawning compassion. I realize how extraordinary it is that she finished school, built a career, and helped thousands of other people. Yet, unable to bear her anguish, shame, and guilt, I had left her to suffer alone. Not only had my father, Bob, and Gladney abandoned her, so had I.

I see her looking at me with faint hope in her eyes and tell her I won't leave her alone any more. I hold her, glad at last for our companionship, the two of us vulnerable together.

The sound of water splashing down the hall draws me up. I stagger to the bath. "I just re-birthed my baby," I tell Dave. He washes my back with the soapy terrycloth.

59

RETREAT

Silence is the language of god, all else is poor translation.

—Rumi

2004

Dave and I have signed up for a five-day silent Buddhist retreat at a monastery just outside of Santa Rosa. Most of my friends recoil in horror when I tell them.

"Silent? For five days?" they stammer.

"Well, there are dharma talks and group interviews," I explain. But, in truth, the prospect of almost a week under a self-imposed cone of silence frightens me, too. I have been in day-long retreats without the distraction of talk and activities and know that the apparent calm and peace on the faces of the group participants often hide strong emotions within. Whatever our busy lives kept at bay emerged when sitting in silence, eyes closed, hands resting in our laps. Breathing, just breathing.

More than that, as a lifelong night owl, the retreat schedule intimidates me. At six a.m., volunteer participants will roam the halls, clanging a heavy metal triangular bell with a mallet to awaken us. We'll rinse our faces and forego any makeup or products with artificial fragrances. We'll pull on long pants and simple tops, making certain not to wear anything provocative. Just reading the rules, I already dread the experience.

Still, staying home alone for five days while Dave goes on an adventure to seek enlightenment doesn't sound appealing either. Besides, the teachings of compassion, kindness, and generosity to ourselves and to others have already helped me. Each time I meditate, noticing my thoughts, feelings, and body sensations, I can observe myself judging, disapproving, wanting things to be different, craving what I don't have, or resisting what I do have. The more I just notice without pushing away these unpleasant parts of myself, the more I feel myself letting go into a greater peacefulness.

The Buddha in his Four Noble Truths teaches that everyone experiences "dukkha," in Sanskrit translated as "suffering." He also taught that we can free ourselves from that suffering. By letting go of aversion to the conditions of our lives and craving for them to be different, we can be at peace in even very difficult situations. We cannot avoid pain in life, but we can avoid adding to our pain and creating suffering. I could see I needed that.

Still, arriving at the retreat, critical judgments clog my mind. With those judgments come "dukkha," suffering. On the second day of the retreat, about forty silent men and women hurry to the meditation hall before breakfast. We keep our eyes downcast to avoid socializing with others through eye contact and smiling. Those with still-flexible joints spread blankets at the front and perch on firm cushions, legs folded into the lotus position and hands resting lightly on their knees. Behind them, we who are middle-aged with knees and hips that protest being folded into pretzel positions sit in straight chairs, throwing light wraps over our shoulders and preparing to sit motionless for the next forty minutes.

John, our teacher, sits on his cushion at the front center of our group. Only an occasional cough or clearing of a throat interrupts the silence that envelopes the room. I close my eyes and count my breaths, "One, two, three, four, five," hoping peace slips over me. Then John begins intoning a metta, a simple recitation of good wishes for ourselves and for others.

Generally, a metta begins with, "May I be happy; may I be peaceful; may I be safe from inner and outer harm; may I be well; may I be free."

Free is interpreted to mean liberated from suffering, including our own negative thoughts and feelings that detract from internal peace. After the well-wishing to oneself, this metta is extended to others we know in a gradually widening circle, until finally, the well-wishing is extended to "all sentient beings, known and unknown, in all worlds, known and unknown."

I approach John's metta that morning with resistance. It's too early for me. The prayer can become tedious. I only managed to gulp down half a cup of coffee. It will be a miracle if I don't fall asleep in the dim light at 6:30 a.m. Aversion and its opposite twin, desire, the prime causes of suffering, grip me. I hope my empty stomach won't growl before we have breakfast. I'm looking forward to oatmeal topped with maple yogurt, stewed fruit, and almonds.

John's metta that morning is like none I've ever heard. His voice reaches across the hall. "If I have ever knowingly or unknowingly harmed myself, I offer myself forgiveness." His words speak directly to me, slicing into my heart like the sharp blade of a steel knife cleaving a hard-shelled coconut with one whack.

Tears pour out and funnel down my cheeks, creating damp paths I yearn to scratch but cannot without moving. I tighten my throat, but behind my closed eyes, my twenty-year-old young woman has returned again. She is a pitiful sight, pale, weak, and still bleeding from childbirth. She can barely stand. Her complexion is gray, her expression lackluster. Seeing her, my heart opens and softens. Tears flow faster.

Holding back my sobs, I manage to arise with my blanket. I step carefully over the bare toes of the other meditators. Once outside, I hurry to an isolated grove of oak trees, where I collapse. During most of the remaining retreat, I lie on my blanket in dry grass under webs of leaves defoliated by tent caterpillars. As much as possible, I join the others in the meditation hall. Occasionally, a fellow participant passes by my private sanctuary, but my continuous sobbing discourages any from staying.

My young-woman self and I weep together. I look into her despairing eyes and see the misery sealed on her face when I turned away from her mute grief. Now, I face her and offer compassion. "It's okay," I whisper. "I forgive you. You were a motherless girl who didn't know what else to do." Resurrected, she raises her eyebrows and looks at me with a questioning gaze, then a hopeful smile. I brush gentle fingers across her cheeks to dry her tears.

Later, I take her with me to our dormitory bath where we sink beneath the steaming water. I hold her with tenderness. She relaxes. I snuggle with her, her warm body a spoon with mine, and assure her she is a good person. I lift her from the bath, dry her slim limbs with warm towels, and see her color return. I lay her between clean white sheets to rest. She closes her eyes in relief. Soft white light suffuses our whole blissful experience.

Later that night, at our silent dinner, I sit next to Dave and feed her warm spoons of vegetarian broth, feeling her revive. As we participants silently return to our single rooms, Dave and I slip into a dark alcove. I cling to him in a wordless hug, drawing strength from his silent support.

Throughout that week, unable to meditate quietly, I continue to lie in my sanctuary under the oak trees, an occasional dry leaf drifting down onto my skin. Neither I, nor my young-woman self, have the energy or desire to stop our tears. We weep together, friends in grief; and as friends do, I come to understand.

She did not freely choose to give away our baby. The young Linda I was had neither the support nor confidence to push Bob into marriage. She was alone, abandoned, and desperate. Her entry into the unwed mothers' home sealed her fate when the agency presented one option and one only; release for adoption. No information or alternatives, legal, social, or financial, were offered.

Like millions of unmarried pregnant girls of my generation caught in the cultural expectations of that time, I allowed myself to be sacrificed. No ceremony, no ritual, no consolation was offered to assist us in this catastrophic loss. Only a deep, unspeakable sorrow, wrapped in silence and cloaked in shame, filled the emptiness of our wombs.

At the end of that retreat week, Dave drives us home to Davis. I invite young Linda to sit next to me in the passenger seat. Erect and strong, we look out together, unashamed.

60

SAY GOODBYE

If you love somebody, let them go, for if they return, they were always yours. And if they don't, they never were.

—Kahlil Gibran

2004

The next week, I sit outside on our deck under the fig tree. It's dusk. Cool fall air announces the coming of winter. Gray doves coo, flying to their evening perches above me. Their calls echo mysteriously, full of melancholy.

An image of my baby lying in a miniature black coffin arises, his tiny body still and gray against its white silk interior, my infant, hidden away these four decades. His little body, just the form, not quite solid, an outline only, but mine. I reach out and lift him up. I feel a faint stirring in his limbs. I cuddle him against my breast, absorbing his infant sweetness, soaking it in. No psychologist with pen in hand is here to pressure me to finish the relinquishment paperwork, just my baby and me. I rub his spiky black hair and smell his milky breath.

For the next few weeks, I do my best to carry him around, snuggle him against my heart, and croon into his hair. I experiment with putting him to my breast, as I did with his brothers, encouraging him to seek out my nipples and suckle.

I feel him squirming and pulling away. He won't nurse the way his brothers did. He won't bond. He becomes impatient. I can feel him leaving me. I have no choice but to accept the truth. It's too late. I can't go back. Whatever bonding we achieved while he was in utero has long been overridden by our separation. His life will continue without me. I can feel his eagerness to go into his own future.

With reluctance and sorrow, I tell my baby goodbye. His shadow still rests in my arms, a faint apparition of my infant I will never know. I lift my arms and release him. I watch as his shadow drifts into space and disappears.

PART 5

61

POWERLESS

Your children are not your children. They are the sons and daughters of Life's longing for itself. They came through you but not from you and though they are with you, yet they belong not to you.

—Khalil Gibran

JANUARY 2005

Lee sends me a "thank you" email for my latest holiday cookie tins I mailed him at Christmas along with a letter describing my excitement about our upcoming trip to New Orleans. He writes:

> "The only thing I really want to avoid is some sense of obligation to shake things up here during your visit. Yes, I would like to see you and learn some more about you, but I am wary that you are making spending time with me the primary purpose of your visit. I would hate to think that you are coming with a certain set of expectations and have made your time with me the entire impetus for coming to New Orleans, but it seems to me that you place an extraordinary amount of importance on forging some type of relationship, which I am not really focused on. I hope you can understand my hesitancy."

I am a little taken aback. I try to understand. I write back:

> "I already realized long ago that I am more motivated to develop a relationship with you than you with me. It's true that I put a good deal of focus on relationships in general and I recognize that could be experienced by you as onerous or burdensome. However, I have a lot of other wonderful relationships and supports, so I think I can balance my desires with yours and take things as they come. It's true that seeing you in the flesh in July brought up new strong feelings, but I'm now reconciled to the reality that every new stage or contact will introduce new challenges for me to deal with in our reunion. I'm committed to not placing my expectations or needs on you."

My words are fine-sounding and sincere. But the gulf between us is wide and deep. My need to repair our broken connection drives me.

What if Lee doesn't include his children in our visit to New Orleans? I don't dare ask. I don't dare to presume entitlement to anything. I am reduced to the terrible powerlessness of my twenty-year-old self.

Still, Lee's concerns about my expectations are valid. I have no right to push myself onto him. His words should have given me more pause than they did.

62

NEVERLAND

There is a candle in your heart, ready to be kindled. There is a void in your soul, ready to be filled. You feel it, don't you?

—Rumi

March 12 - 19, 2005

The day before our flight, I receive an email from Lee. Joy rushes through my grandmother's heart like a flight of birds into sunrise.

"Oh my God," I rush to tell Dave, "The kids are coming! We get to meet the kids!"

I toss clothes and items willy-nilly into my suitcase. I make sure to remember the gifts Terra and I selected. Terra longs to meet her new cousins, and we had searched the store aisles in San Francisco's Chinatown the week before for presents young children would like.

Lee's restaurant is in an old house with a peaked roof. On the deep front porch hangs the wide swing I'd seen on his website. Palm branches partially shade the area and the front door has a stained-glass window in the center that Lee tells me later his father made.

It's Sunday, March 13th, 11:45 a.m. and Dante's is already bustling with the din of hungry diners when Dave and I arrive. Lee stands at the entrance greeting brunch guests. He is sweating in the heat, his dark curly hair limp. His blue and red checked shirt clings to his back.

I'm dressed in my best short-sleeved, flowered silk top with matching oyster shell locket and earrings. Lee and I lean into a light embrace. He brushes a feathery kiss across my cheek, then leads us up short stairs to a long table in a back space he refers to as "the blue room." The walls are a deep cerulean with a brighter blue trim. Flowered blue curtains dangle on the single window.

After seating us, Lee turns us over to a young waitress who brings coffee and water. My heart pounding, my coffee cup threatening to slip out of sweaty hands, I straighten my skirt and blouse and apply a fresh coat of lipstick.

A young woman with a dignified air comes toward us. I recognize her from the pictures; Ellen Kaye, Lee's now-estranged wife. She wears a simple white round-necked top and skirt. A ribbon at the nape of her neck ties back her dark blond hair. Holding her mother's hand is a little girl with similarly blond hair, wearing a blue and white striped T-shirt. Gwendolyn, five and a half, my youngest granddaughter. Next to her is Madeleine, no taller than her sister though two years older. A little shy perhaps, a bit reserved, Madeleine wears a blue-green headband that matches her puckered top and holds back her long brown hair. Both girls share Lee's and my round faces and high foreheads. Meeting them feels unreal. Am I caught in one of my fantasies?

I want to lean down and put my arms around them. I hold back. It seems too soon. I don't want to appear presumptuous. After all, perhaps they just learned of my existence. Dave and I rise to greet them.

I bring out their little gifts - black stuffed monkeys that squeal when their long arms are pulled and birthstone earrings Terra and I found -- a deep blue sapphire pair for Madeleine and a milky-white opal pair for Gwendolyn. Neither girl has pierced ears.

My new granddaughters love the screeching monkeys. Pulling the arms to make the toy animals scream, Maddie makes a growling monkey face, scrunching up her eyes and nose and threatening us with a simian smile, her front teeth ready to bite.

I chat with their mother. I hope Ellen Kaye realizes that she'll always be family to me, no matter what her relationship to my son. "Your girls are so adorable," I tell her.

"They look just like my sister," she replies.

Observing the two sisters eating their breakfasts, I see two little girls who appear like carbon copies of me and my sister at their ages. Maddie finishes all her scrambled eggs and leaves her toast. Gwen eats everything in front of her. That fits my family of hearty eaters.

"I met a woman who gave up her baby and then couldn't get pregnant again and adopted another woman's baby," Ellen Kaye confides.

I know about secondary infertility. The pain of losing my own child to adoption had shattered me. How could I live with that while knowing the pain of another mother whose child I would adopt? I change the subject to something safer.

After brunch, we all gather on the swing on the front porch of Dante's Kitchen. Lee has just arrived, his hair curling damp on his forehead. "I want to sit by that one!" Maddie exclaims, running to me. Lee sits on my other side.

"It's been a hot morning for you," I comment.

"Yes," he acknowledges, taking Gwen onto his lap.

As I sit sandwiched in the swing between Maddie and Lee and Gwen, my years of waiting and longing recede.

It rains buckets the next day, the kind of downpour where drops bang onto the pavement and bounce back up. After lunch, Lee, Dave, the two girls, and I retreat to Lee's bachelor pad not far from his restaurant. He plops into his dark blue vinyl recliner and Gwen pitches herself on top of him.

> They peer towards me in the photo I snap, Gwen's pale right cheek pressed against Lee's darker one. She's smiling. He has his beefy arms wrapped around her. His hazel eyes gaze out unruffled, a picture of satisfied fatherhood.

"So, what should the girls call me?" I ask.

"Well, I guess they're your grandchildren," he answers, in a slow, puzzled drawl.

"Okay," I release my breath cautiously. "Okay, then, I guess we're their grandma and grandpa."

"Sure," Lee answers.

I feel the same wariness I had with my father. I hurry to go play a game with Gwen in the girls' bedroom, not wanting to risk Lee's changing his mind if I hang around.

When I start to win the game, I notice Gwen's discouraged whimper and make sure to start losing. I savor her satisfied giggle. Next, Maddie and Gwen perform for Dave and me. They put on a CD and dance side by side with delighted grins. Crossing their arms, clasping hands to their tummies, raising their arms to the ceiling, all in synchrony with, "I'm Bringing Home a Baby Bumblebee," they hold the bee with cupped hands until it stings them. "Ouch!" Maddie's blue jeans sparkle with gold, red, and blue star appliques. Gwen's long blond tresses whirl as she bends and twists.

Dave and I take photos with the girls, Grandma and Grandpa holding Maddie between us, our faces pressed against hers, all of us smiling. Next a photo with Gwen in the middle, my arms clasped around the little girl who now can call me "Grandma." Then each of us holding our grandchildren, who make funny faces, mouths wide open or sucked in, eyes rolled up or downcast, tongues stuck out or lagging limp. Finally, my favorite picture is of the two girls perched each on one side of me, their small sweet faces pressed against mine, snuggling into my arms.

As we leave, I happen to walk by the open door of Lee's bathroom and notice the shower curtain pulled aside to reveal a brown soap on a rope hanging from the nozzle. I have a sudden impulse to touch that soap. I remember bathing baby Chad, then Jared, delighting in the warm water as I rubbed a soapy washcloth over their tummies, chests, backs, and bottoms.

Another experience lost.

I go on down the hall and out the door.

Our last day we take the St. Charles Avenue trolley to Danneel Park. Booths manned by parents offer activities for children and raise funds for Gwen's school. Lee's booth sells French bread and caramelized onions from his restaurant. His shirt and cap with a decal of a goose in flight coordinate perfectly with the green awning that shades him. Maddie brings him a beer with the $10 I gave her. Do friends of his permit her to buy it? Perhaps he's already finished it when I snap his picture, arms akimbo, hands on his hips, a broad smile on his face. Lee's cheeks and forehead turn pink the way mine do with alcohol. Dark curly chest hairs peek out from his shirt collar, reminding me my baby has become a grown man.

Dave, the girls, and I go from one exciting activity to the next. Gwen paints me a large blue tulip with poster paints. I'll fold it to fit into my suitcase. I'll open it the next day when we arrive home and shake out the dried blue paint chips scattered over my clothing. Maddie, attached to a rock-climbing harness, propels herself fearlessly up a large fake boulder. Then she races to another booth, cloaking herself in a feathered Indian cape and beating a large leather drum. In another booth, she wraps a deep blue feather boa around her neck and shoulders and coyly fluffs the boa against one cheek like a glamor girl. The girls and I stick our faces into cutouts representing characters from the children's classic, *Madeline*. In the cutout, Gwen's chubby, pink face glows under a yellow broad-brimmed hat. Gwen, in her brown cowboy boots and pink, navy and blue top over her short black skirt, could have passed for one of the little French girls in the book. Maddie spots Gwen's kindergarten French teacher and drags us across the grass to meet her.

Before we leave, "Take our picture," I tell Dave. The little girls clutch my hands, the imprint of their sweaty little palms on mine. They raise their faces to mine, and we smooch light mouth-to-mouth kisses with each other.

63

EPIPHANY

He who cannot forgive destroys the bridge upon which he must pass.

—George Herbert

2019

We might have ended up foundering on disappointments and confusions. So many adoption reunions don't last. I saw my father in Lee and that kept me fearful. Some of my fears were real, some projected, some exaggerated, many created by me, all of them carried into our tentative reunion.

Disrupting that reunion; that I could not bear. The peril of that poisoned my courage, shut down my assertive honesty, and made it harder to overcome misunderstandings. Losing my son again - that I couldn't risk. The decades of our separation meant the love I felt for him – real, true, and essential – also drove me to strive to retrieve our lost attachment, imposing myself on Lee.

Scientists are telling us now that we mothers carry our babies' fetal cells in our bodies. "Fetal cells remain in a woman's body into her old age. The cells of that child stay with her, resonating in ways that mothers have known intuitively throughout time." [31] The son of my body pulled at me and would not let me go. How could I ever forget him?

Once, Dave and I visited during Mardi Gras. Lee and I plunged into New Orleans' most legendary party event, finishing off a long Fat Tuesday in the French Quarter at the Crescent City Steakhouse, "The best in New Orleans," Lee rightly claimed. That Tuesday set a record with its frigid temperatures and we kept warm all day with scotch and bourbon, making for unguarded conversation at dinner in our little curtained booth. Whatever criticism Lee spoke that night that made me burst into sobs, I no longer recall. I do remember leaning across the table, elbow propped, hand supporting my forehead. "Maybe I shouldn't have opened this up. Maybe it was too much. For you, for me, maybe for all of us," I looked up intently at my big boy and told him.

Lee stared across our dining table, raised his right arm, and gave me the finger. He might as well have said it. "Fuck you." His lewd gesture told me his truth; that it was too late to renege, that my finding him was good. I was good. Good for his girls, good for him. He was up to our struggles; he liked a good challenge. My finding him had increased his support, added to his family, and brought the love of another mother. Yes, my unwavering commitment, my love and attention, made him special.

On the last day of that visit, Lee and I sat at the Bourbon House bar sipping cappuccinos. In the bar mirror, our faces reflected calmness and exhaustion.

"I love you," Lee said. "It took me a long time, but now I love you. You've helped me more than I ever could have imagined."

"I love you too, Lee. Your letting me into your life has helped me so much. I'm so much more peaceful now."

"I see that my children love you, too."

"And we love them. They're very important to us; for Dave as well as me."

---

[31] Laura Grace Weldon, "Mother & Child are Linked at the Cellular Level", June 12, 2012, *lauragraceweldon.com*, https://lauragraceweldon.com/2012/06/12/mother-child-are-linked-at-the-cellular-level/.

Lee doesn't reveal himself easily. Over our nineteen years together, like the tender buds of spring, I cherish Lee's kind and gentle qualities. These buds more and more emerge and bloom. I endeavor to be cautious. I don't always succeed. Fortunately, Lee is forgiving.

Friends who know nothing about adoption, when they hear my struggles, say, "Oh yeah, I've had the same problems with my child." They don't grasp the effects of our separate histories and experiences. I did not raise him and that has made all the difference.

"I don't want you to be my mother. I want you to be my friend," Lee said finally, offering me the best rare gift of friendship any parent of an adult child is fortunate to receive.

My heart needed to find the one I lost. His cells are still in my body. I feel him. At every visit, he tugs at my core. My body feels his movements. My bones know his. My cells vibrate with his. My DNA recognizes his DNA. He's in my blood. There's a river of connection coursing through my body to his that has never stopped flowing.

Once, after we arrived home from a difficult visit with Lee, Dave and I were watching a movie. I no longer remember the name of the movie. It must have been something about the search for love and the pain of disappointment. I don't know. Somehow the movie made me see myself and see what my son saw.

After the movie, Dave, who'd heard more than enough of my reunion drama, escaped to bed. Determined to prevent sleep from erasing the insight that had pierced me, I sat down in front of my computer and typed out my epiphany that I would not mail:

> It has been said that inside every birth mother lives a time bomb.
>
> When I discovered Lee, the time bomb exploded in me. An overpowering need to retrieve what I'd lost took over me.
>
> It was like being possessed, not by an evil spirt, but by a hunger that took over my life. I imagined it was outside of me. If I could just know my son and his children, if I could meet them, if we could get back together. That must be the answer.

When I opened that sealed-up lost baby box, I turned on the timer and set off my grief bomb. It blew and I was virtually helpless. I had no idea, not the slightest idea, of all the grief that bomb inside me contained. It poured out of every place I'd had it locked up. All of that pain like a tsunami just bowled me over. I got rolled over and over and over by that wave that just kept on coming. I tried to save myself by grabbing onto a ghost of my lost child, chasing after a baby who hadn't existed for thirty-five years.

God, this is it! It wasn't even exactly about him. Lee's almost just a bit player. Not that I don't care about him. But it's really been what's inside of me. I'm grateful, very grateful, for having a relationship with him, but this is *my* story. Pain can be so selfish and hungry, hungry, needy, needy. That's what I've been suffering.

What Lee wants, what he really needs is for me to free him from my obsession. I see it. I need to free him. I can only do that if I free myself. I feel so relieved. I must be ready. The door to my house of grief just blew wide open and a cool wind is passing through.

I don't know what comes next. I only know the walls have cracked open. The debris is settling. Light is coming through the cracked ceiling. I can stand. I can walk out.

I can let go to become the only mother I still can. Now, in gratitude.

64

MOTHERS' DAY

MAY 13, 2018

Lee calls. "Happy Mother's Day!"

"I just called to tell you I love you and I'm glad you're my mom."

"Oh, that's so sweet!" I reply. "Thank you! That means so much to me and I'm glad you're my son!"

"Thanks! Yeah, it's good," he says.

"I'm awfully glad I found you," I answer.

"Yeah, me too; it's good."

PART 6

Enjoying this book?
The best way to thank an author
is to post a review on Amazon.
Thank you!

65
EPILOGUE

2019

Opening my long-ago adoption loss presented me with the need and opportunity to heal as much as possible the pain and grief left in my son's absence. It also became the impetus for me to become educated about and reconsider the situation, beliefs, and decisions – my own and others – that led to my loss of my first-born. My ability to consider this is enhanced by the fact that I have also been a Licensed Clinical Social Worker for almost forty years, though I never did, nor would have, worked in the field of adoption. Placing children for adoption was and remains a primary specialty for social work professionals. I believe my experience as a mother who lost her son under the influence of social workers, as well as the predominant punitive culture of that time, makes me uniquely qualified to address some of the deficits many of my colleagues still operate under. I also believe this is critical, because adoption promoters continue to convince vulnerable young mothers to give up their babies even today. International adoptions continue, though fewer than in the recent past, and many adoptees describe devastating pain.[32] Of course, previous experiences in their home countries may contribute

[32] Janine Myung Ja, Michael Allen Potter, Allen L.Vance, *Adoptionland from Orphans to Activists, Against Child Trafficking* USA, 2014

to their difficulties after being transplanted onto American soil [33] and this applies also to children adopted out of foster care.[34]

Despite growing evidence from first/birth/natural mothers, adoptees, and professionals of adoptions' lifelong, harmful consequences, adoption remains widely idealized, approved of, and assumed to be a "normal" way to provide for the needs of children in our American culture. I no longer accept this idea. Adoption is neither normal, nor is it natural. It is normal for a mother and her child to stay together. Situations do and will occur where this is impossible, but they are always the result of a problem and those problems are often temporary or reparable. Adoption, which requires permanently separating mothers from their babies, is highly unnatural.

Merriam-Webster's Collegiate Dictionary defines unnatural as:

1) Not being in accordance with nature or consistent with a normal course of events.
2a) Not being in accordance with normal human feelings or behavior.
2b) Lacking ease and naturalness.
2c) Inconsistent with what is reasonable or expected. [35]

There is a multitude of evidence for the destructive effects of adoption loss for first mothers, for whom the adoption, especially a closed one, is comparable to the loss of a child through death. Evidence exists that this can be somewhat lessened through the

---

33 Yanhong Liu, Richard J. Hazler, "All Foreign-Born Adoptees Are Not the Same: What Counselors and Parents Need to Know," *The Professional Counselor,* TPC, Date Accessed 2/12/2019, http://tpcjournal.nbcc.org/all-foreign-born-adoptees-are-not-the-same-what-counselors-and-parents-need-to-know/

34 Dawn Davenport, "9 Surprising Facts About Adopting a Baby from Foster Care," *Creating a Family*, 7/24/2017, https://creatingafamily.org/adoption-category/9-surprising-facts-about-adopting-a-baby-from-foster-care/

35 "Unnatural." *Merriam-Webster*, Merriam-Webster, Accessed 2/15/19, www.merriam-webster.com/dictionary/unnatural.

current approach of open adoption.[36] However, the fact that mothers help select the adoptive parents does not prevent their lifelong grief, especially because most "open" adoptions are not very open and many are closed after a few years, rendering great distress to the first/birth mothers.[37] Research shows first/birth mothers suffer from grief which does not remit and often increases over decades producing depression, anxiety, trauma, anger, fear, alcohol and drug abuse, and affecting every following relationship with partners and children.[38] [39] I recall my intense fear of losing either of my two subsequent sons. As I described in my memoir, the grief of adoption loss created depression, which I know affected my sons and marriage. I was acutely aware of feelings of differentness and separation from others while I kept my secret.

First/birth mothers are rendered at increased risk for chronic sadness, increased physical and psychological disabilities, dissociation to the point of loss of memory of the traumatic separation, and ongoing post-traumatic stress. Evidence exists of higher risk for severe illnesses such as heart attacks, pleurisy, and pneumonia, hypertension, and other physical disorders, especially with anniversary of loss reactions, including suicides and phobic fears. First/birth mothers report ongoing feelings of powerlessness and betrayal, inability to mourn their lost child, and damaged self-esteem and feelings of worthlessness.[40]

---

36 "Are birth mothers satisfied with decisions to place children for adoption?" *Science Daily*, **Science News** from research organizations, Baylor University, June 8, 2018, https://www.sciencedaily.com/releases/2018/06/180608131605.htm

37 Lorraine Dusky, *hole in my heart: memoir and report from the fault lines of adoption* (Sag Harbor, New York: Leto Media, 2015) pgs 131-35.

38 Evelyn Burns Robinson, *Adoption and Loss: The Hidden Grief*, (Christies Beach, South Australia: Clova Publications, 2000, revised 2003) pgs. 101-111.

39 Lorraine Dusky, *hole In my heart: memoir and report from the fault lines of adoption* (Sag Harbor, New York: Leto Media, 2015) pgs.32-60

40 Sister Mary Borromeo, R.S.M., B.A., Dip. Soc. Wk. (1968) in "Adoption: From the Point of View of the Natural Parents," reprinted in "Effects of Adoption on the Mental Health of the Mother: What Professionals Knew and Didn't Tell Us, *Origins Canada*, Accessed 2/15/19, https://www.originscanada.org/adoption-trauma-2/trauma_to_surrendering_mothers/effects-of-adoption-on-mental-health-of-the-mother-what-professionals-knew-and-didnt-tell-us/

Secondary infertility occurs for many, and natural mothers may be forty to sixty percent more likely to experience it.[41]

I was first introduced to the notion that most people see adoption as a win/win for all parties by Evelyn Burns Robinson, a natural/first mother and a social worker, in her book *Adoption and Loss: The Hidden Grief.* Robinson wrote that the grief of the natural mother for her child is disenfranchised in that there is no social recognition of her grief and no rituals or social support to allow her to process it. It is often assumed that the original mother is relieved, the adoptee is rescued, and the adoptive parents are happy to have a child. In fact, mothers of adoption loss suffer in silence, especially when the relinquishment was done in secret and required to remain hidden. As Robinson pointed out, there is no adoption without grief – the grief of the first/birth mother who has lost her child, the adoptee who has lost his or her original mother and family, and the adoptive parents, for whom adoption is usually a last resort when they are unable to conceive their own children. Everyone involved in adoption suffers grief, even when it is not conscious.[42]

Adoptees experience many of the same symptoms as their mothers, though much complicated by the fact that infants are pre-verbal and therefore unable to form any cognitive understanding of the trauma foisted upon them in their initial moments after birth. Many adoptees report feelings of rejection, abandonment, loss, grief, lowered self-worth, loss of a sense of security. Their grief, too, is disenfranchised, as they are expected to be grateful to adopters and are denied recognition of their grief and rituals or support to process it. Probably because of this, many remain unaware of their underlying loss issues and deny negative results.[43]An article reported in The Adoption Quarterly stated: "The risk of adoptees experiencing psychiatric disor-

---

41 Kate Dahlquist, "Costs of Adoption: Increased Secondary Infertility Rates Infographic," Adoption and Birthmothers, Building Bridges to Adoptions Truths, *Musings of the Lame,* October 15, 2013. http://www.adoptionbirthmothers.com/secondary-infertility-among-birthmothers/

42 Evelyn Burns Robinson, *Adoption and Loss: The Hidden Grief,* (Christies Beach, South Australia: Clova Publications, 2000, revised 2003) Introduction and pgs. 101-111.

43 Ibid, pgs.112-122.

ders, contact with mental health services, or treatment in a psychiatric hospital was approximately twice as high as that of non-adoptees. Elevated risks were observed for attention-deficit/hyperactivity disorders, anxiety disorders, conduct disorders/oppositional defiant disorders, depression, substance use disorders, and psychoses."[44]

Female adoptees are at risk of repeating the tragedy of their first mothers by becoming pregnant and relinquishing their own child. Lorraine Dusky in h*ole in my heart* tells how her daughter she gave up for adoption did this and cites statistics that adoptees give up their own babies at *seven* times the rate of non-adoptees. This is referred to as an instance of "repetition compulsion" in psychology and speaks to the adoptee's identifying with her first mother by repeating her act, even though she is unknown. It is further evidence of the probably unconscious need of the adoptee to connect with her missing natural mother. As Dusky says, "One adoption begets another." [45] In a smaller way, I saw this with one of the granddaughters I found with my son. As a young teen, she opined that giving up a baby for adoption is a good and generous act to help an infertile couple. Being a close daughter of her adopted father, I believe my granddaughter identified with his experience. Likely she also resisted the objections she knows I have. Still, I feared my action of relinquishment might pass on to her as we know generational cycles of abuse are transmitted. I hope and imagine she may have changed her opinion as she's matured.

David Kirschner in *Adoption: Uncharted Waters* writes about the over-representation of adoptees who commit serial murders and coined the term "Adopted Child Syndrome" to connect the incidence of increased anger, especially towards women, of adoptees that sometimes,

---

44 Anika E. Behle and Martin Pinquart, "Psychiatric Disorders and Treatment in Adoptees: A Meta-Analytic Comparison with Non-Adoptees." *Adoption Quarterly*, Volume 19, 2016 – Issue 4, pgs. 284-306, received 21 July 2015, accepted 25 April 2016, Accepted author version posted online: 23 June 2016, published online: 13 Jul, 2016. https://www.tandfonline.com/doi/abs/10.1080/10926755.2016.1201708?src=recsys&journalCode=wado20

45 Lorraine Dusky, *hole In my heart: memoir and report from the fault lines of adoption* (Sag Harbor, New York: Leto Media, 2015) p.84

though rarely, erupts into violence.[46] The term is now cited in cases of murder, especially of adoptive parents by their adult children, described by Mirah Riben in her article on adoptees who kill. [47]

In her article, "Toward Preventing Adoption-Related Suicide," Mirah Riben cites statistics that adoptees are four times more likely to attempt suicide than non-adoptees and almost twice as likely to have problems with drug abuse. "Adoptees far outnumber non-adopted youth in all types of treatment facilities," says Riben.[48] She quotes adoptee, Elle Cuardaigh, describing the basis of her considering suicide:

> "We weren't born, so death is of no consequence. There is a certain detachment to adoption. Being 'chosen' rather than 'born to' does it. Because we did not arrive by natural means and so much mystery (or outright lies) are our baggage, we often feel not only that we do not fit in, but that we are disposable. That's the thing about being chosen, you can be unchosen. And some adoptees aren't going to wait for the dismissal; they are going to finally take control of their life by ending it."[49]

Adoptees do not like to be and should not be pathologized. Very few adoptees are violent and when they are, it is far more commonly tragic violence toward themselves in the form of suicide. Most become fully functional adults. Riben is careful to say that adoptees are not the problem. Rather it is the *institution of adoption* and, specifically, the *separation of mother and child* that is inherent in adoption and that is the underlying reason for adoptee trauma.[50]

---

46 David Kirschner, Ph.D. *Adoption: Uncharted Waters.* Woodbury, NY, Juneau Press, 2006

47 Mirah Riben, "Adoptees Who Kill: Examining the Psychological, Societal and Criminal Justice Ramifications of Adopted Child Syndrome," *Crime Magazine,* April 7, 2014. http://www.crimemagazine.com/adoptees-who-kill-examining-psychological-societal-and-criminal-justice-ramifications-adopted-child.

48 Mirah Riben, Contributor, "Toward Preventing Adoption-Related Suicide," *Huff Post,* 12/6/17. https://www.huffingtonpost.com/mirah-riben/toward-preventing-adoptio_b_8127882.html.

49 Riben, "Toward Preventing Adoption-Related Suicide."

50 Riben, "Toward Preventing Adoption-Related Suicide."

Nancy Verrier, an adoptive and biological mother and psychotherapist, has, I believe, been the most prescient in identifying the underlying cause of the symptoms and problems described above. In her book, *The Primal Wound*, Verrier describes the separation of the child from the biological mother as "the primal wound" which "causes pain so profound as to have been described as cellular by those adoptees who allowed themselves to go that deeply into their pain."[51] Verrier describes the connection between a biological mother and her child as "mystical, mysterious, spiritual, and everlasting"[52] and goes on to say, "When this [bonding] natural evolution is interrupted by a postnatal separation from the biological mother, the resultant experience of abandonment and loss is indelibly imprinted upon the unconscious minds of these children,"[53] causing what Verrier calls "the primal wound." Verrier quotes statements by adoptees who report not only feeling loss of the mother but loss of their very selves, leaving "a feeling of incompleteness or lack of wholeness"[54] which is carried through life. Of course, not all adoption separations occur at birth. Yet, even children endangered by their parents and in the foster care system continue to love them and resist separation. What can this signify except the inherent sacred connection nature designed? Verrier writes about the "fear of rejection, lack of trust, fear of intimacy, loyalty, shame and guilt, identity, and power or mastery and control"[55] issues that stem from the adoptees' original feelings of abandonment and rejection. She also describes the now well-known adaptive responses which many adoptees make, some choosing to rebel and act out, while others become overly compliant and "people pleasing."[56]

Sharing some of her own experience as an adoptive mother, Nancy Verrier says that no matter how loving an adoptive mother is, she

---

51 Nancy Newton Verrier, *The Primal Wound: Understanding the Adopted Child,* Baltimore, MD, Gateway Press, Inc., 1993, Twenty-seventh printing 2018, preface xvi, p. 44.

52 Ibid, preface xvi

53 Ibid, p.1.

54 Ibid, p.38

55 Ibid, p. 83

56 Ibid, p.63

cannot make up for or heal this initial severe trauma of the unnatural separation of a baby and his or her mother.[57]

I believe the connection between a mother and child operates on an energetic level as well as manifesting physically and emotionally. I have experienced and heard from other natural mothers that we carry a traumatic parallel trauma that also produces lifelong damage, though we natural mothers are, of course, far less vulnerable than our infants were. I speak to my found son regularly now, as I do to my two sons I raised. I notice, though, a difference. When my rediscovered son and I get off the phone, I always feel our conversation wasn't enough, even though we had run out of things to talk about and were ready to hang up. My feeling of "not enough" isn't about the phone call. It harkens back to our original separation, the wound left by our physical, emotional, spiritual, and energetic split in the moments after his birth when we were ripped apart. It is not coincidental that Lorraine Dusky, another natural mother, titled her memoir, *hole in my heart: memoir and report from the fault lines of adoption.*[58] This is how it feels. There is a hole, a space that can never be filled. With my reunion with my found son, that hole is smaller, much smaller; but it is not gone. I don't believe it ever will be.

If the general public grasped Nancy Verrier's premise that adoption loss leaves a permanent primal wound and an experience of loss of self in a child removed from the natural mother, perhaps they would begin to subscribe to this saying from Family Preservation Movement: "When we preserve a family, we strengthen a society."[59] Perhaps people would no longer tell me of the successful adoptions of their friends and family without at least considering there may be serious pain below the surface. Perhaps the acceptance of adoption would turn into efforts to prevent it and preserve original family units instead because people would see it as in their own best interests.

I attended a workshop in which the organizers put forth a motto: "Adoption is a Way to Form a Family." Attendees appeared surprised

---

57 Ibid, p. 53-67.

58 Lorraine Dusky, *hole in my heart: memoir and report from the fault lines of adoption* (Sag Harbor, New York: Leto Media, 2015)

59 FP365, a family preservation movement, *Familypreservation365.com*, accessed Feb. 15, 2019, https://familypreservation365.com/about/

when I pointed out that every adoption also results in the destruction of the original family. I have noted since I began revealing my adoption loss experience that most people show little reaction when I share my position as the birth mother. These people are not lacking in empathy. Rather, they accept adoption as a normal and good phenomenon. Some compliment me for giving my baby to better parents than I. Others express surprise that it would still bother me. They are as unaware as I myself was when I participated in the institution of adoption.

Under adoption, our babies' original birth certificates were and continue to be sealed, hiding our identities. Most remain sealed today. Many of our grown adoptee children come looking for their birth information and find it still locked away from them by antiquated laws, regressive adoption-promoting organizations, and ignorant law makers who continue to believe natural mothers need to be protected from their own children and discount the needs of adult adoptees to know their own origins. Only nine states – Alabama, Alaska, Colorado, Hawaii, Kansas, Maine, New Hampshire, Oregon, and Rhode Island -- currently have moved to open original birth certificates to adult adoptees without restrictions at this point.[60] Not only adoptees are outraged at this denial of their civil rights. Natural mothers can feel further violated by the obliteration of our own identities as the mothers of our children. The replacement of our names as the natural mothers of our children by adoptive parents' names is a legal fiction that does not remove our emotional relationship as parents. When I added my found son to my family trust, the attorney's comment, "He's not related to you!" hurt me. Unfortunately, legally, she is right. This is the modern system of adoption, "The legal act of permanently placing a child with non-biological (adoptive) parents other than the biological (natural) parents." [61]

People understand that the loss of a child is one of the most devastating tragedies possible for parents. It is extraordinary then that

---

60 "Adult Adoptees' Original Birth Certificate (OBC) Access," *American Adoption Congress: Educating, Empowering, Evolving*, Accessed 2/12/2019, https://www.americanadoptioncongress.org/state.php.

61 "Adoption (disambiguation)", *Wikipedia*, accessed Feb. 15, 2019, https://en.wikipedia.org/wiki/Adoption_(disambiguation).

there is very little recognition that the loss of a child by adoption represents a comparable tragedy. Nature designed mothers and children to remain together. Scientists have discovered cells of a mother's children living in her brain and other organs.[62] Evidence supports the notion that these fetal cells play a part in keeping her healthy, even reducing her likelihood of contracting Alzheimer's disease. Many mothers carry the fetal cells of their babies for their entire lifetimes. Even when our babies leave our bodies, we mothers carry their traces in our bloodstreams. Is it any wonder we never forget them or truly recover from their loss?

It is now known that, by seven months gestation, babies can hear their mothers' voices. In the last ten weeks of pregnancy, they are actively listening to our voices. As newborns, they are drawn to and soothed by our voices above all others.[63] They are soothed by the familiar sound of the mother's heartbeat. A baby recognizes her mother's smell even before birth. A newborn is drawn to the smell of his mother's breast milk and prefers her scent to anyone else's.[64]

"A close attachment can prevent diseases, boost immunity, and enhance IQ in your baby," says Deepak Chopra, M.D. "Mother-child bonding has evolved to become a complex physiological process that enlists not just our hearts, but our brains, hormones, nerves, and almost every part of our bodies."[65]

"A single-cell embryo divides only fifty times to become one hundred trillion cells, which is more than all the stars in the Milky Way galaxy," said Dr. Chopra. "Once your baby is born, all the cells in

---

62 Robert Martone, "Scientists Discover Children's Cells Living in Mothers' Brains," *Scientific American*, December 4, 2012, https://www.scientificamerican.com/article/scientists-discover-childrens-cells-living-in-mothers-brain/.

63 The Baby Center Editorial Team, "Is it true that babies can recognize their mother's voices at birth?" *babycenter*, accessed Feb. 12, 2019, https://www.babycenter.com/404_is-it-true-that-babies-can-recognize-their-mothers-voice-at_10323727.bc.

64 Anita Sethi, Ph.D, "Your Baby's Sense of Smell," *Parenting*, Accessed Feb. 12, 2019, https://www.parenting.com/article/your-babys-sense-of-smell.

65 Patty Onderko, "The New Science of Mother-Baby Bonding," *Parenting*, Accessed Feb. 12, 2019, https://www.parenting.com/article/the-new-science-of-mother-baby-bonding.

both of your bodies act in secret synchronicity to create those simple but incredible connections between the two of you."[66]

This is natural. This is in accordance with nature. What relationship in nature is as profound as that between a natural mother and her baby? What can be more unnatural than rupturing, as adoption does, that relationship? How is it possible that so many in our society unquestioningly accept adoption as a natural, normal process?

It is hard for today's generations of young people to even imagine the situation of the '50s, '60s, and early '70s. Today, 40% of births occur to unmarried women, though most are living with the fathers, and many will marry them.[67] The moral proscription against single mothers has almost faded from most people's consciousness. Though some people still use the old-fashioned term, "born out-of-wedlock," to describe such babies, only one or two percent of their mothers now give them up for adoption.[68] Most raise them themselves and some choose to terminate their pregnancies through abortion, legal since the Roe v. Wade Supreme Court decision of 1973. Adoption is regularly touted as the solution to abortion by politicians, by those who call themselves pro-life, and by the Christian Right. There are around two thousand (2,000) crisis pregnancy centers connected to pro-life and religious groups advertising "Pregnant? Scared? Call 1-800-000-0000," on highway signs throughout the entire country.[69] An article in the AMA Journal of Ethics pointedly titled, "Why Crisis Pregnancy Centers Are Legal but Unethical." discussed how most of the vulnerable young women who call them believe they are abortion clinics or medical clinics and don't realize the center's goal is to

---

66 Ibid, Deepak Chopra, end of article

67 Amanda Marcotte, "Surprise! Unwed Birth Rates Are Going Down," *Slate*, May 11, 2015, https://slate.com/human-interest/2015/05/the-number-of-unwed-women-giving-birth-is-in-decline-not-that-you-d-know-it-from-debates-about-single-motherhood.html.

68 Evan B. Donaldson Adoption Institute, "Safeguarding the Rights and Well-being of Birthparents in the Adoption Process," p. 7, November, 2006, Revised with forward January, 2007. https://www.adoptioninstitute.org/old/publications/2006_11_Birthparent_Study_All.pdf.

69 Jay Hobbs, "10 Numbers You Should Know About Pregnancy Help Centers," *Pregnancy Help News*, Dec.20, 2017, https://pregnancyhelpnews.com/phc-10-numbers.

convince young girls to release their babies to adoption if they are not going to parent them.[70] The Supreme Court ruled in June 2018 that these clinics do not have to provide information on state-funded abortion services, though many receive both state and federal funding.[71]

Even with all of these efforts to promote adoption, not many frightened teenaged girls agree now. The Evan B Donaldson Adoption Institute's report of 2006/2007 states only 13,000 to 14,000 babies are voluntarily relinquished domestically annually.[72] I have met a few of those young women and heard the grief and trauma they are suffering, notwithstanding their smaller numbers and the fact that most met and helped select the adoptive parents of their babies.

Since the demand for adoptable children far outstrips the availability of the domestic supply, international adoptions have become much more common, even with some countries sharply limiting them in the face of scandals and corruption. Kathryn Joyce in her book *The Child Catchers: Rescue, Trafficking, and the New Gospel of Adoption* writes how evangelical Christians seek to adopt from poor and war-ravaged countries, seeing themselves as following the Biblical mandate from James 1:27, "to look after orphans and widows in their distress".[73] It appears, though, that these evangelicals have divorced the care for widows from their mission to save presumed orphans, many

---

70 Amy G. Bryant, MD, MSCR and Jonas J. Swartz, MD, MPH, "Why Crisis Pregnancy Centers Are Legal but Unethical," *AMA Journal of Ethics*, Mar 2018, https://journalofethics.ama-assn.org/article/why-crisis-pregnancy-centers-are-legal-unethical/2018-03.

71 Robert Barnes, " Supreme Court says crisis pregnancy centers do not have to provide women abortion information," *The Washington Post*, June 26, 2018, https://www.washingtonpost.com/politics/courts_law/supreme-court-says-crisis-pregnancy-centers-do-not-have-to-tell-women-about-abortion-information/2018/06/26/d2b9f5c2-7943-11e8-80be-6d32e182a3bc_story.html?utm_term=.e2d260e9ba00

72 Evan B. Donaldson Adoption Institute, "Safeguarding the Rights and Well-being of Birthparents in the Adoption Process," p. 4, November, 2006, Revised with forward January, 2007. https://www.adoptioninstitute.org/old/publications/2006_11_Birthparent_Study_All.pdf.

73 Kathryn Joyce, *The Child Catchers: Rescue, Trafficking, and the New Gospel of Adoption,* New York, Public Affairs, 2013, preface x.

of whom in fact have at least one living parent.[74] Some evangelicals are suggesting their fellow Christians would do better to work to reduce the poverty and social instability that leads to most of these adoptions, but such would not further their dual goal of offering children a new life in America as well as to "bring children out of darkness and suffering into faith and life in Jesus Christ."[75]

Much of the continuing American pro-adoption narrative appears to be maintained by the unquestioned messages promulgated by these conservative religious, political, and anti-abortion groups. Jesseca Boyer, Senior Policy Manager of The Guttmacher Institute states: "Social conservatives in the U.S. Congress are not just antiabortion but increasingly anti–family planning. The harmful policies these lawmakers are pursuing are based on falsehoods, and would severely undermine the health, rights and autonomy of women around the world."[76]

Despite public misperceptions, most women getting abortions already have at least one child, are in their twenties, and are disproportionately women of color living in poverty.[77] Roughly 1.2 million US women have abortions each year and half are twenty-five years or older, with sixty percent having at least one child already.[78] The Evan B. Donaldson report states most American women relinquishing babies also are in their twenties, have graduated from high school, and often have other children. Only 13,000 to 14,000 mothers voluntarily relinquish - a tiny minority.[79]

---

74 Ibid, preface xiii.

75 Ibid, p.28.

76 Jesseca Boyer, Senior Policy Manager of the Guttmacher Institute, accessed Feb. 12, 2019, https://www.guttmacher.org/united-states/abortion.

77 "Abortion is a Common Experience for U.S. Women Despite Dramatic Declines in Rates," *Guttmacher Institute*, Oct. 19, 2017, https://www.guttmacher.org/news-release/2017/abortion-common-experience-us-women-despite-dramatic-declines-rates.

78 "Who's getting abortions? Not who you'd think," *Women's Health, NBC.com,* 1/8/2008, http://www.nbcnews.com/id/22689931/ns/health-womens_health/t/whos-getting-abortions-not-who-youd-think/#.XGOOIzNKjIV.

79 Evan B. Donaldson Adoption Institute, "Safeguarding the Rights and Well-being of Birthparents in the Adoption Process," p. 4, Nov, 2006, Revised with forward

The saying, "Prevention is worth a pound of cure," comes to mind. Were pro-life groups to advocate *for* sex education, birth control measures, and services to reduce poverty and support families, most abortions *and* domestic adoptions might become unnecessary. Yet the answer most often promoted by social conservatives is to resist family planning and glorify the "loving" solution of relinquishment for adoption, which also conveniently supports the American market demand for children, especially infants.

In my field of psychiatry, there is a saying: "Suicide is a permanent solution to a temporary problem." This is true; and it is now often said of adoption. Many, if not most, adoptions could be prevented were there the will to individually and societally act to support natural families. Organizations and programs working toward family preservation are Child Welfare Preservation Gateway,[80] National Family Preservation Network,[81] and Seneca National Institute for Permanent Family Connectedness,[82] all of which work to help prevent separation and promote services toward reunification of family units. A beautiful online video from Nat'l Family Preservation Network shows their commitment to involving natural fathers in parenting their children, in addition to other kin.[83] Were society to widely support such programs, how many foster care placements could be prevented? How many children could be protected from the trauma of loss of their original families? Could not the expense of such programs be offset by savings in foster care and other expensive outcomes of family unit destruction? Even when that may not be possible, systems of permanent guardianship are now being recommended to replace

---

January, 2007. https://www.adoptioninstitute.org/old/publications/2006_11_Birthparent_Study_All.pdf.

80 "Supporting & Preserving Families - Child Welfare Information Gateway," Childrens' Bureau, Dept of HEW, Accessed 2/12/2019, https://www.childwelfare.gov/topics/supporting/

81 National Family Preservation Network, Accessed 2/15/19, https://nfpn.org/

82 "What is Family Finding and Permanency?" *National Institute for Permanent Family Connectedness*, Seneca, Accessed 2/15/19, http://www.familyfinding.org/.

83 Priscilla Martens, "Introduction to the National Family Preservation Network, 5 years ago, Accessed 2/15/19, https://vimeo.com/70371182.

the total and permanent separation that adoption creates.[84] [85] Some would argue that guardianship may not give children a strong sense of belonging in a family, but many adoptees inform us they never really felt they belonged in their adoptive families anyway. Belonging cannot be mandated legally.

A major problem in achieving family preservation lies in the fact that adoption in the United States is big business, about 1.4 billion dollars annually.[86] [87] "American Adoptions" reported online about a survey by *Adoptive Families Magazine* of 1100 families who adopted in 2012-2013 and paid between 34,000 and 40,000 dollars each.[88] The Gladney Center for Adoption, where my son was placed, reports online their current cost for a domestic infant adoption as $47,500.[89] In addition, the troubling reality of adoption is that it almost always involves the transfer of children from women with lower socioeconomic status to economically privileged adoptive parents.[90] The parents chosen for my son both had PhDs, were thirty-five and forty

---

84 Mirah Riben, Contributor, "Family Preservation," *Huff Post*, 04/05/2016 01:29 p.m. ET **Updated** Dec 06, 2017, https://www.huffingtonpost.com/mirah-riben/family-preservation_b_9614136.html

85 Janet Snell, "Adoption isn't the only placement route to a happy childhood," *The Guardian*, 1/18/2012, https://www.theguardian.com/society/2012/jan/18/adoption-placement-route-social-care.

86 Jessica BelBalzo, "The Case Against Adoption: Research and Alternatives for Concerned Citizens," *Baby Scoop Era Research Initiative*, Accessed 2/13/19, http://babyscoopera.com/adoption-articles/the-case-against-adoption-research-and-alternatives-for-concerned-citizens/.

87 Darlene Gerow, "Infant Adoption is Big Business in America," *CUB Communicator*, Accessed 2/13/19, http://www.adoptingback.com/infant.pdf.

88 "Comparing the Costs of Domestic, International and Foster Care Adoption," *American Adoptions*, Accessed 2/13/19, https://www.americanadoptions.com/adopt/the_costs_of_adopting.

89 Financial Info Domestic Infant, *Gladney Center for Adoption*, Accessed 2/10/19, https://adoptionsbygladney.com/i-want-to-adopt/domestic-infant/exploring-adoption/financial-info.

90 Steph Herold and Gretchen Sisson, "Evidence-Based Advocacy: Poverty, Adoption, and Inequality in Perspective," *Rewire*, 11/5/12. https://rewire.news/article/2012/11/05/evidence-based-advocacy-what-are-connections-between-adoption-and-poverty/.

years old respectively when they got my baby, and were established economically.

Perhaps if a system of guardianship replaced adoption it would be possible for non-kin people of average means who desire to raise children to participate. I am not the first person to claim that adoption, in favoring the wealthy and better-resourced over the poor, represents a little-recognized social justice issue. Kathryn Sweeney makes a further point that this discrepancy in financial status perpetuates the culture of poverty arguments -- the American social conservative beliefs which attribute poverty to individual laziness and irresponsibility. Hence, adoption is treated as a solution to poverty; both in this country and internationally. This argument, of course, makes it easier to blame the individual mother than to mobilize to improve systems and services that might allow her to raise her own child.[91]

The fact that adoption involves the transfer of large sums of money also encourages corruption that places greater emphasis on meeting the desires of couples for children rather than the needs of children for parents. The Special Rapporteur, United Nations, Commission on Human Rights, said in 2003:

> "Regrettably, in many cases, the emphasis has changed from the desire to provide a needy child with a home, to that of providing a needy parent with a child. As a result, a whole industry has grown, generating millions of dollars of revenues each year..."[92]

The United States has more adoptions than the entire rest of the world combined.[93] Adoption has become normalized in our American

---

91 Kathryn Sweeney, "The Culture of Poverty and Adoption: Adoptive Parent Views of Birth Families," *Michigan Family Review,* Volume 16, Issue 1, 2012, pp. 22-37, https://quod.lib.umich.edu/m/mfr/4919087.0016.102/--culture-of-poverty-and-adoption-adoptive-parent-views?rgn=main;view=fulltext

92 Mirah Riben, Contributor, "Family Preservation," *Huff Post*,_04/05/2016 01:29 p.m. ET Updated Dec 06, 2017, https://www.huffingtonpost.com/mirah-riben/family-preservation_b_9614136.html

93 Asher Fogle, "Surprising Facts You May Not Know About Adoption," *GH (Good Housekeeping),* 12/8/15, https://www.goodhousekeeping.com/life/parenting/a35860/adoption-statistics/.

culture. As a result, I believe that we have become deadened to the unnaturalness of the system of adoption. We have come to treat adoption as normal and desirable. There is a majority view that adoption is a win-win solution. Until we question this false narrative, little is likely to change.

Adoption causes lifelong trauma and grief. Sometimes children may require the care of non-family parents, but we must recognize that this is *never* the best option. Family preservation is critical to the well-being of children as well as to their mothers, fathers, and kin. Recognition of the inherent and irreplaceable connection between mothers and their children must replace the idea that caregivers are somehow interchangeable. All efforts must be made to preserve the original family unit. Permanent guardianship can be put in place when required. All children deserve to retain their original names, identities, parentage, and heritage. They deserve honesty and removal of secrets. Making a profit on their placement promotes corruption and allows children to be treated as commodities.

Increasing voices call for an end to adoption as we know it. I add my voice to that chorus.

www.ingramcontent.com/pod-product-compliance
Lightning Source LLC
Chambersburg PA
CBHW031118020426
42333CB00012B/139

9781949642155